Meaningful Making:
Projects and Inspirations for Fab Labs + Makerspaces

volume 3

Edited by Paulo Blikstein, Sylvia Libow Martinez, and Heather Allen Pang

Constructing Modern Knowledge Press

This work is licensed under the Creative Commons Attribution-NonCommercial-ShareAlike 4.0 International License. To view a copy of this license, visit creativecommons.org/licenses/by-nc-sa/4.0/ or send a letter to Creative Commons, PO Box 1866, Mountain View, CA 94042, USA.

All marks are the property of their respective owners.
All photos are credited to the article author unless otherwise noted.

Edited by Paulo Blikstein, Sylvia Martinez, and Heather Allen Pang
Series cover designed by Ria Kawaguchi.

Published 2023 by Constructing Modern Knowledge Press, Torrance, CA USA
cmkpress.com

This and other Constructing Modern Knowledge Press books may be purchased for educational and other use at cmkpress.com. See the website for information on bulk purchases, volume discounts, and purchase orders.

Paperback book ISBN: 978-1-955604-12-3
Hardcover book ISBN: 978-1-955604-13-0

EDU039000 EDUCATION / Computers & Technology
EDU029030 EDUCATION / Teaching Methods & Materials / Science & Technology

Contents

About the FabLearn Fellows Initiative vi
About the FabLearn Labs vi
About this book vii
Acknowledgments vii
Meet the Contributing FabLearn Fellows viii
Foreword by Paulo Blikstein xiv

Reflections: Gears of My Childhood 2

E ala! E alu! E Kuilima: Up! Together! Join Hands!
    by Toni Marie Kaui 4

Gears and Fears
    by Greg Houghton 7

Gears of Learning
    by Ridhi Aggarwal 10

Remote Gears
    by Ed Bringas 12

Papert Reloaded
    by Federica Selleri 14

What Makes a Project Meaningful?
    by Lina Cannone 16

Who Killed Our Inborn Maker Culture?
    by Martin Oloo 18

Finding My Gear at Twenty-Three
    by Nadine Abu Tuhaimer 21

Making Means Head and Heart, Not Just Hands
    by Lior Schenk 22

Stop Waiting to Love Learning Again
    by Kristin Burrus 24

Motivation
    by Charles Pimentel 26

Time to Tinker
    by Lars Beck Johannsen 28

Freedom! It Is Easy to See
    by Michael Mumbo 30

Finding Gears Late
    by Rafael Vargas 32

Between the Garage and the Electronics Workshop
    by Mouhamadou Ngom 33

Reading "The Gears of My Childhood" Again
    by Nusarin Nusen 34

Find Your Unique Gear
    Xiaoling Zhang 35

The Gear of Innovation
    Débora Garofalo 37

Making Do: Adaptations for COVID and Remote Learning 38

Six Little Lessons Learned from COVID-19
    by Federica Selleri 40

Online Teacher Training in Mathematics Education: A Maker and STEM Approach to Promote Active Learning
    by Charles Pimentel 42

Lessons Learned from Hosting Virtual Innovation Challenges in Kenya
    by Brenda Nyakoa 46

Tea Sippers & TurtleStitch
    by Kristin Burrus 49

Making Remotely: Sending Embroidery Kits Home and Teaching on Zoom
    by Heather Allen Pang 52

In Your Hands: The Emancipation of Manufacturing
    by Martin Oloo 55

The AI Club: The Importance of Student Agency in the Teaching of Artificial Intelligence
    by Charles Pimentel 58

Making for All ... 64

- Special Needs Lab
  - by Lars Beck Johannsen ... 66
- Garotas STEM: A Project to Encourage Girls to Pursue STEM Careers
  - by Charles Pimentel ... 68
- Let's Think, Build, and Code!
  - by Michael Mumbo ... 73
- Game of Drones: The Beauty of Mistakes
  - by Lars Beck Johannsen ... 75
- SenFabLab: Our Robotics Workshop for Children
  - by Mouhamadou Ngom ... 78
- Reflecting on the Teachings of Gary Stager and My Work with Robotics with Scrap Materials
  - by Débora Garofalo ... 80
- Curiosity Heals at the Repair Café
  - by Mathias Wunderlich ... 82
- Encouraging Diversity in Computer Science
  - by David Malpica ... 85
- Emancipatory Maker Practices in the Global South
  - by Renato Russo, Leah Rosenbaum, Paulo Blikstein, Yipu Zheng, Anisa Bora, Yue Liu, Brenda Nyakoa, Ridhi Aggarwal ... 87

Change ... 92

- How FabLearn Changed My Perspective Towards Technology in the Makerspace
  - by Ridhi Aggarwal ... 94
- Contemplating Education Reform
  - by Toni Marie Kaui ... 96
- Is ChatGPT a Threat to Education? For the Banking Model of Education, Yes
  - by Charles Pimentel ... 100
- Education in the Age of AI
  - by Lars Beck Johannsen ... 102
- Technology is a New Kind of Trojan Horse: Reflections on a Text by Professor Paulo Blikstein
  - by Charles Pimentel ... 104
- Having Financial Resources Does Not Guarantee Learning
  - by Débora Garofalo ... 107

Quilts: Collaboration, Coding, & Culture ... 110

- Digital Quilting Around the World
  - by Greg Houghton ... 113
- Teaching Collaborative Programming: A Creative Adventure Using Lynx
  - by Débora Garofalo ... 114
- Create a Quilt That Wraps the World
  - by Lina Cannone ... 116
- Experiencing a Powerful Mathematical Idea
  - by Ridhi Aggarwal ... 118
- Quilting the Young Coders
  - by Michael Mumbo ... 121

Cultures of Reuse & Recyling ... 122

- Robótica com Sucata: Por uma educação criativa para todos
  - by Débora Garofalo ... 124
- Robotics with Scrap: Creative Education for All
  - by Débora Garofalo ... 127
- Recycling 3D Printing Plastics
  - by Lars Beck Johannsen ... 129
- Interview: Coffee Grounds to Bioplastic
- Interview: Repurposing Projects at Nā Hunaahi
- Interview: Upcycling an LED Racing Game

Maker and Makerspace Culture ... 144

- Children's Lived Experiences: An Integral Part of the Makerspace
  - by Ridhi Aggarwal ... 146
- Why Teach Maker Education?
  - by Lars Beck Johannsen ... 150
- Culture and Making: A Strong and Powerful Connection
  - by Federica Selleri ... 153
- Maker Culture: An Ally in Education and Curriculum Reform
  - by Débora Garofalo ... 155
- Makerland: Exploring the Connections Between Makerspaces and Seymour Papert's Mathland
  - by Charles Pimentel ... 157
- Weekend Makercamps for Students
  - by Mathias Wunderlich ... 162

Projects in Depth 168

Cultural Making: Storytelling through Kalamkari
    by Safoura Seddighin 170

Making in China or Made in China?
    by Xiaoling Zhang.................................... 173

Robot Art
    by Lars Beck Johannsen 180

Biotinkering 101
    by Lina Cannone 182

Stitching Roots: Exploring Family History through Biomaking, Coding, and Stitching
    by Lina Cannone 184

Cherokee Language Syllabary Using 3D Design in Tinkercad
    by Josh Ajima 186

Making Puppets Come Alive
    by Ridhi Aggarwal 188

Imagine Anything: 3D Design without a 3D Printer
    by Lars Beck Johannsen 192

GoGo Board in Brazil: The Engine of Digital Inclusion
    by Charles Pimentel 195

Ideas about America: Making in History Class with Fabric Collage
    by Heather Allen Pang................................200

Found Object Puppetry
    by Ridhi Aggarwal 202

Mole Day in the Makerspace
    by Josh Ajima 204

About the FabLearn Fellows Initiative

The FabLearn Fellows program was created in 2013 and housed at the Transformative Learning Technologies Laboratory (TLTL), then at Stanford University's Graduate School of Education and now housed at Teachers College, Columbia University.

The Fellows program brings together experienced educators from all over the world to contribute to research about constructionist learning, maker education, physical computing, and computer science education in schools to create an open-source library of curricula and best practices.

To date, there have been three cohorts of FabLearn Fellows, a diverse group of sixty educators and makers. Many Fellows from the first cohort have continued to contribute to the FabLearn program as Senior FabLearn Fellows. Together the Fellows represent twenty countries, including sixteen states in the United States, and work with students from a wide variety of demographics at public and independent schools, community organizations, museums, and nonprofits.

The FabLearn Fellows program was created as part of a larger project sponsored by the National Science Foundation entitled "Infusing Learning Sciences Research into Digital Fabrication in Education and the Makers' Movement" (NSF Award 1349163, Division of Information & Intelligent Systems). Some Fellows have been supported by the Lemann Foundation (Brazil) and the Suksapattana Foundation (Thailand).

FabLearn Fellow goals

Despite the recent popularity of the maker movement and fabrication labs in education, most teachers work in isolation, cut off from other practitioners doing similar projects and disconnected from learning sciences researchers. One of the main objectives of the FabLearn Fellows program is to bring researchers and practitioners together to help bridge these gaps, learn from each other's experiences, share these lessons with their local community, and together create educational materials for the rest of the teaching community.

Through this project, we hope to answer four major questions:

- How can we scale up maker education without losing its transformative power?
- How can we generate an open-source set of constructionist curricular materials well adapted for makerspaces and fabrication labs in educational settings?
- How are teachers adapting their own curriculum in the face of these new "making" technologies, and how can they be better supported? What challenges do teachers face when trying to adopt project-based, constructionist, digital fabrication activities in their classrooms and after-school programs?
- How are schools approaching teacher development, parental/community involvement, and issues around traditional assessment?

About the FabLearn Labs

FabLearn Labs (formerly known as FabLab@School labs) are physical makerspaces in K–12 schools developed by TLTL and managed in collaboration with US and international partners. While today there are a growing number of fabrication labs in school settings, in 2009 FabLab@School was the first such program designed from the ground up specifically to serve grades 6–12.

There are currently FabLearn Lab installations on the Columbia University campus (US), and in East Palo Alto (US), Palo Alto (US), Moscow (Russia), Bangkok (Thailand), Barcelona (Spain), Melbourne (Australia), Sobral and several municipalities in the state of Rio Grande do Sul (Brazil), and Espoo (Finland), with partner labs in many other cities.

The intellectual roots of FabLearn extend back to the work of Seymour Papert, a pioneer in the field of educational technologies, and his collaborators at the MIT Media Lab. Papert, Cynthia Solomon, and colleagues developed Logo, a programming language designed for children and the first systems for educational robotics. Their constructionist perspective (a belief that children learn most effectively when they build artifacts and share with peers) is at the heart of the FabLearn program. A second important component is the work of Paulo Freire, a Brazilian scholar who was a pioneer in highlighting the importance of culture, equity, and social justice in education.

The original Fab Lab was conceived in the early 2000s in the Media Lab at MIT by Neil Gershenfeld (in collaboration with Bakhtiar Mitkak) as a creative space for university students. Within five years the concept had been transplanted successfully to community centers and entrepreneurial centers around the globe under the banner of the Fab Foundation. In this book, the spaces that are affiliated with the Fab Foundation are called Fab Labs, while those not associated are called fab labs, fablabs, makerspaces, or their own unique name based on the preference of the organization and author.

Paulo Blikstein was a student at the MIT Media Lab when the very first Fab Labs were being created. He began researching digital fabrication in education in 2004 as part of his doctoral work, created the FabLearn Lab concept when he joined the Stanford faculty in 2008, and designed the first-ever digital fabrication lab at a school of education which still operates at Stanford University. Blikstein is currently an associate professor of Communication, Media & Learning Technologies & Design at Teachers College, Columbia University.

About this book

This book is a compilation of some of the work of the FabLearn Fellows and Senior FabLearn Fellows. Included are articles about making and fabrication in many different learning spaces, ideas for projects, reflections, curriculum integration strategies, and much more. Many of the articles and projects include resources for additional reading and exploration, and every FabLearn Fellow has a page on the FabLearn website (fablearn.org) where more projects, details, and contact information can be found.

Acknowledgments

Contributing FabLearn Fellow authors

Nadine Abu Tuhaimer, Ridhi Aggarwal, Josh Ajima, Lars Beck Johannsen, Ed Bringas, Kristin Burrus, Lina Cannone, Debora Garofalo, Greg Houghton, Toni Marie Kaui, David Malpica, Michael Mumbo, Mouhamadou Ngom, Nusarin Nusen, Brenda Nyakoa, Martin Oloo, Heather Pang, Charles Pimentel, Lior Schenk, Safoura Seddighin, Federica Selleri, Rafael Vargas, Mathias Wunderlich, Xiaoling Zhang,

Editors

Paulo Blikstein, Sylvia Libow Martinez, and Heather Allen Pang

Editorial guidance and section introductions

Sylvia Libow Martinez

FabLearn Fellows project principal investigator

Dr. Paulo Blikstein, Associate Professor of Learning Technologies & Design, Teachers College, Columbia University

FabLearn Fellows principal advisor

Sylvia Libow Martinez, coauthor of Invent to Learn: Making, Tinkering, and Engineering in the Classroom, and president, Constructing Modern Knowledge

Special thanks

Leah Rosenbaum, Renato Russo, Yipu Zheng, Livia Macedo, Jonathan Pang, Tamar Fuhrmann, Alicja Żenczykowska, Diana Garcia and the students and postdocs at the TLTL.

Transformative Learning Technologies Laboratory

The Transformative Learning Technologies Laboratory (TLTL) is a multidisciplinary research group creating and investigating new technologies for project-based STEM education. Within the realm of digital fabrication in schools, the TLTL conducts research and disseminates findings through four main programs: FabLearn Labs (educational makerspaces in K–12 schools developed in collaboration with US and international partners, formerly known as the FabLab@School project), FabLearn conferences, FabLearn training programs, and the FabLearn Fellows program.

Constructing Modern Knowledge Press

Constructing Modern Knowledge (CMK) Press is a publishing company dedicated to producing books supporting modern learner-centered approaches to education.

Caution

Some of these projects call for tools and materials that can be dangerous if used improperly. Always follow manufacturer's guidelines and safety rules, and use common sense.

Meet the Contributing FabLearn Fellows

Brenda Nyakoa

Brenda Nyakoa is a delivery advisor at the Airbel Impact lab for the International Rescue Committee (IRC) where she manages the design and implementation of Education Technology (EdTech) Programs for children living in communities affected by crises. Previously she worked as an associate at Global Minimum Inc., a non-profit that implements innovative hands-on programs for youth in Africa through STEM education. She has worked with over 1,000 high school youth in Kenya through innovation boot camps and maker workshops to help them create innovative solutions to challenges in their communities. She holds a BSC in Electrical & Electronic Engineering from the University of Nairobi.

David Malpica

David Malpica is a CTE Graphic and Interactive Design and Computer Science teacher at TIDE Academy, a small public high school in Menlo Park, California, United States. At TIDE, Malpica serves a diverse community of emergent bilinguals, students with disabilities, and native speakers, while teaching dual credit courses in partnership with Foothill College. Prior to TIDE, Malpica has worked at startups Piper and LightUp, and has worked with students from fifth to twelfth grades at Bullis Charter School, The Girls' Middle school, and Skyline High School with a focus on integrated subject matter projects. He holds a bachelor's degree in Game Art and Design from The Art Institute of California; a master of arts in Learning, Design, and Technology from Stanford University, and a Career Technical Education CLEAR teaching credential from UC Berkeley Extension.

Charles Pimentel

Charles is a MYP Design, Robotics, and Math teacher at the American School of Rio de Janeiro (www.earj.com.br), an international institution that delivers high-quality education within the International Baccalaureate curriculum. He holds an M.Sc. in Informatics and a Postgraduate degree in IT in Education from the Federal University of Rio de Janeiro (UFRJ). His work focuses on the inclusion of Artificial Intelligence teaching in K-12 Education through Educational Robotics.

He has also developed a Maker Math course, which aims to introduce robotics, automation, physical computing, digital fabrication, and AI to K-12 schools. The course explores the mathematical skills and competencies involved in the process of building automated prototypes, with the purpose of creating solutions to real-world problems through a STEM approach. Currently, he is a D.Sc. student in Informatics at UFRJ, focusing on Data Literacy.

Debora Garofalo

Débora Garofalo is a public school teacher in São Paulo, Brazil. In 2015, she started the Robotics with Scrap (Robótica com Sucata) project to teach robotics and computational thinking to children and young people in the city of São Paulo, using recycled materials and trash from the neighborhoods the students came from. Since 2015, over 2,000 students have been directly involved in this project, and today the work has become a public policy of the State of São Paulo which impacts 2.5 million students. Currently, she is the Innovation Director of Multirio, an enterprise attached to the Municipal Secretary of Education of Rio de Janeiro, responsible for innovative public policies. Débora has received several awards including Teachers of Brazil 2018, the MIT Creative Learning Challenge 2019, a UN Peacekeeper Medal 2019, and she was named one of the ten best Teachers in the World by the Global Teacher Prize 2019.

Meet the FabLearn Fellows

Ed Bringas

Ed has been in the maker education field for over 15 years. Currently, Ed is a STEAM learning specialist and classroom teacher at Fannie Lou Hamer Freedom High School in the Bronx, NYC. Prior to that, Ed worked in the nonprofit sector writing, implementing, and designing STEAM curriculum. During that time, he co-authored an award-winning National Science Foundation grant that worked on bringing Fab Labs to high school students in the South Bronx. He has written books around robotics curriculum and articles for MAKE Magazine. Ed is a graduate of the Interactive Telecommunications Program at New York University and holds a Master's degree in Special Education from St. John's University. Ed lives in Brooklyn with his wife and daughter.

Federica Selleri

Federica Selleri is a learning designer and PhD candidate. Passionate about education, technology, and design, she is one of the founders of FabLab Valsamoggia (Bologna). Since 2016 she has designed and made workshops and courses about 3D printing, 2D and 3D modeling, coding for local schools, children, teachers, and retired and unemployed people. Selleri has collaborated with the Reggio Children Foundation about play and learning and with the Andrea Bocelli Foundation about digital technologies in pediatric hospitals. She is also a PhD candidate in "Learning Sciences and Digital Technologies" at the University of Foggia. Selleri holds a BA in Graphic Design and Visual Communication (ISIA Urbino), an MA in Eco-Social Design (Free University of Bolzano/Bozen) and is a graduate of FabAcademy.

Greg Houghton

Greg Houghton is an experienced media developer based in Newcastle Upon Tyne. Greg is project lead at Foundation Futures Make Stuff, a new makerspace to inspire young people to explore technology creatively through community workshops and online maker activities. Foundation Futures supports disadvantaged young people and their families to access and train alongside employers and local businesses on practical activities. During the Covid pandemic, Make Stuff has provided free online and 'unplugged' computing activities to local residents in the northeast of England.

Heather Allen Pang

Heather Allen Pang teaches history and making to eighth graders at Castilleja School, a grade 6–12 private school in Palo Alto, California, United States. She herself is a graduate of the all-girls school (class of 1984) and serves as the school archivist, 8th-grade dean, and History-Social Science Discipline Lead. Castilleja's Bourn Idea Lab is closely associated with Stanford University's Transformative Learning Technology Lab. Before joining the faculty at Castilleja, Pang taught at the University of California, Davis; Santa Rosa Junior College; and American River College. She holds a bachelor's degree in European history from Wesleyan University; a master of arts in teaching in European and American history from the University of California, Davis; and a doctorate in American history from the University of California, Davis.

Josh Ajima

Josh Ajima is the Makerspace Facilitator at the Academies of Loudoun, a public STEM magnet high school in Loudoun County, Virginia, United States. He was awarded the VSTE Innovative Educator of the Year award in 2017 for his work integrating maker education into the content area. He has a passion for digital fabrication, has won the FormLabs 3D Design Awards for Top Educational Model, and served as a reviewer for Make: magazine. Ajima shares his work on making in the classroom on his blog (designmaketeach.com) and YouTube channel (youtube.com/designmaketeach). He holds a bachelor's degree in chemistry from the University of Virginia.

Kristin Burrus

Kristin Burrus has 23 years of experience in education. From 2017 to 2019, as a FabLab Specialist in a K-12 public magnet school, she developed and facilitated problem-based learning and design thinking units for elementary, middle, and high school students, integrating digital fabrication into content classes. In August 2019, she became the Digital Fabrication Ecosystem Lead at STEM School Chattanooga, providing professional development and support for digital fabrication teachers in the district. Currently, Kristin is the Innovation Manager and Lead teacher in the Global Center for Digital Innovation (GCDI), the first K-14 educational Fab Lab in the Nation. She is a National Board Certified Teacher and holds a BS in Biology and a Masters of Education.

Lars Beck Johannsen

Lars Beck Johannsen is a Fablab manager at Fablab Skanderborg, where he facilitates workshops for schools, runs after-school programs, educates fellow teachers and runs a weekly openlab. He has a background as a K-12 teacher, teaching math, arts and music from 2003 – 2018. In 2014 he discovered maker-technologies through the fablab@school project in Denmark, and they became an integrated part of the subjects he taught. At the moment he is engaged in establishing new makerspaces in local schools and developing an after-school project around the concept of escape rooms. Further, he works closely with researchers from University of South Denmark (SDU) around different areas of investigation e.g., the use of tangible objects as a mediating means for Computational Thinking and problem-solving.

Lina Cannone

Lina Cannone is a primary school teacher and the Makerspace manager at IC Orazio in Pomezia, Italy. She is the founder of "Let's STEM," a blog for teachers and educators about tinkering and making projects. She is the co-founder and president of We Make Lab, a non-profit organization whose mission is to bring children and young people closer to creative learning, coding, making and tinkering topics. In her town, she also runs a CoderDojo club with other volunteers to help kids expressing creativity. Lina is a trainer for teachers and educators, she has taught several courses, and she facilitates the development of educator's skills and professional networks. She holds a bachelor's degree from the University of Bologna, in Management Engineering.

Lior Schenk

Lior is captivated by both science and the arts as ways of knowing the universe and thus merges both subjects as an interdisciplinary teacher at Pittsburgh's Environmental Charter School. From themes of surrealist portraiture to Anthropocene speculative fabulation, Schenk aims to engage students in making as a liberatory force for social and planetary justice. In this critical moment of disconnect, he is a staunch advocate for creative learning and making, perhaps our most crucial and forgotten, human practice. Schenk is a graduate of UC San Diego and the University of Pennsylvania, with a B.S. in Physiology & Neuroscience and an M.S.Ed. in Science Education. He also partners closely with institutions such as the Green Building Alliance, the MIT Presencing Institute, and the National Writing Project in pursuit of thriving learning ecologies.

Martin Oloo

A graduate of FabAcademy, a social impact entrepreneur, and founder and CEO of Fablab Winam, Martin serves on the Board of the Association of Countrywide Hubs, Kenya. A social worker, but has a great passion for STEAM education and has been promoting its hands-on approach through Fabkids in partnership with Global Kids Day, SHE-Builds, and Jua Kali Plus programs. With over 15 years of ecosystem building, Martin has also been instrumental in founding of Lake Basin Innovation and Investment Week and supporter of African Makerspaces Network and AfricaOSH. Martin also has longstanding interest on the financial sustainability of Fablabs, makerspaces, and other innovation hubs where he has worked on the development of the Open Catalogue of Business Models for the mAkE project.

Mathias Wunderlich

Mathias Wunderlich is a teacher at the Freie Aktive Schule Wuelfrath in Germany near Düsseldorf. This is a K-13 school with deep roots in the pedagogy of Maria Montessori as well as Rebeca and Mauricio Wild. The school offers students the opportunity to work, invent, and tinker whenever they want. It gives students maximum freedom of choice for what they want to learn, when, with which classmates, and in which chronology. Wunderlich runs a dedicated makerspace there, with all kinds of tools and materials for crafting, making, electronics, and more. He's responsible for a number of school activities: a Repair Café, kids workshops at maker fairs, participation in science competitions, different student companies, and more.

Michael Mumbo

Michael Mumbo is an educator deeply rooted in Mathematics and IT. As the Co-founder and Director of Edutab Africa, an EdTech enterprise in Kenya, he orchestrates both facilitation and the creation of coding activities and educational resources for STEAM courses. His true passion lies in constructionist learning, particularly Math maker learning, driven by the belief that math's riches are within everyone's grasp through discovery, not just for the academically inclined. Michael leads in various virtual Maths Circles under The Global Maths Circle, USA, furthering math education. He's also a finalist in the Falling Walls global summit, dedicated to kindling children's scientific curiosity. Beyond education, Michael explores uncharted territories through mountaineering and cycling, seeking new connections and inspiration.

Mouhamadou Ngom

Mouhamadou Ngom, known as Modou, is a member of the team that installed the first FabLab in Senegal. He founded Senfablab in 2018, a digital fabrication laboratory located in Grand-Yoff, Senegal, and is part of the MY Human Kit network. This space is dedicated to fostering creativity, learning, prototyping, and sharing, as well as promoting digital technologies and hands-on learning. Senfablab also operates as a mobile lab, catering to students from suburban and rural areas, providing training in computer science, robotics, and 3D printing. Modou organizes training sessions on e-waste recycling and digital embroidery for seamstresses. Thanks to Senfablab, digital embroidery is now certified in Senegal. Senfablab played a pivotal role in the establishment of Senegal's first FabLab led by young women, the "Linguère Fablab," which is also known as Queen Fablab.

Nadine Abu Tuhaimer

A computer engineer, a digital fabrication specialist, and a passionate maker, co-founded menalab — a startup acclaimed for its product design services and comprehensive training in design, prototyping, and digital fabrication. Her contributions within the 3Dmena team reshaped Jordan's technological landscape, advocating passionately for fablabs and 3D printing. Nadine's legacy flourished with the inception of Jordan's first Fabrication Lab and Manufacturing Incubator, Shamal Start/FabLab Irbid. At its helm, she channeled expertise from the Fab Academy Diploma, guiding startups to materialize their visions. A founding member of the Fab Arab Network, Nadine pursues a Master's degree in Engineering Management from Princess Sumaya University in Jordan, and the University of Arizona in the USA. Nadine aspires to champion access to quality education for marginalized communities.

Nusarin Nusen

Nusarin Nusen teaches programming and invention at the Constructionism Consulting Center (CCC) within the Darunsikkhalai School for Innovative Learning (DSIL) in Bangkok, Thailand. Her previous experiences includes curriculum design, facilitating project-based learning for students in grades 2 through 6, as well as designing professional development workshops for teachers and adult learners centered around the design process and FabLab pedagogy. Nusen has a bachelor's degree in industrial computer technology and master's degree in computer engineering from Chiang Mai University.

Ridhi Aggarwal

Ridhi co-founder of Swatantra Talim, a non-profit working in alternative education in India with a vision to co-create every village as a "Center of Innovation" and every child as an "Innovator." Passionate about working with children and devising contextual engagement tools that co-create a learning environment for their joyful experience, Ridhi is a puppeteer and an origami lover. She has been instrumental in co-creating maker-spaces in public, private schools, and non-formal learning centres. A graduate of Lady Shri Ram College (Delhi University) and a post-graduate in education and commerce from Tata Institute of Social Sciences, Mumbai, and Delhi School of Economics. She has been a Wipro Seeding Fellow 2017-23, Vital Voices Visionaries Fellow 2022 and Young & Emerging Leaders Forum 2023-24.

Rafael Vargas

Rafael Vargas is an architect and multidisciplinary designer. He directs the Fab Lab at the University of Puerto Rico, where he teaches and manages research projects for graduate students dealing with digital prototyping and design. Rafael created the Emergent Tools initiative, which delivers technology training to diverse communities around the Puerto Rican archipelago and other Spanish-speaking territories through physical and online courses. He is involved in creating educational experiences dealing with various technologies, such as 3D printing, parametric design, digital fabrication, 3D modeling, and most recently, virtual reality. He pioneered the development of the first maker spaces in schools in Puerto Rico. Rafael often provides professional design services and consultancy related to emerging fabrication technologies and their applications for architecture, design, engineering, and product development.

Safoura Seddighin

Safoura is the co-founder of Fabinnov, the first educational fablab in Iran, located in the city of Isfahan. As the manager of the educational outreach program of the fablab (named Fabinnov Skills School), she and her team design, develop and implement programs and products that would slowing spread the maker culture and innovative learning practices considering the context of education in Iran. During her 14 years in the US, she studied and worked in designing, implementing and using new technologies for human development and related fields. Fabinnov serves both the industrial and educational sections. Fabinnov Skills School activities are designed based on two main themes which are mostly missing from the formal educational system: "joy of making and courage" and "digital design and fabrication."

Other Contributors

Toni Marie Kaui

Toni Marie Mapuana Kaui is the Founder of Nā Hunaahi, an independent competency-based high school in East Hawaiʻi. Nā Hunaahi perpetuates the Native Hawaiian language and cultural practices through design-based integrative STEAM curricula and in partnership with community organizations. Kaui models innovation to promote student development of creativity and imagination. She champions increased engineering and technology education and opportunities for underserved and underrepresented student populations and works toward achieving these goals as a Society for Science Innovation Education Fellow, a Department of Defense STEM Ambassador and a Code.org facilitator. She holds a Doctor of Philosophy in Integrative STEM Education, a Master of Education in Education Leadership, a Bachelor of Arts in Architecture, and a Bachelor of Science in Business Administration.

Renato Russo

Renato Russo is a Brazilian doctoral student at Teachers College, Columbia University, and a researcher at the Transformative Learning Technologies Lab (TLTLab). Renato graduated from Stanford University's Learning, Design, and Technology (LDT) Master's program. At TLTLab, he partners with local organizations and schools worldwide to investigate how maker education intertwines with local socio-cultural practices to create uniquely relevant and meaningful learning experiences. At Teachers College, Renato is also part of the teaching team for Beyond Bits and Atoms, a graduate-level course that teaches students to design, build, and critique constructionist educational technologies. Besides his work associated with maker education, Renato has presented and published work on disinformation and its close connections to cognitive processes associated with learning.

Xiaoling Zhang

Xiaoling Zhang is a Secondary teacher at The ISF Academy (Hong Kong SAR, China). She teaches IB MYP and DP courses as well as school-based self-initiative courses. She has run projects of Making+learning Chinese ancient poems, Making + history learning and Scratch+book reading with students from various language level groups across different grades. Her passion is to integrate Making and Technology into classes to provide students with a comprehensive type of learning experience and foster their understanding, creativity and interdisciplinary learning ability. She holds a Master's degree of Education in Teaching Chinese as a Second Language from The University of Hong Kong, and Bachelor of Arts in Teaching Chinese as a Foreign Language from Shanghai Normal University.

Foreword

by Paulo Blikstein

Shaping and combining materials transcend cultures and geographies, and even species — beavers also build exquisite nests and dams. Most of what we know about ancient peoples comes from objects they made, from everyday items such as pottery and tools to ceremonial objects like jewelry or religious icons. Humans took making to unprecedented levels of complexity, going far beyond basic needs or utility to reach for expressions of spirituality, customs, and aesthetics. A clay pot might look purely functional — meant for carrying water or cooking food — but its production is often deeply embedded in cultural practices that carry emotional and symbolic weight. An heirloom quilt might be made of simple fabrics, but its value comes from the history and love embedded in its stitches. Passed down from generation to generation, it becomes a family artifact that holds stories and memories.

But when objects started to be mass-produced, our relationship with them changed. Walter Benjamin's 1935 essay "The Work of Art in the Age of Mechanical Reproduction" discusses how industrial reproduction altered how we consider the authenticity of art. Benjamin suggests that the *aura* — the aesthetic authority of artistic works — is lost when we copy paintings or sculptures *en masse*. Would a similar process apply to the made objects around us? Is an industrially produced clay pot devoid of authenticity or history?

Research in Material Culture has pointed out the puzzling relationship between the urban dwellers of the 21st century and authenticity. In an age dominated by automation and mass production, the quest for the authentic has paradoxically become both more elusive and desirable. As we consume industrial objects on a daily basis, we decorate our homes with hand-woven tapestries, artisanal pottery, and traditional artwork sourced from remote communities. The stark juxtaposition between mass-produced goods and these handcrafted items is not accidental. Companies go to great lengths to assure customers that their products indeed contain elements of hand-craftsmanship, whether it's a leather bag that's been "hand-stitched" or a wooden chair that's been "hand-sanded." This complex relationship reflects one of the key tensions that define modern life in industrialized regions — a pull between the efficient and the meaningful, the generic and the unique, and the machine-made and the handcrafted. How could maker education help us better understand this tension and engage youth in this discussion?

The answer to that question could be a way to conceive our work in the next decade. As the maker and digital fabrication movement celebrates its tenth anniversary in schools, let us focus less on the latest and greatest digital fabrication machines, or clichés such as "getting kids to follow STEM careers," and more on inquiring into the relationships we create with objects when we construct, destroy, share, love, and critique them. We are drowning in objects, yet we barely have time to develop relationships with them. It is common to hear people talk about how making their own bread, cheese, or chairs changed their lives. It was clearly not about the efficiency of the process or even the quality of the product (both possibly inferior) but about the relationship that was established between the maker and the materials, processes, and products, the successes and failures, the moments of sharing with others, the experiments, and learnings along the way.

So, what does it mean to "make" when everything can be made by machines faster and better? This book brings many examples of how this conversation could go — from making household appliances using found materials in India to repairing them in Germany to repurposing them in Italy. Those examples suggest some more nuanced ways to look at these different contexts. For example, girls in India used found materials to make a clothes washing machine because new materials were not available. In Germany, the concept of a Repair Café connects generations and gives young people opportunities to be useful in their community (even though material availability is not an issue). In an Italian example, repurposing organic materials provides lessons in thrift, ecology, and material science. In Hawaii, using non-native, invasive species as building material for projects is a statement about taking back the land. How do we conceive these radical differences despite the fact that these groups were all using found or recycled materials? It is less about creating a "recycled materials" curriculum that could work everywhere, but about understanding how these ideas and materials can be appropriated and transformed locally.

Makerspaces could be, thus, more than just the place to make objects, but the locale in schools in which these rich discussions happen — it should be both about making, its context, and its critique. It is the perfect place to discuss consumerism and programmed obsolescence, inequality, design inclusiveness, sustainability, ableism, corporate greenwashing, or what objects mean to people and their families. But even more fundamentally, maker education could give students a space to examine these issues from a unique perspective — that of someone who is engaged viscerally in the construction and deconstruction of objects rather than following a recipe to make keychains or participating in a merely theoretical exercise in social critique. As Edith Ackermann would say, the most powerful aspect of creating things is the "cognitive dance" of diving in and "being one" with your creation, and stepping out, taking some distance. Making objects should also be about making meaning, and understanding how they relate to our lives, our planet, and all the social issues of our time.

The objects we create serve as reflections of our lives and societies, capturing a myriad of functions, emotions, and purposes. They are time capsules that allow a glimpse into our world, helping reconstruct the values, technologies, and everyday lives of societies. From the most mundane household item to the most sacred religious artifact, objects hold a wealth of information that can help us better understand who we are and where we want to be.

But in addition to these conversations about the future of maker education, this book celebrates those who are the true engine behind maker education: teachers. All over the world, from Senegal to Brazil to Hong Kong to the United States, maker teachers accomplished a once-in-a-generation school reform project — they created a new type of space and a new culture in schools, making constructionism part of the students' day in ways that have not been seen in decades. And they did this often outside of the official routes, with amazing stamina, creativity, and initiative. In this volume, we have many examples of this, such as holding maker camps in the face of COVID lockdowns, starting an AI club run by students (attracting international expertise), teaching other teachers how to teach design and making, establishing a scrap robotics project that has become public policy, finding ways to teach making remotely, establishing thriving makerspaces in unexpected places, and many more.

This book also documents a unique period in history, the global COVID-19 pandemic. Almost at the same time this third cadre of FabLearn Fellows was announced, schools began to close around the world. The focus of this cadre was going to be "cultural making," but this slightly changed as the Fellows, like all educators, grappled with the immense challenges they faced both personally and professionally. As you read the articles in this volume, you will see the ingenuity and determination to support young people displayed by these educators. Aspects of our attempt to investigate cultural making remain in these articles, but as happened with many things during the pandemic, we had to adapt and include other topics and kinds of activities.

Granted, maker education has a long way to go to be truly democratic and transformative, but we need to celebrate and elevate the efforts of the maker teachers of the first decade of this movement, who did what many thought impossible: fundamentally change how people think about teaching and learning.

Reflections:
Gears of My Childhood

The first section of this book is a collection of articles by the FabLearn Fellows reflecting on an essay by Seymour Papert called, "The Gears of My Childhood" which appears as the foreword to Dr. Papert's seminal book, *Mindstorms: Children, Computers, and Powerful Ideas* (1980). Dr. Papert's theory of learning, constructionism, is a pillar of FabLearn as it presages how the digital fabrication and maker movements can be combined with a compelling, modern vision of learning.

Papert writes about his own love of gears as a child, and how both the love and understanding of gears allowed him to learn other things.

"What an individual can learn, and how he learns it, depends on what models he has available. This raises, recursively, the question of how he learned these models. Thus the 'laws of learning' must be about how intellectual structures grow out of one another and about how, in the process, they acquire both logical and emotional form."

The FabLearn Fellows offer their personal recollections of how both logic and emotion must be present to foster deeper understandings and connections with powerful ideas.

E ala! E alu! E Kuilima: Up! Together! Join Hands!

by Toni Marie Kaui

Teachers are at the heart of my fondest memories of my primary and secondary education. Ms. Neet, Ms. Kala, and Mr. Akana were my fourth, fifth, and sixth grade teachers, respectively; Mrs. Harbottle taught music in grades four through eight; Mrs. Melahn taught me seventh and tenth grade math; I had Mrs. Huch for ninth grade English; and Mrs. Powers for eleventh grade English. These classes also happen to be the classes I learned the most in and whose content I can readily recall. Papert, in his essay, "Gears of My Childhood," highlights the relationship between affect and learning, and was what these teachers provided for me — memorable classroom experiences leading to well-learned content.

As I embarked on a new adventure of opening my own high school, Nā Hunaahi, I took to heart the relationships I developed and nurtured with my primary and secondary teachers. I aimed to create learning environments that supported knowledge acquisition and retention, which meant implementing practices beneficial to creating memorable classroom experiences. I recalled my memories of how these teachers and their classrooms made me feel and asked colleagues and friends and family to do the same in an attempt to find commonalities and central themes of teachers who positively impacted learning and the learning environments they created. These trips down memory lane confirmed the importance of the affective domain in learning, specifically a "sense of belonging – when one feels a part of a particular group" (Trujillo & Tanner, 2014).

A signature pedagogy of Nā Hunaahi is "learners engaged in the construction of an artifact or shareable product" (Hay & Barab, 2001) in order for the learner to build his/her knowledge. However, attention must also be given

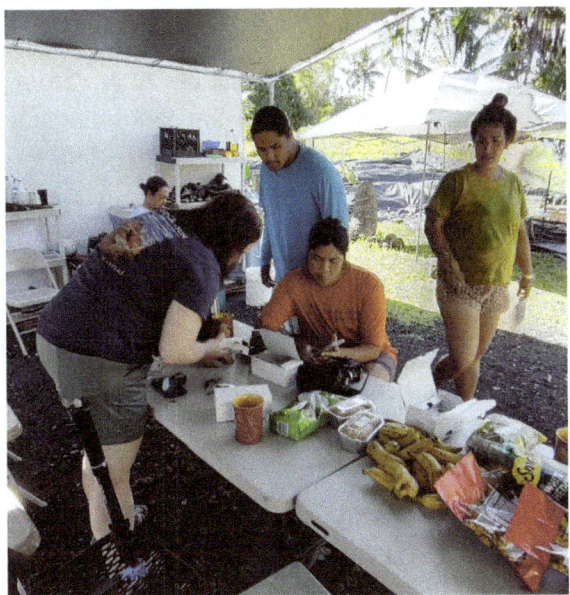

to the development of practices that imitate the positivity, joy, and happiness felt by students with memorable classroom experiences in which knowledge was acquired and retained. In "Gears of My Childhood," Papert suggests the need for "a positive affective tone that can be traced back to … experiences that connect with joyful and optimistic memories and prior experiences" (1980). I might add to his suggestion by also inspiring teachers to create positive affective tones through relationship building. Baumeister and Leary define "a need to belong, that is, a need to form and maintain at least a minimum quantity of interpersonal relationships" (1995), and teachers, as persons with significant time spent with students, can create a sense of belonging by purposefully and intentionally choosing to form quality interpersonal relationships. Additionally, numerous studies connect a student's academic success with his/her sense of belonging, and that sense of belonging can be developed by an individual and/or the school (Brooms, 2019; Korpershoek et al., 2020; Master et al., 2016; Museus et al., 2017; van Caudenberg et al., 2020; van Herpen et al., 2020). Regardless of who or what supports the development of a sense of belonging in students, doing so helps create memorable relationships that foster learning and achievement and creates an anchor students can set and navigate back to throughout their lifetimes.

In Hawaiʻi, we like to say, "It's a *kākou* thing," meaning it is the responsibility of all. *Kākou* is the first-person inclusive plural pronoun used to denote three or more persons including the speaker. The beauty of *ʻōlelo Hawaiʻi*, the Native Hawaiian language, as with many Polynesian languages, is its "distinctions in its pronouns between inclusive and exclusive forms and between dual (2) and plural (3 or more) referents" (Saft, 2017) allowing the speaker to clearly orient "the number of people being referred to and whether their interlocutors are going to be included or excluded in the content of the speech. An inclusive form, then, can serve as an immediate signal that all of those involved are (or are not) part of one inclusive group or community" (p. 96).

Beyond its use in speaking and writing, *kākou* also evokes images of togetherness and unity and supports the development of a sense of belonging. In addition to the use of language, *ʻōlelo noʻeau*, or Native Hawaiian poetical sayings, are used to remind students of their connection with each other, their teacher, the school, and the community. "*Pūpūkāhi i holomua*, unite in order to progress" (Pukui, 1983), is referenced often by teachers, coaches, community leaders, and government officials to remind us of our connectedness, and that progress comes through our combined efforts. At Nā Hunaahi, we use *ʻōlelo Hawaiʻi* and cultural practices and quality time to build strong adult-youth relationships. These relationships also demonstrate our commitment and dedication to the student as a person, to his/her family, and to his/her learning and achievement. It also contributes to developing a sense of belonging for the student.

When looking to support student learning and achievement, in addition to allowing students to build knowledge through construction of learning artifacts, we must also address the affective domain of sense of belonging. By creating a sense of belonging, we help students develop a context around their content of learning.

References

Baumeister, R. F., & Leary, M. R. (1995). The need to belong: Desire for interpersonal attachments as a fundamental human motivation. *Psychological Bulletin*, 117(3), 497-529.

Brooms, D. R. (2019). I was just trying to make it: Examining urban black males' sense of belonging, schooling experiences, and academic success. *Urban Education*, 54(6), 804-830.

Hay, K. E., & Barab, S. A. (2001). Constructivism in practice: A comparison and contrast of apprenticeship and constructionist learning environments. *The Journal of the Learning Sciences*, 10(3), 281-322.

Korpershoek, H., Canrinus, E. T., Fokkens-Bruinsma, M., & de Boer, H. (2020). The relationships between school belonging and students' motivational, social-emotional, behavioural, and academic outcomes in secondary education: A meta-analytic review. *Research Papers in Education*, 35(6), 641-680.

Master, A., Cheryan, S., & Meltzoff, A. N. (2016). Computing whether she belongs: Stereotypes undermine girls' interest and sense of belonging in computer science. *Journal of Educational Psychology*, 108(3), 424-437.

Museus, S. D., Yi, V., & Saelua, N. (2017). The impact of culturally engaging campus environments on sense of belonging. *The Review of Higher Education*, 40(2), 187-215.

Papert, S. (1980). Gears of My Childhood. In *Mindstorms: Children, Computers, and Powerful Ideas*. Basic Books.

Pukui, M. K. (1983). Ielo noʻeau: Hawaiian proverbs & poetical sayings. Bishop Museum Press.

Saft, S. (2017). Documenting an endangered language: The inclusive first-person plural pronoun kākou as a resource for claiming ownership in Hawaiian. *Jourrnal of Linguistic Anthropology*, 27(1), 91-113.

Trujillo, G., & Tanner, K. D. (2014). Considering the role of affect in learning: Monitoring students' self-efficacy, sense of belonging, and science identity. *CBE-Life Sciences Education*, 13, 6-15.

van Caudenberg, R., Clycq, N., & Timmerman, C. (2020). Feeling at home in school: Migrant youths' narratives on school belonging in Flemish secondary education. In *European Educational Research Journal* (pp. 428-444).

van Herpen, S. G., Meeuwisse, M., Hofman, W. A., & Severiens, S. E. (2020). A head start in higher education: The effect of a transition intervention on interaction, sense of belonging, and academic performance. *Studies in Higher Education*, 45(4), 862-877.

Gears and Fears

by Greg Houghton

When reading Papert's essay I was fascinated by the way that Papert creates the link between his earliest childhood memories to his own learning and how these experiences shaped the way he would forever interpret the world around him.

In the essay he describes how his love of automobiles helped him to give context to the gears in a construction set. The gears then became a "comfortable friend" for him to experiment and explore mathematical ideas. This concept of building on learning and developing strong abstract representations to think with really interests me and is something I would like to explore further here.

My own personal gears story began with music, in particular the Yamaha VSS30, a sampling keyboard used primarily by my brothers to play expletives in 8bit samples across 32 polyphonic keys, but for me, there was more. I was fascinated by the way that audio could be looped and manipulated using effects to create new and otherworldly sounds.

The Yamaha VSS-30

I loved electronic music. I would spend my pocket money on records and cassettes with no concept of how this music was created. At no point did I consider that the sampling keyboard had anything to do with this futuristic soundscape I enjoyed so much. Something so obvious now seemed impossible to understand then. I would watch the BBC music show *Top of the Pops* religiously, and try to figure out what was going on. I would write to my favorite musicians to try and find out how they created their sounds, but if I was lucky the PR staff would only send me a signed photo of the act.

The Shamen – 1993

Computer technology and music were two things that I had not linked. Around this time I would visit the local Bainbridge's department store to see the latest tech gadgets. I was amazed at the computer's ability to display a photograph, but still, the idea of the machine's full potential was not clear to me. It wasn't until a few years later that I managed to sneak into a nightclub one Tuesday evening after school that I was awakened to this connection. I had recently bought the album *Homework* (ironic, right) by Daft Punk and they were headlining. That evening was the best homework I would ever have. I stood in the balcony in amazement as I watched visuals played via the MIDI keyboard connected to an Apple Mac computer. On stage, Thomas Bangalter and Guy Manuel played an array of electronic instruments the likes of which I had never seen before but most importantly, I saw people enjoying and interacting with technology in ways I had never considered possible.

Daft Punk – Daftendirektour 1997

From that day I was hooked. At that time, digital musical instruments were relatively inexpensive and they weren't too hard to come across. I built a small setup of my own and began to learn about waveforms, patterns, synchronization, and sampling through play. I was inspired to learn about video, animation, and sound. To this day I apply these principles to my work and not just in the context of music.

At the same age that I found my love for sound, Papert "developed an intense involvement with automobiles." At this young age, we both had found our favorite pastime.

Returning to the essay, I was intrigued as to what an "Erector Set" was so I decided to take the risk of Googling it. An Erector Set advertisement from the 1930s reads, "*Hello Boys! SEE WHAT MIGHTY MECHANICAL MARVELS YOU CAN BUILD WITH The Great new Erector!*"

I was confronted by an uncomfortable thought. What if my experiences had been determined by my sex, race or gender?

When considering Papert's essay "The Gears of My Childhood" and reflecting upon my own experiences my initial thoughts were — what if Papert wasn't exposed to cars as a child or didn't have the opportunity to play with toy gears, or even, what if he wasn't a "he," what then? Would this alternate identity have developed an "intense involvement" with automobiles, or gears, or even become a mathematician?

Erector set – 1930s advertising

Of course, we can look at this advertisement today and think that it's of its day or things were just like that back then, but have things really changed that much? Do we still see gender bias in transitional objects? Of course we do! How many people have missed learning opportunities by not being given a toy that might have become a transitional object to a passion or a deeper understanding or something because of their sex?

If you were to walk into any major toy store you will see a pattern, the pink aisle and the blue aisle. Where would you most likely find a Meccano set or an engineering toy?

In 2019, research conducted by the Royal Academy of Engineering found that just 12 percent of engineers in the UK are women and they earn on average 11 per cent less than their male counterparts.[1]

I don't want to oversimplify the issue or suggest that toys are to blame for this, but through my own experience, electronic music has the same issues. In 2020 the top 15 highest paid DJs in the world were all men.[2]

Papert said in "Gears of My Childhood" that "a modern-day Montessori might propose, if convinced by my story, to create a gear set for children."

I think this could be a positive conclusion — let us build a gear set, let us create a sewing set, let us create a whatever set! But let us not impose gender stereotypes upon these objects.

8-Bit Cross Stitch – Make Stuff North East Activity

Nostalgia plays a pivotal part in Papert's story, without his experience of automobiles and with gears and the Erector Set Papert may never have discovered his "comfortable friend" that helped him become the person he became. Some of us may never find our own "comfortable friend."

I hope that as an educator I can help others find their own "comfortable friends" and not be constrained by the vision that our modern patriarchy imposes.

Notes

1. Closing the engineering gender pay gap (2019) raeng.org.uk/media/nsgnbjah/raeng_gender-pay-gap_web.pdf
2. djcity.com.au/blog/the-worlds-highest-paid-djs-electronic-acts/

Gears of Learning

by Ridhi Aggarwal

The essay "The Gears of My Childhood" by Seymour Papert raises many questions and sparks as I reflect on my own life experiences, both my own childhood experiences and those of being an educator experiencing my student's learning experiences.

To me, the word *gear* metaphorically means a *slight push* that puts things in motion for you to learn from your own experiences. As John Dewey pointed out in his book *Democracy and Education*,

> "An ounce of experience is better than a ton of theory simply because it is only in experience that any theory has vital and verifiable significance. An experience, a very humble experience, is capable of generating and carrying any amount of theory (or intellectual content), but a theory apart from an experience cannot be definitely grasped even as theory. It tends to become a mere verbal formula, a set of catchwords used to render thinking, or genuine theorizing, unnecessary and impossible" (1916).

The nature of these experiences should be to drive inquiry and demand thinking. But what is there to inquire? Well, it can be about everything and anything in life that children have curiosity and open-ended questions about. Children should be given the opportunity to explore their questions like babies explore the world around them. Babies drop things to test their strength and sound, and form theories about the world by experimenting.

These kinds of experiences, exploring things, and playing games have been the gears of my life as they have provided opportunities for me to think, reflect, and learn.

As a child I loved playing games. But the major question back then was — *how can I possibly possess all those games or toys I see?* The constant urge to play pushed me to make new games on my own.

Hence, I started making games from old cardboard boxes, newspaper, and twigs. The games I saw at my friends or relatives' homes, I made on my own and iterated the rules to suit the material or the structure. These self-made games were not only exciting to play but actually created a lot of my mental models around problem solving, generating ideas, and resource optimization. I didn't realize this until I studied these concepts in economics and management later on in university.

These models are not just facts and concepts, but they gave me perspective to find a way through the maze if I got stuck. This was apparent one year when an accident left me with steel rods in both arms. Writing exams seemed impossible and I was advised to drop out. But I started thinking of all the possible ways I could write my exams, and I found the answer in *making*. As I was making something I realized that I still could easily cut using scissors with both of my hands. This gave me the idea to try writing with both my hands simultaneously to compensate for the loss of control in my arms. In the end I passed my exams and my perseverance and problem-solving skills were validated.

Problem solving and *learning-by-doing* had always been an integral part of my learning. But in spite of knowing and experiencing it, it was very hard to internalize it as a teacher. A lot of reflection was needed to understand how I could facilitate the kind of learning I valued in my own life. When I started to teach, I understood that the focus of my lessons should be on *doing*, and *learning* would happen as a result.

I designed many such *tasks* but in the end, they were mere *tasks*. While the children were experiencing *making*, I questioned the nature and extent of their learning.

For example, in a class where children were learning about alternative sources of energy, they made windmills and solar cookers. But there was no connection to *why* we were making them. They were busy completing the task but had no chance to incorporate what they were doing into a larger understanding. Every child followed the same process incorporating the same design. There was no opportunity to alter the course of the task to fit the *meaning-making* of any individual student.

This made me think and reflect on my experience of observing my students doing and learning. Was the making actually resulting in any kind of deep learning?

The question stayed me for a long time until one day my co-teacher and I were working with students on a project about the workings of a hand pump. I had made a working model of the hand pump to explore the nuances with students, but they seemed to be disinterested in the discussion. This was an unusual thing. On probing them, I found out that my design was flawed, and they were not sure if they should challenge my thinking and knowledge. Thus, the children NOT raising questions was answer to my question. Children would learn by doing only when they make things that are answers to their own questions. Based on this idea, we started a Question Hour in which children could just share their daily curiosities about anything and everything. They raised questions and discussed possibilities, and then they explored the ideas by making things.

In one such conversation a child raised a question about alternative sources of energy. They asked that if it's that effective, can it be used to charge a mobile phone as there was no electricity in the village and they had to walk 5–7 kilometers to a shop to charge it. To investigate the question, they read some books and did some trials before coming up with a plan to make a solar mobile charger, which they then built. It worked perfectly. This not only gave us the answer to our questions and a useful tool, but seemed to me to be the proof that questions and thinking are closely related to doing and making and learning results from inquiry.

Since then, there have been many such instances where children's questions have led to their exploration and tinkering as well as finding answers. This has led everyone in our organization to make it a priority to provide opportunities for students to do things and make things with both body as well as mind using hand and senses. Tinkering and making develops a sense of resourcefulness, a discipline of working and exploring with different types of materials and tools, even when the students attempt to construct something out of their imagination. In this process the student finds a space for creative expression instead of being a passive learner.

Aligned with children's driving curiosity, asking questions and finding answers by exploring and doing drives meaning-making in any field of knowledge. And when it is in the context of the individual child it evokes further questions. John Dewey said that experience has two core characteristics, *continuity* and *interaction*. Thus, for knowledge to be relevant it has to remain alive, and we have to make and re-make the connections rather than treating information as a finished product to be held in memory.

I believe in this maxim from John Dewey, and it has been the gear which keeps me motivated and has made me a more reflective teacher.

> "Give the pupils something to do, not something to learn; and the doing is of such a nature as to demand thinking; learning naturally results" (1916).

Reference

Dewey, J. (1916). Democracy and Education: An Introduction to the Philosophy of Education. Macmillan.

Remote Gears

by Ed Bringas

I've been engaged in Maker education now for about 16 years and I truly believe that learning should be done through an array of modalities. I find that in my own life, I tend to learn better when I hear things and make things based on what I see and touch. I also know that I'm a visual learner, I like seeing things in front of me. I like to play with objects and ideas to see how they work or relate to other ideas.

My personal "gear" story happened when I was in graduate school. I took a generative art course where we used computer programming to make animated pieces of art. There was one project where I started to play around with sines and cosines to make my animations grow and shrink to make the piece look like it was breathing. It was through that tinkering that I understood what cosine and sine were. It was also my first glimpse of what I wanted to achieve in my career, taking math that is so beautiful and finding ways to teach it in a way that made sense to others. Learning trigonometry in my junior year of high school was rather bland, it was just going through the motions of solving problems but not understanding what the point was or having an experience to ground my ideas.

Currently I co-teach a class called Trig Functions with Kate Belin. We start with students building a Ferris wheel and looking at the motion between the bottom of the ride and the top of the ride. This provides a guidepost for the experience to study the concepts. It wasn't until I started making art with trigonometry did I feel like I really understood the concepts.

Everyone has a different experience latching onto different interests and ultimately different ideas. Dr. Papert spoke of this when he said, "I fell in love with the gears." The visual representation of sine and cosine in my animation was the vehicle for me to understand the concepts deeper. But not everyone is going to understand math through Ferris wheels, gears, or generative art — but I think this diversity of understanding through experience is why I enjoy teaching Making in the classroom.

Making is an experience that connects different ways of learning to make both new ideas and objects. There's something mystical about the moment when an idea just clicks into place through the experience. What makes it very special is how intimate these ideas are to each individual. When people are Making, they are engaging with the materials all the while they are forming new ideas. Everyone is making their own connections and meaning through the process. I believe that if Dr. Papert could see a Maker classroom he would appreciate the work being done. His ideas about the computer are how I see Making, "Because it can take on a thousand forms and can serve a thousand functions, it can appeal to a thousand tastes."

As I write this and think about Making and Papert's constructionism learning theory, I think back to my daughter's parent teacher conference we just had. She is in second grade and in a week she will have been learning remotely for a whole year. She has done more remote learning than in-person instruction in her entire elementary school career. She is a lovely person, of course a parent would say that, but in truth, she loves to learn, create, and imagine. Sadly, we spoke with her teacher about how the science lessons are not engaging her. All her science lessons are watching videos. Her class is learning about simple machines and will ultimately create a bridge from these experiences, but they are learning about simple machines only through watching videos.

We chose this school not for any promises of "academic rigor" but for the holistic curriculum and the level of project-based experiences in the classroom. As a teacher, I also know the challenges of trying to do engaging remote instruction and stretching one's own creativity to include hands-on work. I wanted to communicate to the teacher that something was missing in the remote instruction. Both my wife and I believe it's the lack of engagement and socialization but how could this be improved in a remote situation? What would get my daughter into learning simple machines? What is her "gear" in all of this?

It dawned on me today after she went to a friend's home, a girl that she visits every Thursday to do science and socialize. She came home so happy to show me her Catmobile that she built with recycled boxes, straws, and bottle caps after studying wheels. She was proud to show me the charms she made with yarn, bottle caps, and hot glue.

At that moment I realized what was missing, the constructivist piece that attracted us to attend this school. With remote instruction, she was missing the hands-on learning and the magic of making connections between new ideas through the hands-on approach.

I wholeheartedly believe that she learned more about wheels today than she has the entire time watching videos about wheels. Watching her light up, beaming proudly, at what she made helped me see the glimmer of her love of learning again and of her own gears turning.

"Catmobile" By Zoë Bringas

Papert Reloaded

by Federica Selleri

Italy, March 2021. We are in the middle of a pandemic, schools are closed and, as a technology teacher, seeing children every day in Google Meet boxes is both hard and fascinating. Hard for obvious reasons — everyone is trying to talk, chatting, using the tool they have in their hands (and are forced to use), exchanging ideas, organizing online playtime together, and looking at the games others have at home — all while the teacher tries to get them to do something.

However, it is fascinating to note the children's great resilience. Their ability to always turn what they have into a way to do what they want. They have learned that every Google Meet has a code, so if the teacher has one they can create another, and get together online to talk and be together. Wanting to do something at all costs has, in some ways, "forced" them to adapt the medium to their needs, going above and beyond to help each other.

This situation reminded me of my first experiences with computers when I was a child. In my parents' house there was only one desktop computer, because my father, an IT specialist, had his own personal laptop, so he had assembled a desktop one to use at home for schoolwork, not for games. In the afternoons after school, my brother and I wanted to use the computer to play games, but without getting caught. I looked for solutions to keep us undetected, and that's how I learned to clear history and cache, open anonymous windows, put everything on my portable USB stick, change passwords, etc. It was fun watching streaming series, chatting, playing videogames, and then deleting (most of) the traces I left behind!

Of course, I was convinced that I always deleted everything, but today I can imagine that my father knew a lot more than I did and was able to see what I was up to.

But more than the practical skills I acquired, the most important lesson I learned was to analyze the problem in front of me and try many small solutions until I found a way to solve (or get around) it. It's the same thing I try to make my students understand. As a new teacher, I'm still learning many things, but I think it's fundamental to start from a "constructivist" approach to education.

In teaching technology, it is essential to develop a flexible and resilient approach, so students do not get knocked down by the first difficulty they encounter in using an app, a device, a program, a tool, etc. I'm experiencing firsthand the effort and passion it takes to support students as they learn. It's especially hard to help children at a distance, to explain to them that they don't have to give up if the program doesn't start or if the connection is slow.

The way I have found to do this is very simple and can be summed up in the word LISTENING. When you approach a digital tool you have never used before (whether it is a computer, Scratch, Google, Arduino, etc.), the first impression is often disorientation due to not knowing exactly where you are in the process or what to do. This feeling risks irreversibly conditioning any future experience of approaching technology.

Design process – from paper to prototype in schools
(Workshop designed by FabLab Valsmaoggia)

As Papert said, we need to create and take care of the conditions in which the learning process takes place, because the creation of cognitive models is closely linked to the experience associated with them.

Therefore, it is important to pay particular attention to the context in which the experience takes place, and to design it in such a way that it can be about generating ideas and not about running into obstacles. This means thinking about the tools you want students to use, and trying them out for yourself to evaluate their possibilities, but listening to the students' hypothesis about how things work and supporting their investigations.

Papert rightly declares that the computer is a tool that offers countless possibilities. However, as with gears and mathematics, it can be hated right from the start if we don't listen to students so we can create the conditions for students to be able to experiment in a constructive way.

When we approach a tool with children that they don't know, the first thing I try to do is engage their curiosity. By creating a challenge or a problem, I try to make them find their own way to the solution, supporting them when they ask for help or explanations. Exploring unknown tools in a creative and playful way creates a positive model linked to that type of experience, which will become an essential foundation for future learning processes.

What Makes a Project Meaningful?

by Lina Cannone

I have read Seymour Papert's article "The Gears of my Childhood" before and it always inspires the same questions. What is meaningful? What triggers the sense of involvement that allows children and adults to "fall in love" with a project? At this moment, I have only found partial answers to these questions.

I remember exactly when I discovered computer programming. I was 6 years old, and my father had given me a Commodore 64 for my birthday. It was not easy for me (I had just learned to read), but I found a guide to the BASIC programming language in the box with the computer. Following the instructions, I was able to write a program that would print (the printer ... such a wonderful thing!) some recipes for my mother.

I experienced a great satisfaction in creating working code that did precisely what I had imagined. I also remember that I tried to draw with asterisks, a dog as I recall. After that we had other computers with other operating systems and there was no longer the need to write programs to write a text or draw.

Commodore 64 (photo by Bill Bertram CC BY-SA 2.5)

Love blossomed again at university with a computer science class. The exercise of imagining scenarios in my head where I can foresee and imagine how to realize them has helped me in different areas of my life. I still use these skills daily, for example using recursive cycles to break down complex activities into simple structures or a routing algorithm to organize daily activities.

Now I teach in a primary school in a city near Rome. I try to offer my students different experiences so that each of them has the opportunity to find what is meaningful to her or him. In my school we are lucky to have a makerspace and I often find myself wondering what activity to propose. A few years ago, I noticed that depending on the project, not everyone felt involved. Some dedicated time to their project, carried out research, and constantly improved their artifact. Others, on the other hand, were sloppy, working in a hurry to be able to move on to the next activity. It was a difficult balance, because a too well-defined project might not emotionally involve the whole group, yet my very young students (about 6 years old) could not be expected to have the skills necessary to start from scratch.

Papert's explanation of how Logo was designed gave me new insight into this dilemma. The Logo programming language has a "low floor," allowing children to engage with minimal prerequisite knowledge, and a "high ceiling," offering opportunities to explore more complex ideas. I think this aspect is what fascinated me about computer programming in my own life, the possibility of being able to approach a challenge even as a beginner, yet having the possibility of future understand that was more complex — low floors and high ceilings.

Now I always try to suggest activities that can be accepted, adapted, or declined according to everyone's interests. Other goals are to offer a space that can be explored with a relaxed timeline, while asking stimulating questions to help them find their project idea. Sometimes we start from the materials, for example glitter or rainbow straws, other times from an idea found on Pinterest or seen the day before on YouTube ... who knows!

Another interesting aspect that I found in the article is in the following sentence: "Anything is easy if you can assimilate it to your collection of models." This construction of models happens when people have good, creative experiences. I believe that our mission as teachers and educators is to offer opportunities to our students, and to propose experiences, challenges, and learning environments that can allow everyone to discover their own version of Papert's gears. No one knows what it is until they meet them.

So, what actions can a teacher take to facilitate this meeting? I believe that a synergy between teacher and learner must be nurtured. We must abandon pre-planned activities and projects that ignore the participation of the learner. We must give way to the co-planning of activities.

I remember that when I was in front of my Commodore 64 I did it by choice, no one ever asked me to do it or told me what to do. I believe that the choice to start a project and the enthusiasm in designing and deciding what and how to do it is an important detail that makes the work meaningful.

Who Killed Our Inborn Maker Culture?

by Martin Oloo

Across Kenya, over 50,000 engineering students graduate annually from universities. But we should ask — does this translate to actual productivity? The answer is — it doesn't. This is no different from most African countries. Very little manufacturing is taking place locally and this, I believe, is directly due to the lack of practical experience in our education system. Most graduates can explain the theory of how things work, but are not confident enough to try to make things.

Growing up in the rural Africa can be the most exciting experience one would want to have as a child. Kids in these regions have no choice but to build their own toys. Resources are so scarce, and the urban life of going to a store to buy toys is just a fantasy. The culture of making was all around us, born of necessity.

I grew up in the rural parts of Western Kenya in Africa and this was my story too. When I started school, the entrance test was being asked to fold your hands over your head to touch the ear on the opposite side. The school was far away and so as

What kind of toys do your children play with? Who chooses those toys for your child?

a little boy I had to rely on joining older people to walk to school. Some of the classwork I remember from my early days included drawing lessons where we were taken out of the classroom to draw on the bare ground. Other lessons included making toys — animals, houses, cars, and household items.

As I grew older and more experienced, my peers and I started building things that mattered to us. I could spend many hours making toy cars using wires, or tangle (a plant bearing lots of round fruit) which we used as wheels. We also built more useful items, such as a wheelbarrow-like tool made of recycled automobile parts and waste materials. These could be used for transporting farm harvests to stores, enjoying the rides at no cost, or ferrying water which had to be fetched from a long distance away.

When sent to a shop, I could take my *nyangee*–a hand-made ring that you roll on the ground as you tap it, chasing it just like you roll a car tire. On this journey you would hear me reciting the items I was sent to purchase — *sukari kwota, majan gi change* — meaning ¼ kg sugar, tea leaves, and the rest of the list until I reached the shop. This was to ensure that I would get to the shop faster and avoid distraction by my friends on the way. When I reached upper primary level, I had more lessons which pushed us into more making. They included building musical instruments, making mosaics, stitching, and others, but that seemed to end with primary school. Going to high school, there were no practical subjects offered, even though as an individual, I remained interested in making and repairing things.

My life took a different turn when I became a community social worker fighting gender violence and promoting children rights. I remember one day when I was working at a childcare center and a volunteer from Ireland bought LEGOs for the kids; this became my one of primary responsibilities to play with the kids and help them make various toys out of LEGO.

Later while working to establish a Gender Violence Recovery Centre (GVRC), we decided to do a survey and I went to the field to collect data. I spoke to so many girls and young women in their early twenties who were single mothers, divorced, or married but all suffering Gender Based Violence (GBV).

As a social worker, I did not have much to give other than counseling and hope. But they were suffering and they needed more help than that. They were in a vicious cycle of poverty and most of them had dropped out of school. Their spouses were often also very young school drop-outs — frustrated men who had turned to drug addiction and domestic violence. What kind of support do they deserve? They all agreed that they needed hands-on skills that would help them generate their own income.

I relate to this quote from Seymour Papert's "The Gears of My Childhood,"

> "What an individual can learn, and how he learns it, depends on what models he has available. This raises, recursively, the question of how he learned these models. Thus the 'laws of learning' must be about how intellectual structures grow out of one another and about how, in the process, they acquire both logical and emotional form."

This vision inspired me to enroll in the Fab Academy Digital Fabrication Course in 2016[1] which rekindled the maker fire in me.

This then led to the establishment of FABrication LABoratory Winam, an innovation makerspace where makers can share both tools and knowledge to learn to custom-make things they want and need.[2]

Working in Fablab Winam with different makers, learners, professionals, and kids has provided me with a unique opportunity of seeing how making and Papert's learning theory of constructionism are applicable in the real world.

Even with the number of innovation hubs growing quickly in Africa, there are still many questions. Will the efforts of makers who are focused on working with children revive our dying culture of making and self-sufficiency? Can teaching people to make things spark cottage industries that help people, especially women, escape poverty and violence?

This maker culture can have impact on individual lives and our whole country. I am hopeful that maker culture may turn around the economy of our country and encourage a lot of local manufacturing. These cottage industries could have an impact on the multiple crises currently facing the country. When more young people get a chance to make things not just in their early lives, but as a respected part of all education, maybe we can answer these questions and change this story.

Notes

1. archive.fabacademy.org/fabacademy2016/fablabgearbox/students/163/
2. fablabwinam.org/

Finding My Gear at Twenty-Three

by Nadine Abu Tuhaimer

After reading Dr. Papert's "The Gears of My Childhood," I realized that I found my gear long past my childhood.

As a kid I used to love tinkering with anything I could get my hands on, whether it was an old toy with a mechanical movement, an old computer, or even random household objects.

Luckily, I grew up with a mom who loved tinkering herself and a father who as a mechanical engineer, had every tool there is to help me in this hobby of mine.

When I finished high school, I thought my passion was programming. I had a knack for writing programs and analyzing how the digital world works. I was lucky enough to be born at the time where I was young enough to know the internet but was still able to play in the streets. So naturally I decided to study something related to my love for the digital world, which is why I studied computer engineering. After graduation, I realized that my love for tinkering with objects outshined my love for programming, I love to see the tangible results of what I do and not have them confined to a computer screen. That's when I stumbled across the Fab Lab world.

I was like Willy Wonka walking around in my own version of a chocolate factory. I was 23 when I first learned what a Fab Lab was, which is a space with different tools that enables people to build customized solutions to problems. There was no lower or upper limit to what the problem can be, whether you wanted to just customize a mobile stand or build cutting-edge products that could be turned into viable businesses.

At 24, I decided to take the "Fab Academy – How to Make Almost Anything" course. This is a six month long intensive program that teaches the principles of digital fabrication. With a background in programming, I do admit that it was easier for me than some of my colleagues.

Since then, I've been teaching in the Fab Academy program and trying to incorporate what I learned with the different educational programs I run at the Fab Lab where I work, the first Fab Lab in Jordan.

I incorporate hands-on practical learning methodology in almost all the Fab Lab educational programs. I believe in the importance of engagement, if kids are engaged, it is more likely they will develop an interest and a passion for whatever they are learning.

Although I know there is truly no age limit to finding your gear, I still aim to maximize the exposure of youth to as much as possible at a young age to enable them to find their passion and their own gear as quickly as possible.

Jordan's first Mobile FabLab, "Luminus Mobile FabLab Sponsored by Orange".

Making Means Head and Heart, Not Just Hands

by Lior Schenk

Can you recall the secret thrills of your childhood? The deep fascinations that enraptured you? We might call them obsessions, fixations, or phases — as doomed to end as the passing of seasons — for even as I was filling my room and imagination with dinosaurs, I never became a paleontologist. Neither did Seymour Papert who "developed an intense involvement with automobiles before the age of two," become an automotive engineer. The deep fascinations of our childhood are but infantile experiences — and so we are quick to forget them in the grounds of our becoming.

For Papert, however, these pastimes of playing with car parts — turning gears with his hands, rotating all manner of circular objects against each other, learning the stories of their functioning — fostered within him a deep love for gears that transcended innocent playthings. The gears instead served as material medium to the universe's most poetic distillations. *Car child* did not become *car professional* — he became a mathematician.

He also became a cyberneticist and renowned learning theorist, responsible for both the 1:1 computing initiatives and the constructionist movements rippling across education to this day. As a preface to his seminal book on constructionism, *Mindstorms*, Papert reflects on the gears of his childhood. Gears were, he describes, "both abstract and sensory," acting as "a transitional object" connecting the formal knowledge of mathematics and the body knowledge of the child.

As he turned wheels in head and hand alike, the complex patterns of differentials and transmission shafts and mental gear models provided the means for Papert the child to see mathematics in his own world. Multiplication tables and variables and algebraic equations alike were all embedded in the workings of the gears! Thus they were not abstract, but rather "comfortable friends" substantiated and reified in the things he had come to know and love.

This notion of knowing — what it means to know something, to learn, to develop knowledge — formed the central thesis of Papert's career. Knowledge is not merely absorbed through cognitive assimilation, but actively constructed through affective components as well. Papert would assert, in other words, that we learn best when we are actively engaged in constructing things in the world. Real, tangible things. Things you can hold, manipulate, and feel in order to make sense of them.

Look inside schools, however, and you shall largely see a different picture. Rather than learning the world by reading and writing the world, experiencing it with the fullest of our senses, we learn the world by hastily memorizing facts about the world. Or, as Harvard Graduate School of Education professor David Perkins suggests, schools suffer from "aboutitis" — never getting to play the whole game and only learning *about* the game (2010).

Perhaps this is why the so-called maker revolution is surging today. In a school culture where learning has become so rote, so mechanized, and so devoid of meaning, making is an attempt to restore meaning to education. We can also call it hands-on learning or student-centered pedagogy. When going to school means jumping through hoops, and when boredom in the classroom is higher than ever, we as educators are called to shift what it means to learn in school.

But there are problems with these movements as well. Hands-on activities like making slime or crafting Grecian urns can offer the illusion of disciplinary engagement — *this is science, this is cultural literacy, and hey the kids are having fun too!* But following cookbook instructions does not equal scientific inquiry and slapping gluey newspaper on balloons does not equal historical analysis. Similarly, making a model of a cell, whether it is from paper or cake or plastic, lends no further understanding of how cells function if the student is not also thinking how their model works as a model for cells! What are the parts, how are they connected, why do they look the way they do, how are they complex?

Too often we leap into hands-on activities with the belief that because they are fun, they are engaging and therefore students will learn more deeply. But we are mistaken when having fun merely means being entertained. Through the trap of passivity we shall learn nothing.

But I also think a component is often left out, and that is *the heart*. When Papert writes of his involvement with gears, he does not limit his language to just cognitive and sensorimotor actions. He is adamant in describing the *emotional* forms of his play: positive affect, feelings of joy, wonder, magic, and love. And he speaks of *love* quite often — most pointedly, when he asserts that the "essence of the story" is not in the doling out of gear sets for all future generations of children but that he as so poignantly "fell in love with the gears," other people will fall in love with other things. Papert's successes, as he would ascribe, were not due to interacting with gears as objects — rather due to *falling in love* with the gears as *more than objects*, as a conduit across intellectual and emotional worlds.

I think this concept of love is worth further attention in teaching and learning. Not love as a toxic unwavering positivity, and definitely not love as dedication to test scores. I mean love as understanding, interconnection, and interbeing. When we stretch our perceptive faculties through deepest care, expansive listening, and attending to another, it allows us to see people for who they really are. As Dr. Humberto Maturana said, "Love, allowing the other to be a legitimate other, is the only emotion that expands intelligence."

We expand our notions of objects from that of reductive othering *It* to that of fullest personhood *Thou* (Martin Buber) — surely that must be the heart of learning! A change of paradigms made manifest in our very perception of others-in-the-world, down to our most fundamental cognitive and neural architectures. What if, as educators, we invested our energy towards such heart in our curriculum? What do we want our students to *love*, in fullest understanding and appreciation? I think that goes far deeper than, say, *what standards do we want our students to master!*

Making is a vital act. Not because it is assumed to be fun, or entertaining, or an escape from the traditional disciplines of schooling — though all of the above are often true. Making is vital because it *represents* what teaching and learning could and should be. When students are actively engaged in the construction of a meaningful product in order to be shared with the community, THAT is powerful learning! Uncanny, because it seems so obvious. Complex, because it is so difficult to achieve. Yet revolutionary, because it is precisely what is missing in so many classrooms today.

Revolutionary also, because it is a shift in how we relate to things in the world. Making is not just about giving kids things to put their hands on. It's about embracing the agency of children as learners, and their agency over media and the material world. It's about shifting the paradigm from students as receivers of knowledge to students as constructors of knowledge. It's about letting go of the mindset of command and control. It's about liberation. It's about the heart of what it means to be human — fully sensing and making sense of the complex world in which we are bodily immersed.

We live in a time where we are profoundly disconnected from nature, from each other, and our own selves. We are so disembodied, and we yearn to become whole. I daresay that making is not just vital but sacred to being human. Without it, we are lost. So let us come to our senses and make way. This is the way.

Reference

Perkins, D. (2010). *Making learning whole: How seven principles of teaching can transform education*. John Wiley & Sons.

Stop Waiting to Love Learning Again

by Kristin Burrus

I've been a little worried lately. Not about the world, or politics, or COVID-19 — well yes, of course about those things, but lately I've been mostly worried that I've forgotten how to teach. I feel out of practice and out of touch. Everyone in education is a bit out of practice, having spent a lot of time teaching remotely, learning how to use Zoom, learning how to be somewhat engaging for our students online, and learning how to connect with people at a distance.

In the midst of all this I have been transitioning from an established position in a school where I taught for 20 years to a FabLab Lead Teacher role at the Global Center for Digital Innovation (GCDI) in Chattanooga, Tennessee. It's intimidating, exciting, and amorphous.

My job description is all about collaborating with classroom teachers to help integrate maker education and digital fabrication into content areas, inspiring kids of all ages to create prototypes of their innovative ideas, and giving community members a space to try their hand at entrepreneurialism. It is truly a dream job! And so far, I'm still just dreaming about it.

Reflectively, I feel like I am pretty good with change, and I love a challenge. It's the delay that has made me nervous. In the midst of a global pandemic, the building construction stalled, and an opening date of August 2021 has been pushed back all the way back to… not yet. A tentative move-in date of April 2021, has been promised and I am cautiously hopeful. Eight months of planning at first seemed a blessing. But some of my confidence has waned with the passing months. How will I get the space ready for kids in time for summer camp? Do I remember how to use all of the equipment? What supplies do I need to order? How long does it realistically take to put together a full-sized ShopBot? And most importantly, do I remember how to teach?

Of course, I haven't been idle for eight months. I have been working with students the whole time. This year teaching has been more informal and focused on small groups of students who want coaching on soldering, or laser cutting, or Fusion 360. I have facilitated professional development workshops for teachers both in person and virtually. I have been productive and contributed to the school community. In many ways, it has been the best teaching experience of my career. But I just can't shake that feeling of uneasiness while I wait…

Fast forward to about a week ago, when I read, "The Gears of My Childhood" by Seymour Papert. Papert begins by explaining how much he loved cars as a child and how he found an affinity for understanding the interactions of gears, particularly the differential. Honestly, my first thought was, "Oh no, do I need to understand a differential?" Then I realized the story was really about how Papert credits the experience of loving gears and being able to use a differential as a model of learning for his successes in mathematics. He states, "Anything is easy if you can assimilate it to your collection of models. If you can't, anything can be painfully

FabLab under construction. Photo Credit: Betty A. Proctor, Chattanooga State Community College

difficult." I completely agree. When knowledge can be connected to previous experiences or mental models it fits within a student's mind and can be more easily learned. But it must also be loved, like Papert loved gears, to be transformative.

After Papert points it out, it seems so obvious that our ability to learn is tangled up in our emotions. As a child, I found comfort in the natural world. I loved figuring out how bugs and plants and mammals all interacted and needed each other. It is no surprise that my major in college was biology. I loved systems — at first, the only systems I could see were ecological, then I started seeing systems in things like bicycles, and eventually, I started seeing systems in the art of teaching. It became fun to plan lessons for students that sparked inquiry and wonder.

Students aren't aware of all the "strings" holding together a complex unit plan, intertwined like a food web, and designed to lead them toward self-discovery and hopefully a love for learning.

Papert wrote, "The understanding of learning must be genetic. It must refer to the genesis of knowledge." Maybe it is the science teacher in me that wonders if this statement was a bit of a joke, but I like the idea that it is the genesis or beginnings of learning that impacts students the most. It includes the how, when, and where of learning.

Now one of my favorite systems to observe is a group of students highly invested in brainstorming solutions or making a new design, they invest both their minds and emotions when working on a meaningful problem. There is a genuine sense of pride, maybe even love, in creating something out of nothing.

Maker education provides kids with the opportunity to examine how things work, how systems are interconnected, and how they can influence those systems through innovation and creation.

Perhaps the uneasiness I've been feeling lately stems from the fact that I've been in limbo, not really knowing how things in my life are connected or how our pandemic world will adhere to the previous rules of cause and effect. Patterns have changed; interactions are no longer predictable. It's been a dark year and I feel like maybe my fears about teaching are simply a manifestation of my fears about the world.

I am looking forward to awakening a renewed love of learning for myself and my students in the GCDI and creating lessons with intertwined "strings" that lead students to new discoveries about themselves and their world. That's why I see April as a date for change, for moving forward, for taking back some control, and a date to just stop waiting. I know moving into the new FabLab is really only a symbol, however, I need it and I will take it!

Motivation

by Charles Pimentel

Seymour Papert's essay "The Gears of my Childhood" made me think about the ancient story of a young man named David, who defeated the mighty giant Goliath in an epic battle. Maybe you know this story well or maybe you have only heard about it.

David was small, had no resources, and was alone in this fight, but he did something that changed his story — he put his heart into that duel. And he won the battle.

But why did I remember David?

Papert's story, which talks about the way in which he put his heart into his relationship with the gears and how that changed the way he saw the world around him, reminds me of David. This story reminds us that in life what we do needs to have meaning and motivation. That is an important reflection for us, both as educators and as apprentices. Papert's story also reminded me of my own story. Maybe you also have memories of someone, or something, that changed your view of the world.

Some years ago, I had the opportunity to read an article by the Brazilian writer Rubem Alves, which was published in a large newspaper in Brazil. In that article he used a phrase that touched my heart, *"curiosity is an itch in the ideas."* That phrase became the gear of my life as an educator.

As a mathematics teacher, I always hear the same question from my students, *"Where am I going to use this formula in my life?"* — usually related to the Bhaskara (quadratic) formula. It is a valid question, especially if that student has no interest in the field of mathematics.

I would love for my students to create connections between the real world and math. For a teacher of this discipline, it is wonderful to have students who, like Papert, have models that inspire them and help them see meaning in what they do. It is thought-provoking how Papert knew at a young age that he understood the functioning of gears and the structure of differentials so well, including making connections between them and mathematical equations.

I remembered my childhood, how I used to ask so many questions and how curious I was. And I thought: *"How can I create a space that fosters my students' curiosity? How can I help them have ideas that itch?"* I concluded that my classes should be more constructionist, that is, more exploratory.

One of the first projects I developed with my students was the Mousetrap Car, where students build cars powered by the spring of a mousetrap. This project became another gear for me. I started to see different applications for the Mousetrap Car project in math and science courses. I could see that students were engaged and motivated, filming their cars on their smartphones, figuring out the trajectory, and using calculators to estimate the speed of their prototype.

Shortly afterwards, I expanded my activities to educational robotics with LEGO Mindstorms and to the electronic prototyping platform Arduino.

At that point, I also developed interactive math quiz projects with my students, using the visual programming language Scratch, and introducing concepts of computational thinking. What I found was that the "itch in the ideas" that I wished for my students had started to take hold in me. Thus, I became an educator who researches new methodologies and technologies for teaching mathematics.

This new identity led me to new paths. In 2018, I was involved in the implementation of the makerspace at Polo Educacional Sesc, where I was a math teacher. I collaborated with other educators

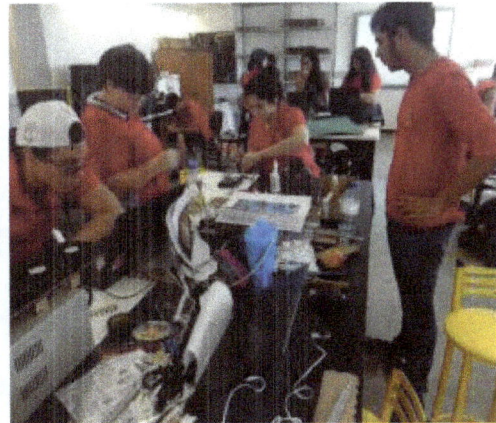

Designer in Digital Fabrication training course

on the creation of the course called Designer in Digital Fabrication, an initiative to empower the students to use the resources available in our new makerspace 3D printers, laser cutter, and other prototyping resources through the Design Thinking process.

I began to participate in makerspace educator training with our network of schools. These actions inspired me even further and became the differential in my professional life.

By merging low- and high-tech resources for hands-on activities, my eyes were opened to a new perspective on math teaching. That was how in 2019 I created the Maker Math course.

Teaching mathematics through digital fabrication, educational robotics, and artificial intelligence is the guiding thread of this course. Mathematics, which exists in all these technologies, allows the student to develop skills and competences through the development of projects of interest.

Stimulating curiosity and promoting incentives for the student to put their heart into what they are learning is a good start for a meaningful and enjoyable classroom. The giant Goliath, for many students, represents their efforts to create a connection between what is taught at school and the real world.

But there is nothing like strong motivation to help learners to move on and overcome difficulties. The term motivation is derived from the Latin word *movere*, which means "to move." Motivation can be defined as "the forces that act on or within a person that cause the awakening, the direction and the persistence of the voluntary effort directed towards an objective."

Papert was moved by his gears, and they reverberated in a life focused on research, innovation, and the inspirational constructionist theory of learning. I found meaning in seeing this come to life in the work of my students and their incredible motivation to learn and grow.

Educator training

Time to Tinker

by Lars Beck Johannsen

Gears!

What comes easy to you?

Love it, show it, share.

Connect, evolve, and have fun!

When Seymour Papert tells the childhood story of his love for gears, he tells a story about a system of tangible objects that became obvious to him, though it would seem complex to others. Through play and love for the turning and interaction between the gears he gained a scaffold to learn other subjects. Papert, for example, mentions an experience where he understood multiplication and variables through his mental image of how gears worked.

The point here is not that every child will learn multiplication by learning how gears work. The learning experience is very personal. We all have our own version of gears. His love for gears, physical objects he could manipulate, and experiment with gave him a mental representation of the mechanics that translated into other concepts.

What can we learn from this?

I think that it is difficult in most classroom situations to see the gears of the individual pupil. Some kids are explicit about their special interest or excel in obvious ways. But many of us might not even be aware of our own gears. I, for one, have trouble naming my own gear. Maybe it is because I am more of a generalist. I don´t know. I have always loved many different things, and would rather learn something new than master what I am already able to do. Of course, that is not true in every aspect. I spend a lot of time teaching, tinkering, and creating music but I will not say that I have mastered them — yet.

I believe that we need to help our students discover their own gears, and help them channel it into their projects whenever possible. I also believe that it is a teacher's task to help students develop new gears. Another task is being aware of the way you learn. If something is easy to you, it is natural to believe that it is also easy for everyone else, but that is not the case. We need to help our kids to discover their strengths!

There are a few things that could make this happen. One is knowing your students! Not just on a factual basis but also on a more personal basis. How would you otherwise discover, what makes them tick, what they love, who they are?

Time, patience and more unsupervised time!

It takes time to build relationships that are genuine. And it takes time for the child to immerse oneself. I sometimes worry about the small amount of unsupervised time that each child has for themselves during a day. In Denmark the school days were recently made substantially longer, basically to perform better in PISA and other tests. Though the intentions were to reform the school system, the reality was more of the same — a lot of instruction. Fortunately, we have solid traditions for teaching using projects but that is a rather small part of the school day. Especially in 8th and 9th grade, which concludes our basic school, teachers often depend on instructional teaching, because they have so much to cover before exams. I know that is the standard argument for not working more with projects.

When I was a child the school days were about 4–5 hours each day including breaks. I had a lot of time after school on my own or with friends. There were no adults present to manage our activities, and we did a lot of tinkering in that time — sometimes rather dangerous things, but that is another story for another time. That extra time is now taken away by our school system and filled with textbooks. I strongly urge all the schools I work with to make time for more project based, constructionist, student-centered learning. The after-school programs, which most kids attend because the parents are working, also need to be a more inspiring place to spend your time. A place to tinker, do what you love, make stuff together with other kids, and have fun! They need to be places where the adults know when to leave kids alone, and when to help and guide them.

Think of your favorite childhood game or activity ... where was the adult?

True, meaningful learning comes from within the child — not from an adult telling you what to do!

Make sure they get time to tinker!

Freedom! It Is Easy to See

by Michael Mumbo

Many times during my childhood, I was misunderstood not only by my caregivers but also by my peers. Even my teachers, who I view as my destiny makers, sometimes misunderstood me. Life and education in rural Kenya back then was an adventurous experience accompanied with the bliss of childhood memories; such as the school bells that reminded us when it's playtime or when class time was over. The sound of the school bell could open a whole new chapter in the day, where playtime went on until dusk. Getting home in the dark however, meant knowing this will not end well, but you still march home like a movie star only to be ushered in to the disciplinary committee.

But blissful childhood memories aside, mathematics was a real "monster" to me.

Math class made me feel like I had thoughts that made sense in my brain, but I couldn't express the ideas verbally or through writing. I know now that I have an inquisitive nature that required patience and deep understanding and above all freedom to think differently, things not found in my village school.

To my parents I was that family lawyer, they called me *okil kamaloka* — the lawyer. I always wanted to see that statements and assumptions made sense. However, I knew I had to be extra careful especially before my mother or else things would be rough at home and also at school, because she was a teacher in the same school I went to. I can vividly recall my nice morning walk to school coming to an end when I was met with the stroke of the cane for incomplete or incorrect math assignments.

It took me a while to realize that the rote nature of math wasn't my favorite cup of coffee. I was curious about numbers, patterns, and whether they made sense. Statistics let me satisfy my curiosity about how things worked.

My high school math career had fun moments

School Bell

and a few instances of strong smashes on my head by my teachers. My math teachers always said that things were easy to see in their eyes, and sometimes I saw them too. It seemed like my math journey was taking a turn from being misunderstood to understanding.

In my work with kids, they have taught me three important things: the art of patience in teaching and learning, to honor the freedom to think differently, and to remember that what is so obvious to adults is not always obvious to kids. I find it awesome, and a moment of pure bliss when one of my students can ask a question that uncovers assumptions about what seems obvious but isn't!

For example, when looking at a grid, why do we count the corner twice while getting the dimensions for length and width? The moment a child innocently asks you to help them understand what you have always found to be obvious is a moment that makes a teacher. Children have this weird ability to not know many things yet! This means that until they experience it or are taught, nothing is obvious to them. As a math teacher, I am learning to be more careful in my assumptions.

Back in my high school days, I was obsessed with logic. This made me think for a moment, maybe I had inherited my mother's prowess in accounting and money matters despite her limited educational background. In business studies, accounting was always a option, and my confidence in my own abilities made me think accounting was my destiny. I was all wrong.

Math started to make more sense when I went to university as a math major. It even became exciting in an introduction to logic, proofs, and refutations class. I felt like my nerve endings were ignited, as I realized that the math monster of my younger days was something I could conquer. I fear so many young people never get past this monster, and as a result, there are so many untapped skills and great minds lost in the pool of conventional learning. I have always found joy and beauty in collegial math discussions and for this reason, I resolved to help and support young learners in trying to regain the long-lost glory of the language of math.

Math is freedom

Finding Gears Late

by Rafael Vargas

Papert's fascination with gears relates to his childhood learning. He developed an interpretation of mathematics in the gears' inherent mechanical properties and function. His fascination with gears had a direct relationship with understanding how automobiles operate, which was a topic of immense interest for Papert when he was young. This assimilation of the model of gears is what engaged him with mathematics and made him feel comfortable with equations.

Being currently involved in various education initiatives in Puerto Rico, I can identify that I did not have that kind of assimilation with specific models related to any learning experience when I was a child. I also disassociated my topics of interest in school and what I was thought to be practical at the moment. Perhaps this is unsurprising, due to how I was exposed to mathematics and sciences in my early childhood.

It was later in my life, when I was studying architecture as an undergraduate student, that I started viewing the buildings and the products that I was designing as systems, meaning structures composed of complex parts. I discovered my fascination with technology and its usefulness as a tool to solve problems. I was ultimately inclined to explore design through science, mathematics, and emerging technologies, and learned topics like programming, parametric design, and digital fabrication. Those tools required me to be proficient in certain skills that I was not interested in learning before, unless it was to pass an exam.

Nevertheless, I was always attracted to the science and mathematics disciplines (in their pure and traditional forms), just not in a playful way that I found interesting. Now, I find it interesting that my inclination towards creative fields was always treated by school as something unrelated to mathematics. It was when I was exposed to having to solve real design problems in my adulthood that I had to revisit and relearn these connections.

While Papert's constructionist theory of learning focuses on the importance of tools, it also stresses the idea of context. The immediate context of the person learning is vital to assimilate cognitive skills and apply actual action to developing knowledge. Learning is an experience of self-reliance, and being a maker becomes an advantageous skill for problem-solving.

I believe that, as an educator, understanding this is essential at a personal level. Curiosity about trying to find out how things operate is something I can observe in students when working on projects in our workshops and classes.

The immediate context of some of the students in Puerto Rico is an economic crisis: hurricanes, earthquakes, and a current pandemic. The significant challenge (and opportunity) is to provide the processes and spaces for individuals to find their "gears" in this context, and not have to wait for adulthood.

Between the Garage and the Electronics Workshop

by Mouhamadou Ngom

My learning story is similar to Seymour Papert's story of learning many things through mechanics. I come from a modest family and I stopped going to school at an early age to help my parents.

When I was 15, I walked into a car garage to learn a trade — mechanics. Being very young, my role was to do some light tasks for the adults.

Two years later, my uncle who worked in a fuel distribution company with a car garage inside, took me under his wing. A year after that, my boss, an employee in this company, opened another garage and I started working for him.

I stayed there for four years before meeting Moussa, an electronics expert who transformed my life. Moussa repaired video games and had a very well equipped shop with generators, oscilloscopes, and other tools I didn't know about.

I began to watch him work, and I listened to his discussions with the other technicians, although I didn't understand a thing. I watched and listened to them religiously without understanding the terms used.

Eventually I would arrive at 6 pm every day after the garage closed and stay until 10 pm, so I spent all morning in the garage and all evening with Moussa.

This is where I made my first electronic creations: a radio made with recycled parts, an intercom installed at the door of our house, and an FM transmitter to broadcast music in the neighborhood.

Two years later I went back to school for training in electronics and computer science.

I repaired a lot of electronic devices and I participated in the installation of the first Fab Lab in Senegal.

To conclude, I would say that the most important part of learning by doing is careful observation.

My secret as a specialist in electro-mechanics is to take careful notes. For example, before disassembling a mechanism, I mark the intersections between the different gears.

This is why I ask learners to observe well, to listen well, and to document their work.

Reading "The Gears of My Childhood" Again

by Nusarin Nusen

After I finished to reading "The Gears of My Childhood" by Seymour Papert, it made me think about what I learned from this article during my master's degree. In Thailand, this article is widely discussed in teacher education programs, especially among constructionists in Thailand.

From understanding what Seymour learned from gears, I found it liberated my thinking about learning. Observation of one's own interests becomes tacit knowledge for that person. New knowledge gets inside your mind and connects with one's existing knowledge. This type of learning is such an individual process. Only the person who experiences it can construct their own knowledge. Moreover, I'm impressed with the power of the computer, and I agree that the computer can help us see concepts such as simulation and feedback very quickly. Troubleshooting is a process of correction that is helpful in acquiring new knowledge.

However, in some school cultures, especially in conventional Thai schools, schools often make students feel insecure about exploring and expressing what they think. The mindset is that everything has only one correct answer. This instills a mindset in our students that being correct is good and mistakes are bad. If someone makes mistakes, the teacher will cross out the wrong answers with a red pen or will give a zero score. This means students can't learn from mistakes because they do not want to make any mistakes and eventually they become a person who lacks the confidence to try things on their own.

From my teaching experience in constructionist schools, I've found that each student connects, understands, and creates their knowledge in different ways and also at different levels. It depends on their background experience, observation skills, and how well they can connect the new knowledge to old knowledge.

For me, the essential parts of learning are not only arranging hands-on learning experience for students, but also providing the opportunity for students to make decisions on their own, to try things, and learn from mistakes. To me, those are the first steps for students to gain confidence and feel comfortable enough to try things and construct their own knowledge.

Find Your Unique Gear

Xiaoling Zhang

There is a Chinese saying: "You may figure out a person's future from his childhood." I think it applies well to the experience that Dr. Seymour Papert shared with us in "The Gears of My Childhood."

It seems that many important events in Dr. Papert's life can be traced back to the gear systems that brought him joy in early childhood. Understanding gears became a starting point which drove his development as a human being, mathematician, and researcher.

Dr. Papert's experience makes me think that it might be a natural human instinct to love fiddling with objects as a prompt to explore the world around us. By building and playing with things, we are also building the connections between ourselves and the physical world. When it happens frequently and reliably, then it becomes a way of thinking. It makes it easier when we see consistency in the world to believe that there are laws behind seemingly superficial phenomena and to discover even more possibilities.

> "By the time I had made a mental gear model of the relation between x and y, figuring how many teeth each gear needed, the equation had become a comfortable friend."

For someone like me who is not that good at mathematics, I am still not able to thoroughly figure out how the equation relates to a mental gear model. However, I can empathize with the thrilling feeling when my students and I discover something new when making a project and it "clicks." It echoes what Dr. Papert says in this essay,

> "Assimilating equations to gears certainly is a powerful way to bring old knowledge to bear on a new object. But it does more as well."

By more, he is saying that it is more than just learning something, it creates a good feeling, a "positive affective tone." For me, this affective aspect of assimilation is the power behind making-based learning.

> "But I was painfully aware that some people who could not understand the differential could easily do things I found much more difficult. Slowly I began to formulate what I still consider the fundamental fact about learning: Anything is easy if you can assimilate it to your collection of models. If you can't, anything can be painfully difficult. Here too I was developing a way of thinking that would be resonant with Piaget's. The understanding of learning must be genetic. It must refer to the genesis of knowledge."

My understanding of this is that every child or every person has their own unique "gear." But can everyone find their gear? Or can we help them to find something that THEY love and can be applied as a bridge to understand more abstract ideas and the world. It seems that unique gear can't be cloned or taught, but must be discovered.

Through making, I found that one of my gears is to be open to discovering new possibilities. While embracing the uncertainty, the projects inspired both myself and my students.

Four years ago, my former students did a mini exhibition project based on the themes of the Chinese culture unit in my Chinese second language class. Despite the limited time and materials, the products that students made surpassed my expectations. That experience gave me the first taste of the charm of making.

What making projects brings to our brains is like the turning of different gears. Some are turning one way, and others are going the opposite way, yet they work together to bring out new thoughts and ideas and in turn, greater enthusiasm in teaching and learning. That's why when I was introduced to the idea of a makerspace, I immediately wished to try for myself and make it "click" into more learning experiences.

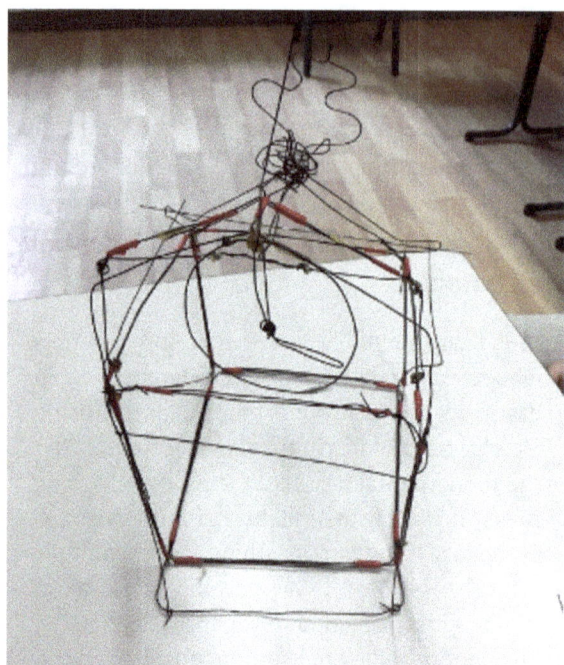 

These images are from a pre-makerspace student building design project. It combines a Western clocktower on one side, while the other side is in the style of a traditional Chinese pavilion.

First trial product in the makerspace with a group of four students.
A Chinese style partition screen interpreting their understanding of an ancient poem.

The Gear of Innovation

Débora Garofalo

When reading the essay by Seymour Papert, "The Gears of My Childhood," the preface to his 1980 book *Mindstorms: Children, Computers and Powerful Ideas*, I couldn't help reflecting on my own purpose and work with education.

For me, the story of the gears is about finding the things that motivate me. I am passionate about finding ways to make it possible for my students to be protagonists of their own lives by having the opportunity for engaging and meaningful learning by using the lessons of constructivism and of Paulo Freire. So, when I started working with scrap robotics for children and young people from underprivileged communities in São Paulo, Brazil, I wanted to provide them with an education that focused on creativity and problem solving, but that also involved academics.

My purpose was to show them that the universe of programming and robotics was also for them. To do this, it was necessary to invent new paths in education so that experimentation, doing, creativity, and meaning had increased importance. The maker movement was instrumental in that transformation.

Like Papert, I believe that the "gears" available to students need to be revised. In our case, the maker movement made it possible to give a new meaning to traditional areas of knowledge, to bring experimentation and playfulness to the teaching and learning process, and to introduce active and innovative methodologies so my students could have new experiences and understandings of the world.

These changes brought solid results. It gave me new understandings as well, as I was learning, teaching, and trying to mediate new processes all at the same time. Therefore, not only did we find new paths for learning, but we have also created a new teaching methodology that today has transformed public policy and impacted 2.5 million students. It has had enduring outcomes such as the creation of the São Paulo Basic Education Innovation Center, an organization that develops methods, practices and technologies to drive innovation in public education.[1]

Notes

1. centrodeinovacao.educacao.sp.gov.br/

Making Do: Adaptations for COVID and Remote Learning

The third cohort of FabLearn Fellows started their journey in early 2020, the same time as the COVID-19 pandemic spread around the globe, changing our lives forever. It would be impossible to ignore the impact of the pandemic both personally and professionally. Educators in schools around the world worked valiantly to support their communities in a scary time when no one really knew what was safe and what could result in deadly infections.

In some schools, tools and materials were simply boxed up and put away for fear of spreading disease. In some, makerspaces were repurposed as classrooms. Other schools worked to provide hands-on materials to students to make sure that the benefits of making could be maintained during times of remote learning. Some schools pivoted to digital making, including programming, as a way to ensure students had creative opportunities even without physical materials.

What we learned during this time should not be forgotten as things return to "normal." We learned, once again, that learning is not contained in a building or bound to the traditional trappings of subjects, bell schedules, tests, and grades. Learning happens in communities that care about each other and want to make the world a better place, no matter the obstacles.

You will see the impact of COVID-19 throughout this book, but this section in particular reveals the ingenuity of real-time adaptations to a changing landscape, the "making do" part of making.

Six Little Lessons Learned from COVID-19

by Federica Selleri

6 Little Lessons Learned from COVID-19.

1- We need more spaces and more nature. Possibly together.

2- In the end, distancing can be somehow useful.

3- It is important to remember this experience. For the future, just in case.

Making Do: Adaptations for COVD and Remote Learning

4- Can we please take back control of our technologies?

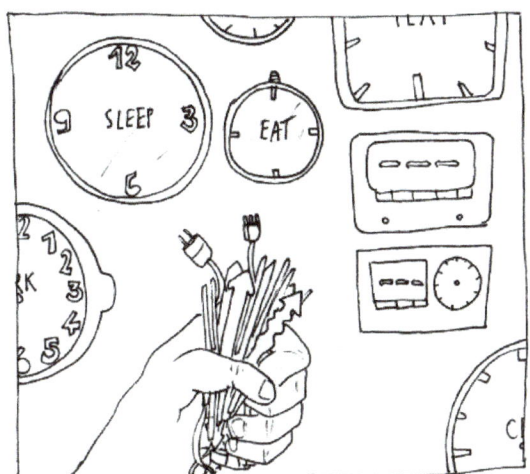

5- We should learn again how to give everything the right amount of time.

6- Creativity works wonders.

*Based on a real story from a primary school in Modena, Italy.

Online Teacher Training in Mathematics Education: A Maker and STEM Approach to Promote Active Learning

by Charles Pimentel

In 2021 in the midst of the COVID-19 pandemic, I was invited to organize two-week long online teacher training workshops for Mathematics teachers from public schools in the Brazilian state of Rio de Janeiro.

I thought it would be a great opportunity to talk about using maker education and an integrated STEM (Science, Technology, Engineering, and Math) approach to the teaching of mathematics. Although I had already given some hands-on courses for math teachers, the opportunity to carry out this type of activity virtually made me very excited.

But I wondered, would it be effective to do maker activities virtually?

Teacher training is the best investment in education

Nothing is more important to education than a well-prepared teacher.

According to Brazilian mathematician Marcelo Viana (director of the Brazilian National Institute for Pure and Applied Mathematics – IMPA[1]), training is the Achilles' heel, meaning the weakest part, of helping teachers teach math in Brazil (Viana, 2017).

Giraldo states that university education can have essentially no effect on teacher's understanding of how to teach math. In Brazil, undergraduate courses in the Mathematics Licentiate favor academic mathematics, without paying attention to school mathematics, nor to the methodologies for teaching the discipline (Giraldo, 2018).

Thus, the classroom reference for educators who graduate from higher education and start working in basic education *are the experiences they had, as students, during their school life* (Cabreira, 2016). This truth leads to a repeated cycle in the educational process, where teachers teach the way they were taught, most often as a passive spectator in the classroom.

To change this situation, the ongoing education of mathematics teachers is important to break this cycle and take new paths (Santos, 2017).

Mathematics with a STEM and Maker approach

This is why I was invited to conduct online teacher training workshops in an initiative called *Rio de Mãos Dadas*,[2] organized by the institution SescRJ,[3] with support from the public and private sectors.

In a partnership with Polo Educacional Sesc,[4] the high school where I was a teacher, we offered a course for public school teachers in the area of mathematics. The modules I proposed and taught were "Collaborative and Hands-On Math" and "STEM: A New Way to Look at Math."

These modules were attended by eighteen K–12 educators and aimed to introduce active methodologies with maker education and an integrated STEM approach.

According to Gavassa (2020), maker education is student-centered as students learn through discovery. Likewise, by promoting the development of multidisciplinary practices, the STEM approach encompasses the understanding of scientific concepts and phenomena by learners while engaging in design and engineering practices (Bevan, 2017), using mathematics as a symbolic language to represent reality.

In the module "Collaborative and Hands-On Math" I asked the teachers to reflect on the importance of the student`s role at school, and the potential of hands-on activities to provide an environment of innovation, collaboration, and creativity, thus allowing the student to leave the

Making Do: Adaptations for COVD and Remote Learning

role of content consumer to become co-creator of their educational process.

I presented different ways to implement maker education through different resources, that is, starting from paper and glue to the new high-tech possibilities available in makerspaces.

The specific objectives of the "Collaborative and Hands-On Math" course were:

- Understand the roots of the maker movement and its connection to maker education
- Recognize of the importance of maker education to develop competences in the mathematics discipline
- Prototype a Learning Object with recyclable resources

The "STEM: A New Way to Look at Math" module, on the other hand, aimed to provide a reflection on education for the 21st century, taking into account that students are digital natives and that they have information, in real time, in the palm of their hands through their smartphones. In this module I highlighted the integration of Science, Technology, Engineering and Mathematics (STEM) subjects as a way to make math more meaningful with real-world problem solving.

The specific objectives of the course "STEM: A New Way to Look at Math" were:

- Present practical examples of how to implement the STEM approach for teaching mathematics in the reality of Brazilian classrooms
- Use recyclable resources for hands-on math activities
- Create a Learning Object that might be used in their classroom

Delivering a hands-on course virtually

I taught the modules entirely online, each was two weeks long. The resources were made available in the virtual learning environment Moodle. In addition, I held two synchronous meetings, one each week, with a total duration of four hours.

Among the resources available were articles, videos, infographics, and articles from scientific journals. All the resources were made available before the synchronous meeting, so that participants would know what would be covered during the interaction with me and other course participants.

The synchronous meetings were held in Google Meet. I sought to provide an environment for exchange and discussion. Participants reported, for example, hands-on experiences they had when they were students in K–12 education, and how this impacted their own education. During the presentation of the slides that guided each workshop, checkpoints were defined to discuss the topics presented.

I proposed collaborative activities such as the Semantic Panel (a type of a mood board to collect initial impressions) on the Canva platform and also used the Padlet tool. The Padlet was used to share the hands-on challenge prototypes.

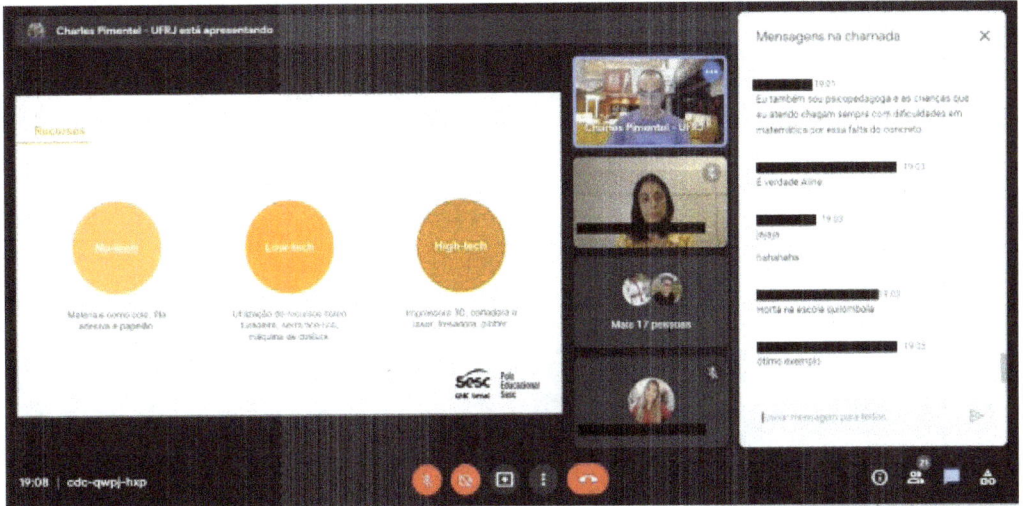

Educators discussing the difference between no-tech, low-tech and high-tech resources

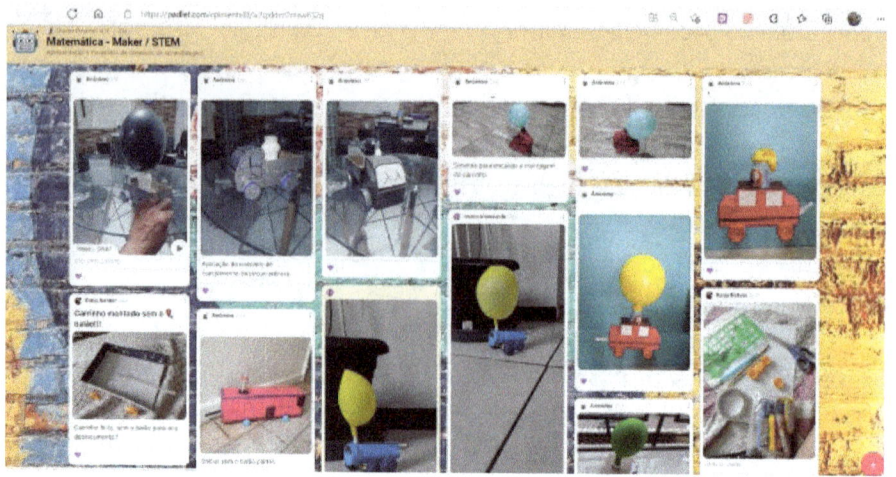

Display of learning objects prototyped by some of the course participants

Learning objects

As part of the course, the teachers were challenged to make a "learning object," something that represented mathematics in the real world and could be used in their classrooms. They were asked to use easy to find recyclable materials to make their prototypes.

To inspire participants, I made a video tutorial proposing a model of a Balloon-Powered Car, but I advised them that it would be important for the project to be their own ideas, and which could be made with materials available in their homes.

Evaluating the process

To assess how the teacher training was received by the educators who participated in the meetings, I sent questionnaires at the end of each meeting.

When asked what most caught their attention in the course, they answered:
- *"Interactivity between the participants. In addition to clarifying the topic addressed"*
- *"The possibility of doing the work at the time of class, energy, proposed challenges, teacher's didactics and exchange between participants"*
- *"These new ways that the STEM model can provide the teaching of mathematics"*
- *"Suggestions of tools we can use in teaching Mathematics"*
- *"The content, mostly. It was new to me"*

At the end of the course, I asked the educators to say in just one or two words what the course meant to them. Here is the word cloud created using Mentimeter, an interactive presentation site.

While all these words show how the course was important in the professional life of these educators, the word "resignification" stands out. It means to give a new meaning to something. As one of the main objectives of the course was to provoke teachers to take a new look at a way to teach mathematics, this signaled success.

I feel that providing a safe environment for dialogue, experimentation, and sharing of experiences was essential for the participants to feel connected with the project's objective.

The participants` engagement and the feedback pointed to the effectiveness of this online training. It shows that discussion about new ways to teach mathematics can be conducted in virtual environments, incorporate hands-on activities, and reach educators who wish to expand their repertoire to promote a teaching of mathematics that fits the reality of education for the 21st century.

Acknowledgments

I would like to thank FabLearn Fellow Débora Garofalo for kindly guiding me on how to start designing online teacher training. I'd like to also thank Gisele Ribeiro, a co-worker and math teacher for giving me support during the workshops and actively collaborating to make the project better.

Notes

1. gov.br/mcti/pt-br/composicao/rede-mcti/instituto-nacional-de-matematica-pura-e-aplicada
2. riodemaosdadas.com.br/714-2/
3. sescrio.org.br/
4. poloeducacionalsesc.com.br/
5. Balloon-Powered Car – YouTube youtube.com/watch?v=mSv0UbDO5mQ

References

Bevan, B. (2017). The promise and the promises of making in science education. Studies in Science Education, 53(1), 75-103.

Cabreira, M. C. (2016). Percepções do professor de Matemática: relação entre formação acadêmica e atuação docente. XX Encontro Brasileiro de Estudantes de Pós-Graduação em Educação Matemática, 1-12.

Gavassa, R. C. F. B. (2020). Educação maker: muito mais que papel e cola. Tecnologias, Sociedade e Conhecimento, 7(2), 33-48. doi.org/10.20396/tsc.v7i2.14851

Giraldo, V. (2018). Formação de professores de matemática: para uma abordagem problematizada. Ciência e Cultura, 70(1), 37-42.

Santos, M. S. (2017). Da formação à prática docente: uma habilidade criativamente inovadora. IV Congresso Nacional de Educação.

Viana, M. (2017). Formação é calcanhar de Aquiles dos professores de matemática do Brasil. impa.br/noticias/formacao-e-calcanhar-de-aquiles-dos-professores-de-matematica-do-brasil/

Lessons Learned from Hosting Virtual Innovation Challenges in Kenya

by Brenda Nyakoa

Since COVID-19 was declared a global pandemic in 2020, learners and educators across the world experienced a shift in their way of learning and teaching.

In Kenya, schools were closed in March 2020 and reopened in October 2020. This meant the parents and guardians stayed home with their children. Some parents explored online learning to keep their students engaged. However, many students who had no access to the internet and digital resources had to wait for schools to reopen.

Many organizations launched remote programs for students to engage with educational activities while at home. At Global Minimum Inc., we shifted to remote delivery of our programs. In this article, I will share lessons learned from facilitating our InChallenge program remotely.

Global Minimum Inc (GMin) is an international non-profit organization that encourages young innovators and leaders in Africa to engage with critical thinking skills and hands-on learning programs to tackle challenges affecting their communities. GMin provides tools, safe spaces, workshops, mentorship, resources, and networking opportunities to African youth, ultimately equipping young people in Africa with unique opportunities to take their future into their own hands. Since 2008 we have worked with over 10,000 youth aged 13–20 in Kenya and Sierra Leone. GMin believes all youth have the potential to learn and create innovative solutions in their communities.

The InChallenge program is a national innovation competition for high school-aged youth in Kenya and Sierra Leone. Every year, participants are invited to identify a social problem in their community and create a project to solve that problem. Fifteen teams of finalists with up to four students each are invited to a week long innovation boot camp where they attend workshops on innovation, human-centered design, entrepreneurship, and responsible leadership. They work with technical mentors to assist them in building the first prototypes of their proposed solution. Mentors are typically young professionals and industry experts in the respective fields in which the participants are building solutions.

Remote workshop delivery

COVID-19 brought many changes to the InChallenge program. Shifting from in-person workshops to virtual workshops meant reorganizing our presentation material and activities. For instance, we redesigned the presentation slides to be more visible when sharing screens via video conferencing and incorporated more visual elements in our presentations to keep our learners engaged.

Unlike in-person camps where we could play games outdoors and provide materials for hands-on activities, virtual camps limited us to online activities, but we were pleased to see that participants were creative in utilizing local materials available to them to build crafts.

For example, we use a marshmallow design challenge to demonstrate the iterative nature of design thinking. In this challenge, participants are asked to build a tower using 20 sticks of spaghetti, one yard of string, and one yard of tape. They are then required to place a marshmallow on top of the tower and the tallest free-standing tower is declared the winner.

In our virtual workshop, since some of our participants were not able to collect all the materials, they used alternatives they could find in their homes. For instance, instead of spaghetti,

Making Do: Adaptations for COVD and Remote Learning

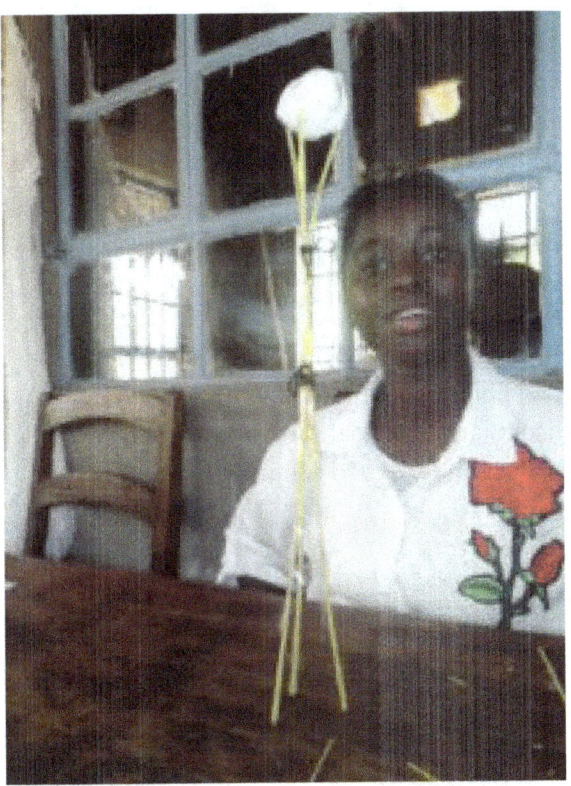

Participant displaying her spaghetti tower

Prepping materials before dispatching to team representatives

they plucked sticks from bushes around their homes. In place of tape and string, they used fibers from banana stalks and recycled old clothes. The flexibility they displayed reminded me why cultural making is important. As educators and makers, we need to account for the needs of all learners when designing activities.

Remote mentorship

When we started hosting virtual innovation boot camps in 2020, one of the major challenges we experienced was the difficulty in delivering technical mentorship remotely. Teams of students lived in different geographical regions across Kenya away from their mentors. Learners and their mentors had limited time to build their prototypes. As a result, many teams expressed frustration over the inability to finish building their solutions.

In April 2021, we hosted our second virtual camp and started utilizing WhatsApp groups to allow mentors to have extra time with the teams and offer consistent technical support. The groups were more accessible as most teenagers who had access to a smartphone were familiar with WhatsApp. With the increased mentorship time, the teams got to work on their solutions and made impressive presentations.

Internet connectivity

Another major challenge was internet connectivity, especially for the individuals who were connecting from remote areas where the coverage is not as robust. Moreover, some of the participants did not have access to a computer that they could use to sign in to the workshops.

One solution that helped was purchasing generic smartphones, which we sent to the finalists' parents to help them prepare for the camp. We further provided data bundles for all the participants who did not have WiFi in their homes. With these adjustments, over 90% of the finalists were able to participate in the workshops successfully.

Online collaboration

Collaboration is a fundamental part of the InChallenge boot camp. Each team of students works together to build a prototype for the solution they have proposed. During in-person boot camps, every team gets a chance to buy materials for their prototype and build them together.

For the virtual camps, teams had to select a member to take the lead in the building process. The team representative received the materials sent from our office in Nairobi to their homes and built the prototype on behalf of the team. Although one team member was building the solution, all other members were supporting the process remotely via video calls. This ensured the participants learned how to work in teams to achieve their objectives. At the end of the ten day boot camp, learners were able to document their progress through video recordings and photographs.

The journey continues

Making remotely has been a rewarding and fulfilling experience. Even though it came with challenges, it also presented us with an opportunity to learn new methods of delivering learning remotely. We continue to explore and utilize available technology to engage our learners and educators to ensure we create enabling environments for our students.

Making resources such as the internet, prototyping material, and electronic gadgets accessible to the students is fundamental to encourage participation from learners especially those in underserved communities.

Tea Sippers & TurtleStitch

by Kristin Burrus

For 24 Sundays in a row, I have set an alarm and jumped on a Zoom at 10 am. Usually, Sunday is the one day a week I choose to sleep in, be lazy, and not do anything productive. I do not like getting up early, but I can't help myself; I just keep doing it. I have Zoomed from all over the place these past six months, including a campsite in Kentucky with very spotty wifi, from the car in nowhere Georgia with an even less reliable signal, on the way to a beach trip with two of my girlfriends, and from a friend's kitchen with two very young kids bouncing around. Most Sundays, however, I have been home in Tennessee in my PJs sipping coffee (ironically, not tea) and absolutely enjoying the heck out of the morning. The craziest part of this whole experience is that I have been learning math and coding on these morning Zoom meetings as part of an amazing group, self-titled "Tea & TurtleStitch."

Tea & TurtleStitch is a first-class group of educators and makers and intellectuals and artists from New York, Boston, Tennessee, Texas, California, Italy, Germany, Sweden, and China. What brings us together is that we are all interested in using coding to make embroidery. Yes, you read that right, we use code to determine the size, shape, type, and color of stitches in an embroidery pattern.

TurtleStitch[1] is a programming language designed for this. It is based on the programming language Snap! However, I have noticed that we have done most of our coding in a Logo kind of way. This is not surprising since Cynthia Solomon, co-creator of Logo, the first computer language for children, is one of our two fearless leaders. Our other leader is Susan Klimczak, Education Organizer at South End Technology Center and Senior FabLearn Fellow. These two are a pretty hilarious duo and bring out each other's strengths each week. Cynthia is the master coder and Susan is the master maker (as well as an amazing coder).

Joining our Tea & TurtleStitch Zoom group from my campsite on a Sunday morning in July.

Susan has inspired me to learn not only how to code for embroidery, but also make finishing touches to the design like adding zippers to pouches and laser cutting frames for display. The group itself is a who's who of maker educators and computer scientists. But the best part is the joy everyone brings to the art and science of TurtleStitch. The simplest achievements are genuinely celebrated on-screen and on Twitter. As a novice coder (and embroiderer for that matter), I have felt included and encouraged at every step.

In conversations with friends of mine over the years who are math teachers, I have realized there are some serious gaps in my math education, and in my spatial reasoning. I could memorize things and pass tests (most of the time), but what I have been lacking is a deeper understanding of mathematical concepts and any real practice in geometry. Calculating the volume of a "cone of corn" may have been part of my college entrance exam, but it never held any meaningful application in my life. I even worked at Baskin Robbins as a teenager and filled waffle cones with ice cream, but I was never asked to measure the volume because folks just wanted the most mint chocolate chip I could squish down inside! Logo and our friend the turtle may have been developed for kids, but I am so grateful for the experience of finding joy in math for the first time in my life.

Best lesson yet — scale! I made a witch based on Ed Emberly's book teaching kids to draw entitled, *How to Draw Monsters and other Scary Stuff*. The first version resembled more of a chicken on a broomstick than a witch (really, check out the picture). What I figured out is that, unlike the Ed Emberly drawing, an equal-sized nose and chin give the impression of a beak especially if it isn't filled in with green color. I also realized after I embroidered the first witch that she was tiny and only about 1.5 inches tall. The design needed to be big enough to make changes to her nose.

My first instinct was to quadruple the size of every shape. While that did allow me to give her a proper nose, now she was too big to embroider with my machine's 4-inch hoop. Darn! The next step was to scale her down by ¼. Because I really did not want to sit and do the math for every step. I thought I was clever and multiplied all the move blocks by 0.75. It worked! Since Turtlestitch.org makes every design public, Susan and Cynthia would check on our progress between Sunday sessions. They would celebrate our successes, remix our projects, and offer suggestions when appropriate.

While the design was cute, Cynthia noticed a terrible inefficiency in my code. During our next Sunday session, she explained how she improved my code by creating a variable called SCALE. Now the witch can be changed easily to any size. In

It took several weeks before I was ready to start using my embroidery machine. Learning how to thread the machine was a whole different learning experience. In the meantime, here is Susan's multicolor (variegated) thread embroidery of my shell2 design.

hindsight, it seems simple and so obvious, but for the mathematically disinclined, it was a revelation. It is the simplest example of why variables are so important in both coding and math, but it took a relevant application to really see it.

This reminds me of my favorite quote by Seymour Papert, "Anything is easy if you can assimilate it to your collection of models. If you can't, anything can be painfully difficult." Well maybe that is why math was always so difficult, I had no models with which to assimilate it. TurtleStitch and these amazing fellow Tea Sippers made learning difficult concepts FUN for me. I am as surprised as anyone that I want to spend hours after our Sunday morning Zoom sessions working on a new design or a new coding concept.

I am the luckiest person in the world to have been led to this group. Thank you!

Notes

1. turtlestitch.org

"Chicken" witch and code with inefficient scaling.

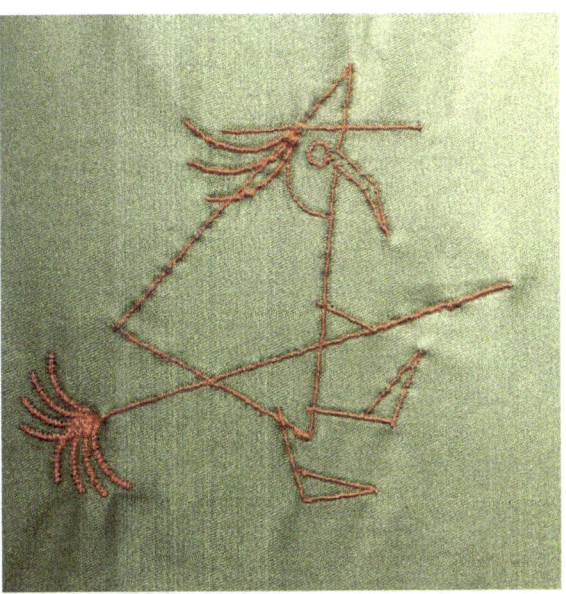

I used Cynthia's improved code using SCALE and designed a final witch with a proper nose.

Making Remotely: Sending Embroidery Kits Home and Teaching on Zoom

by Heather Allen Pang

In the fall of 2021 my school was fully remote, but we had the opportunity to send supplies home before class started. I was ambitious, and I put together two different sets of making supplies as well as some printed materials for my 8th grade US history class.

The two making kits were embroidery and fabric collage.

The embroidery kits included a 6-inch embroidery hoop, a skein of black 6-thread embroidery floss, a needle (DMC size 5), and two pieces of fabric. In late summer, when it still felt like I had all the time in the world to get ready for school, I decided to use up some of the fabric overflowing from my own collection and make drawstring bags to hold these supplies. I stayed up way too late making those bags the night before I had to drop them off at school for sorting. That was my own fault. While my timing was off, I was right that having the supplies in one bag would be helpful for the project. They did not lose the supplies over the several weeks we worked on the embroidery. I also sent home some photocopied pages of simple embroidery designs from a Dover reprint book: *Early American Embroidery Designs: An 1815 Manuscript Album with over 190 Patterns* by Elizabeth M. Townshend (reprinted 1985).

I found some basic embroidery videos online from my favorite sewing instructor on YouTube, the Crafty Gemini,[1] and posted those for the students. (Seriously, she is a great teacher, and her step-by-step project instructions are fantastic for sewing, quilting, knitting, bag making, and just about anything else she puts her hand to).

Over Zoom, I showed the students how to put the fabric into the hoop, and how to do it so that the fabric lines up with the bottom of the hoop so you can trace from a drawing or printout onto the fabric (hold it up to a window and let the sunlight act like a light table).

"To plant a garden is to believe in tomorrow."
— Audrey Hepburn. (Abigail K.)

This is a trick I learned from another great online instructor, Shannon Downey (Her site, *Badass Cross Stitch*, might not be a name appropriate for school, but that is the way it goes sometimes).[2]

The first assignment was just to get some stitches done. I asked them to submit a photo of the hoop set up with some stitches of any kind. We worked on some other things for a while, and I could tell that some of the students were working on their own, since they asked me questions about how to do certain stitches, or what I recommended they try next. Others put the project away in the bag and forgot about it.

I talked about the importance of needlework in the lives of women as we read about Oney Judge, an enslaved woman owned by Martha Washington. When she runs away, she makes a living as a needlewoman, and we talked about the history of cloth and sewing, the importance of making clothing in a pre-industrial and early industrial world, and how the skills were essential to many women being able to make their way in the world in the 18th and 19th centuries.

I had students pick quotations about the United States, history, reform, justice, or related themes in another lesson, and I brought that lesson together with embroidery to create the list of options for the embroidery assignment:

Instructions for all options
- Pick one of the three options listed here.
- Your embroidery should cover (not solid, but filled, decorated, written on) more than half the size of the hoop. It may be larger if you want.
- You may use any of the fabric (or some of your own), any of the floss, in as many or as few colors as you like.
- Embroider your name or initials to sign your piece.
- Turn in a good quality photograph and a one sentence explanation on Schoology before winter break

Option 1: Finish the piece you started with your quotation or design

If you started with a quotation, add a small design from a part of the pattern from *Early American Embroidery Designs (1815)* by Elizabeth M. Townshend.

If you started with a design from a part of the pattern from *Early American Embroidery Designs (1815)* by Elizabeth M. Townshend, add at least 3 words or a full quotation.

You may add anything else you want to the finished piece.

"If they don't give you a seat at the table, bring a folding chair." —Shirley Chisholm
("This quote shows the importance of having one's voice heard." —Zoe L.)

Option 2: A modern pattern with words and decoration

Do a google search for: free embroidery pattern printable and find one you like. Please pick one that has words and patterns or images, or add your own words to one that does not have any. Complete that pattern or modify it to suit your taste.

Option 3: Design your own idea and get it approved.

If you want to do something else, please pitch the idea to Dr. Pang.

Reflecting on this project

We have not done any other embroidery assignments this year, but several of the students have kept going on their own. One mother contacted me to find out what supplies I should get for her daughter's birthday, since she was embroidering all the time.

Looking back on the work, I think this project will stay in my class even when we are back to full-time in-person school. It unites the history of the craft, which is important in American history, women's history, and economic history (and really any period of history, those are just the ones that fit in my class) with practicing the craft. It is an opportunity for students to learn something that might be completely new to them, but is an ancient craft.

Notes

1. craftygemini.com and youtube.com/playlist?list=PLj9jdzKVN1echw6yse5esu2IxMt3CkgFt
2. badasscrossstitch.com

California wildfires

"All is well when flowers grow, because flowers can grow in the most barren of circumstances, and so can one." ,— Flo

In Your Hands: The Emancipation of Manufacturing

by Martin Oloo

"Necessity is the mother of invention" is a famous proverb used across the world. In 2020, it was never more accurate as when COVID-19 disrupted and in many cases completely cut off supply chains in many countries. Everyone wanted to do something, to offer solutions to the problems of COVID-19 including those of us in makerspaces. For a lot of people, this was the first time they saw the need for innovative makerspaces.

Traditionally and culturally, many communities had ways of fulfilling their needs by making products. For example, communities had traditional healers, pot makers, ironworks, weavers, garment makers, and leather tanners among others, but where are places for innovation? Where can you go and turn an idea into reality or share your thoughts and get genuine feedback from people experienced in modern industry?

In the West, many households have a garage. These garages, unlike in Africa where their purpose is

Fablab users consulting with staff

only to keep a vehicle safe, might hold a workshop where repairs and building things takes place. A workshop fitted with tools enables one to build something and liberates people from relying entirely on the others to repair small broken items in your house. The need for such spaces gave birth to Fablabs and makerspaces across Africa which have both traditional tools and modern power and digital fabrication tools while at the same time enjoying the privilege of global connectivity which allows participants to embrace collaborative design from any part of the world.

Fab Labs: Democratization of manufacturing

A FABrication LABoratory (Fab Lab) is described by the founder, MIT professor Neil Gershenfeld as a place where you can "make almost anything." Fab Labs are where an idea is turned into reality, where planning, design, production and fabrication processes are all done in one place. Fab Labs allow people to make things without turning to an outside manufacturer, thus emancipating the manufacturing process, and making it accessible to average people.

This technological emancipation of manufacturing is supported by an array of digital desktop fabrication and manufacturing tools which ranges from cutting, drilling, and molding tools like 3D printers, CNC millers and routers, laser and vinyl cutters, and supported by electronic and power tools. These tools enable makers to turn their ideas to reality by designing and producing at the same place under their full control.

Worldwide, Fab Labs have acted as agents for democratization of manufacturing, since the network of Fab Labs have similar tools and share similar processes. The worldwide need has generated the remarkable growth of Fab Labs, makerspaces, hackerspaces, and innovation hubs which provide shared tools and knowledge for the manufacturing of various items.

In addition to production, Fab Labs provide a unique learning approach borrowed from the work of Paulo Freire which encourages adding new things to familiar practices. This is expressed by Paul Blikstein in "Travels in Troy with Freire: Technology as an Agent for Emancipation" (2008). Paulo goes on to stress the dichotomy between being immersed in one's reality (only being aware of your own needs) and emerging from reality (being active in fulfilling those needs). The learners go from the "consciousness of the real" to the "consciousness of the possible" as they perceive the "viable new alternatives" beyond the "limiting situations."

Humanitarian making in crisis

In the March 2020 when the first cases of COVID-19 were found in Kenya, there a feeling of panic, as everyone was clueless about its causes or treatment. Any ideas for curbing the dreaded disease were welcomed. As the medical health workers were setting up facilities ready to receive patients, the maker community started to figure out what they could build, and the media took charge of relaying correct information (although this became more difficult thanks to freedom in social media).

Around the world, different makerspaces and fablabs like Vigyan Ashram Fablab (India), Shenzhen Open Innovation Lab (China), Kamakura Fablab (Japan), Fablab Oulu (Finland), Fablab Leon (Spain), Kumasi Hive (Ghana), Fablab Rwanda (Rwanda), and many others joined forces. In Kenya, some learning institutions like Dedan Kumathi University of Technology, Technical University of Mombasa, and Nyangoma Technical Institution of the Deaf shared findings and solutions they invented. Other humanitarian organizations like Countrywide Innovation Hubs, Afrilabs, Red Cross, Field Ready, UNICEF, and even small youth-led groups like Kisumu Youth Caucus made an impact in different ways by supporting various programs and disseminating information.

On the 18th of March 2020, just four days after the first case was announced in Kenya, makers at Fab Lab Winam came up with a contact tracing mobile application for passengers of Public Service Vehicles (PSVs).[1] This was in response to the Kisumu governor, Prof. Nyong'o's appeal for PSV operators to keep a manifest of all passengers. This was later improved to include cashless payment and named mSafari.[2] This solution was a way to trace the spread of COVID-19 created by the movement of people in obviously overloaded *matatus* (minibuses) in Kenya and many other African countries whose means of public transport are not so organized.

During the same period, we set up virtual classes for teaching STEM to young people aged 10 to 17. Our approach was peer education. We identified some students who were at home but are good with STEM to offer virtual training to others. So many students benefited from this program.

On June 15th 2020, at the celebration of the Day of an African Child, Fablab Winam hosted a Global Kids Day in partnership with Fab Lab Kids. Global Kids Day is a virtual maker-workshop for children from different parts of the world working and collaborating together. Each workshop has its own strategies for developing values, knowledge, and skills, but they all share the same basic methodological structure. It is championed by team of friends from different countries (Mexico, Qatar, Brazil, Japan, Argentina, Sudan, and Kenya). This particular one focused on African culture and over 500 participants from 10 countries benefited from this workshop. Another workshop benefited about 100 children from Dolphine Korando Educational Centre with support from BetterMe Kenya.

Fablab Winam has continued to work with different people and firms to develop and locally manufacture a number of items, including 3D printed face shields, an elbow-operated tap, mask clips/ear savers for facemasks, an elbow door opener, a foot-operated tap for already installed sinks, constant heat plastic roller sealer, and others.

Production area fitted with digital fabrication machines

Making Do: Adaptations for COVD and Remote Learning

Printing PPEs and other small medical devices.

Some of the products built in other Fablabs in response to the COVID-19 pandemic were ventilators, sanitizers, handwashing stations and foot-operated taps, air purifiers, respirators, face masks and face shields, elbow-operated taps and door openers, gowns, hospital beds, and many more.

Self-reliant, participatory rural development

Rallying people together to identify their own problems and designing their own solutions is the topic of Stan Burkey in his book titled *People First: A Guide to the Self-Reliant, Participatory Rural Development* (1993). Burkey says, "Go to the people live with them, love them, learn from them, work with them, start with what they have, build on what they know and, in the end, the people will say, 'we have done it, have done it ourselves.'"

Our experience during COVID-19 showed that 21st century skills and technology were the main agents for emancipation. This will hopefully continue to bring much needed transformation and give consumers freedom and a sense of ownership over the products they use. Someday, manufacturing will no longer be in the hands of the few, but everyone will be able to make their own contributions in the production process, especially with respect to their environment and the locally available materials; designing globally and producing locally.

Notes

1. kenyainsights.com/two-computer-geeks-in-kisumu-develops-a-mobile-app-to-help-trace-those-exposed-to-coronavirus-in-matatus/
2. msafari.co.ke

References

Blikstein, P. (2008). Travels in Troy with Freire: Technology as an Agent for Emancipation. In P. Noguera & C. A. Torres (Eds.), Social Justice Education for Teachers: Paulo Freire and the Possible Dream (pp. 205-244). Sense Publishers.

Burkey, S. (1993). People first: A guide to self-reliant participatory rural development. Zed Books Ltd.

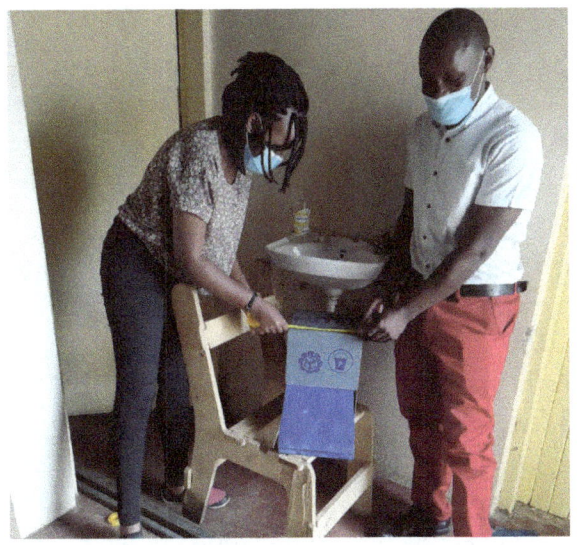

Field Ready staff assessing the quality of FUTAP

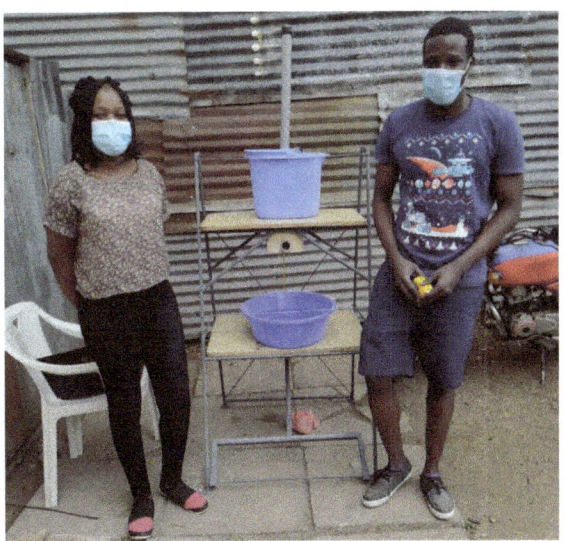

Victor & Angela after assessment of handwashing station

The AI Club: The Importance of Student Agency in the Teaching of Artificial Intelligence

by Charles Pimentel

"Studying is not an act of consuming ideas, but of creating and recreating them." —Paulo Freire

Why teach AI in K–12 education?

Artificial Intelligence (AI) is an increasingly pervasive technology that has expanded its field of action in a short period of time. AI has been applied in areas ranging from marketing, medicine, engineering, politics, and in services related to human and financial resources, and even in leisure activities, including games and social networks.

The ubiquitous nature of this technology has caused people to interact with AI passively without considering, for example, that this interaction exposes their individuality and privacy. As with many user-friendly things, people often neglect the need for caution both in its usage and when granting permission to access their personal data.

One of the ways to raise awareness in young people about this technology is via AI literacy lessons, so that users interact with AI in a critical and less passive way.

There are important reasons why the school should include subjects related to AI in curriculum. Among them, we can point out the impacts that AI has caused on human relations in 21st century (Druga, 2018). In addition, the expansion of the integration of this technology in day-to-day resources points to changes in the professional world, enhanced by the fourth industrial revolution. Just as the first industrial revolution introduced machines into the production system, the second introduced electricity and the third introduced information technology, the fourth revolution encompasses a broad system of advanced technologies such as artificial intelligence, robotics and the Internet of Things.

The 2018 update of the National Curriculum Guidelines for Secondary Education in Brazil,[1] proposes that curriculum units known as Formative Itinerary[2] of the Mathematics and its Technologies include among other topics, studies on AI:

> "Deepening of structuring knowledge for the application of different mathematical concepts in social and work contexts, structuring curricular arrangements that allow studies in problem solving, (…), robotics, automation, artificial intelligence, (…), considering the context and the possibilities of provision by education systems."

According to Libâneo (2004), the school can no longer be an isolated institution, separated from the surrounding reality but should be integrated into a community that interacts with broader society. In fact, the school environment is a space where this topic can be addressed. AI's operating logic can be presented and discussed as a means of clarifying to students what makes smart devices so invasive. Initiatives like this creates a new generation of citizens aware of the benefits, risks, and care related to the use of such devices.

Implementation of AI teaching at Polo Educacional Sesc

In 2019, in order to relate Mathematics, Computer Science, and New Technologies to the high school curriculum at my previous high school, Polo Educacional Sesc, I proposed a course for the Mathematical Formative Itinerary, called "Math Maker."

The course is a STEM (Science, Technology, Engineering and Mathematics) approach that integrates robotics, automation, programming, and AI.

Just as the Brazilian Ministry of Education proposed actions to modernize and update teaching through the Common National Base Curriculum,[3] the STEM approach is a government initiative that emerged in the United States with the aim of improving the learning of these subjects.

In November 2009, former US President Barack Obama presented the "Educate to Innovate" initiative as a collaborative effort between the federal government, the private sector, and the nonprofit and research communities. STEM education was recognized as an integrated approach that brings greater relevance to the teaching of concepts in mathematics, physics, chemistry, and computer science topics.

This approach provides the student with a more modern understanding of the integrated nature of STEM subjects and develops important skills for the 21st century professional. They will be more prepared for a labor market that demands a new set of cognitive skills and abilities, previously only accessible to specialists, promoting the democratization of various tasks.

At the Polo Educacional Sesc, one of the activities that resulted from the Math Maker course was the Artificial Intelligence Club.

The first year of the AI Club

In 2019, the first year of the AI Club, students participated in workshops that promoted the introduction of Machine Learning concepts via educational robotics. Machine Learning is an AI field whose objective is to develop algorithms capable of improving its performance in specific tasks. Machine learning algorithms learn information directly from data without the need for a predetermined equation as a model. The workshops lasted four months, and the students did activities related to pattern recognition, database definition, training, classification and accuracy using the Python programming language.

In the school makerspace, I prototyped a Raspberry Pi-based robot called Frankie (F.R.A.N.K.I.E stands for Fostering Reasoning and Nurturing Knowledge through Informatics in Education). This robot made it possible to teach students the mechanisms behind an artificial neural network, so they could understand what makes AI so important in countless applications. During the workshops, the students taught the robot to recognize geometric shapes and move in a different direction based on the shapes. Realizing that Frankie's AI algorithm sometimes did not properly recognize the image learned and consequently moved in a different direction than expected, students compared it to an autonomous car and raised the following question:

"Whose responsibility would it be if an AI driving an autonomous car makes an inappropriate decision and causes an accident? The owner of the car or those who developed the AI algorithm?".

Robot Frankie prototyping stage

The first year of the AI Club showed us that we needed to go beyond just learning mathematics and computer science concepts. The meetings with the students pointed to the need for a multidisciplinary discussion.

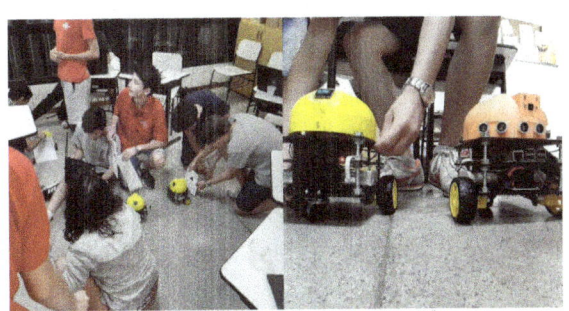

Conducting field activities with the Frankie Robot

Students raised important questions, among them the power that AI has in processing a large amount of data and transforming it into privileged information. One of the participants said that he had read that "data is the new oil," referring to the phrase said by Brittany Kaiser, former director of the extinguished British company Cambridge Analytica. We discussed this and another statement by computer scientist Kai-fu Lee who said, "if artificial intelligence is the new electricity, big data is the oil that powers generators" in his book *AI Superpowers*.

In addition, students showed concern for ethics on the part of those who develop AI algorithms and those who obtain and use personal data through these algorithms. They explored fears about the social impacts of using this technology such as the automation of numerous fields of work and consequent unemployment. It was impressive that young people thought deeply about citizens who would find it difficult to find jobs and reflected about investments in social programs that might become essential if AI is widely implemented.

Through these questions, we can see that the results of the 2019 workshops went far beyond technology learning and provided an important reflection on ethical and social issues regarding AI.

The second year of the AI Club

With the pandemic in 2020, the AI Club continued as best we could with remote experiments and biweekly debates. For the second year of the AI Club, I counted on the partnership of the researcher and co-worker Isaac D`Césares. It is important to emphasize that for entrepreneurial educational actions to find success, establishing partnerships with other educators is essential.

Machine Learning experiments were introduced using free web interaction platforms such as Teachable Machine[4] and QuickDraw[5] and proceeded to hands-on programming activities on the Google Colab platform,[6] which allowed students to collaboratively program machine learning libraries on the web in the Python programming language.

Online workshops explored AI topics such as the Linear Regression Algorithm, Scikit-Learn Clustering, Decision Tree Algorithms, and Neural Networks. One of the workshops, organized by members of the Club, provided experimentation with the WiSARD neural network model.

The debates of the AI Club, now livestreamed, were attended by educators from the Polo Educacional Sesc and professionals from various fields, among them former students of the institution, as well as important researchers like Professor Paulo Blikstein from Columbia University.

Two debates can be highlighted, in which students discussed the ethical, social, and political issues related to the use of AI whose themes were: "Artificial Intelligence and Ethical Implications" and "Power and Politics in the Digital Age".

Online workshops promoted by students

In the "Artificial Intelligence and Ethical Implications" livestream,[7] values and principles involving the implementation and use of AI by technology companies were discussed. A student described the case of an American company called Target, reported in the book *The Power of Habit*, with the title "How Target knows what you want before you know it," highlighting how companies like Target use their customers' personal data to recommend products and boost their sales.

Menstruation apps were also used as an example. In these apps, a user can note not only the date of her period, emotions, and symptoms, but also if she had sexual intercourse and when. Thus, the app can predict her next menstruation or indicate the possibility of a pregnancy. When users approve the "Terms of Use," they allow their data to be used by companies without being aware that it can be shared and sold to other companies. For example, if the user checks in the app that she has dry hair, she can receive ads for hair products. At the center of the debate was ethics and personal data.

In the "Power and Politics in the Digital Age" livestream,[8] it was discussed, among other topics, how AI is used in the dissemination of news, both real and fake, and targeted political propaganda.

During this livestream, the students explored the case of how the now defunct British company Cambridge Analytica managed to influence elections in the United States by using data gained from users taking simple Facebook quizzes.[9] Facebook users didn't realize the quizzes gave permission to the company to gain access to all their likes and even likes from their network of friends.

The students pointed out that with only 270,000 users who participated in these quizzes, the company gained access to the data of approximately 87 million people. Based on their interactions, citizens' personalities were typed to promote political advertisements aimed at these people, with content that caused the polarization of society and influenced the country's political destiny.

In their presentation, the students explored a study that claimed that by analyzing 70 likes, Facebook "knew" the user better than a friend; with 150 likes, better than his parents; and to know the user better than his love partner, only 300 likes were needed. They emphasized the need to control access to this data so that what happened in the American election is not repeated in other elections.

The AI coding experiments and debates proved to be complementary, as the students dealt with the subject through both practical use and thoughtful conversation. According to Paulo Freire, consuming ready-made ideas does not make a person a scholar or a researcher but participating in the process of creating ideas does (2001). This process of creating ideas is supported by action.

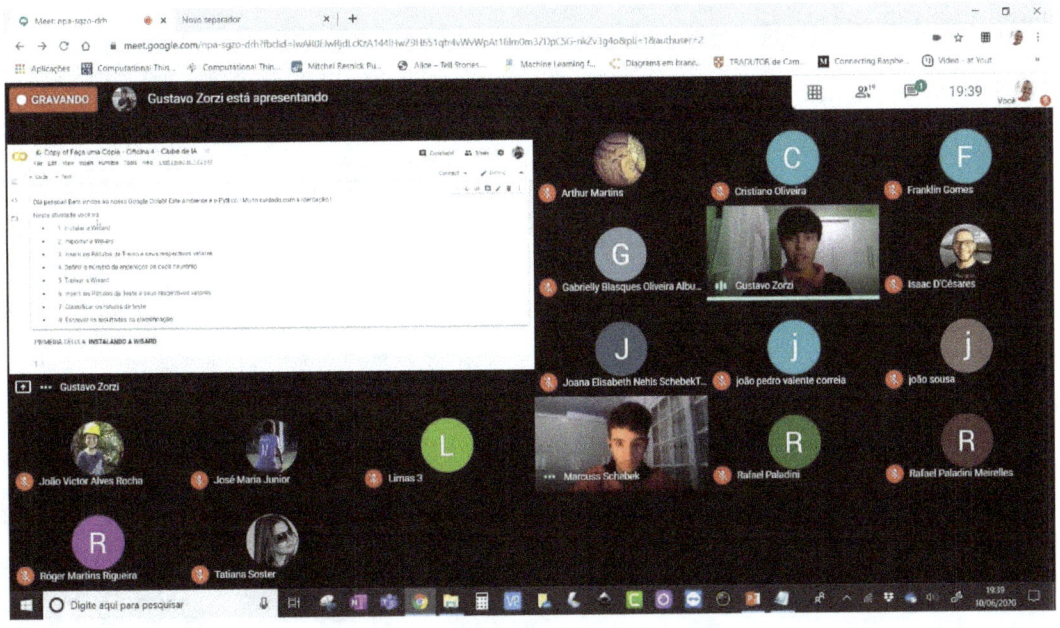

Live online debates

AI Club 2020 Remote Meetings

Meeting 1: Presentation: "Artificial Intelligence Club – 2020"
Meeting 2: Workshop: "Introduction to Machine Learning and the Development Environment"
Meeting 3: Debate: "Artificial Intelligence and Ethical Implications"
Meeting 4: Workshop: "Machine Learning Experimentation – WiSARD Weightless Neural Network on the Google Colab Platform"
Meeting 5: Debate: "Creativity and Artificial Intelligence"
Meeting 6: Workshop: "A Matemática por detrás de predição usando um Algoritmo de Regressão Linear"
Meeting 7: Debate: "Teacher training, Maker Movement and Artificial Intelligence in K-12 Education with Professor Paulo Blikstein – Columbia University – NY"
Meeting 8: Workshop: "Clustering with Scikit-Learn: Working with Unsupervised Data"
Meeting 9: Thematic Panel at the Knowledge Festival of the Federal University of Rio de Janeiro: "Artificial Intelligence in K-12 Education – The teaching of AI, and the teaching through AI. How can the school prepare for this new reality?"
Meeting 10: Debate: "Power and Politics in the Digital Age"
Meeting 11: Workshop: "Classification using the Decision Tree Algorithm"
Meeting 12: Debate: "Artificial Intelligence Contributions to Human Health"
Meeting 13: Debate: "Artificial Intelligence, IoT and Smart Cities: The Contributions of Mathematics to a Society 5.0"

Notes

1. in.gov.br/materia/-/asset_publisher/KujrwoTZC2Mb/content/id/51281622
2. Formative Itineraries are curricular units offered by educational institutions that allow the student to deepen their knowledge and advance in their studies of interest or prepare for the working world.
3. Document that defines the essential knowledge that all K–12 education students in Brazil have the right to learn.
4. teachablemachine.withgoogle.com/
5. quickdraw.withgoogle.com/
6. colab.research.google.com/
7. YouTube video – bit.ly/ia_ethical
8. YouTube video – bit.ly/ia_politics
9. The story can be seen in the documentary *The Great Hack*.

References

Druga, S. (2018) Growing up with AI – Cognimates: from coding to teaching machines. In: Dissertação (Mestrado). Massachusetts Institute of Technology.

Libâneo, J.C. (2004) Organização e Gestão da Escola: Teoria e Prática, 5. ed. Goiânia.

Freire, P. (2001) Ação Cultural para a Liberdade e Outros Escritos. 9ed. São Paulo: Paz e Terra

The AI Club

Making for All

In an ideal world, digital fabrication, making, and makerspaces should be open to everyone — any gender, age, experience, skill level, ability, and any kind of interest. These articles document different makerspaces and activities from around the world that reach out to people and create communities of respect and trust.

When we work to include everyone, the benefits go beyond just making a statement or feeling good about ourselves. Research shows that diverse groups generate ideas that are more imaginative and less constrained. Diversity and acceptance are part of a virtuous circle that results in more participation, more choices, and more confidence.

Creating these kinds of opportunities doesn't happen by magic. These articles demonstrate the thoughtfulness and care involved in making learning environments and practices open and accessible to all.

Special Needs Lab

by Lars Beck Johannsen

This school year a big change occurred in our makerspace. We expanded our space by 400 square meters to start a new school for children with special needs, combining traditional school with our makerspace, and adding 40 students and 12 new teachers to our daily life. The idea of the new school is that the first part of the day is traditional school, and the second half takes place in our different workshop areas, where they can work with metal, wood, ceramics, music, and the different machines in Fablab Skanderborg which has its own dedicated area.

My role in this was starting a 1½ hour long weekly subject simply called "Fablab." The idea was to introduce some of the new teachers and students to maker-based learning. It was a bit of an experiment, but after the first seven weeks the conclusion is simple — it was a huge success!

Here are some of the things that we observed.

Involvement of the special needs students

- Students come by during their breaks to start a 3D-print, lasercut something, or just hang around and have a talk.
- Four out of the eight students have joined my afterschool program "Fablab Freetime."
- Two of the students also continued into our Openlab night, which means that on that day they spend nearly twelve hours in the lab from 12:15 - 21:00. (They attend "Fablab," "Fablab Freetime," and "Openlab.")

Observations

- Our new students needed only a few instructional sessions to learn a bit of Inkscape, 3D-modeling, and coding with the micro:bit microcontroller.
- They have been full of ideas and have worked either on their own or together with one other student.
- Most ideas have revolved around making something for someone else.
- They have mastered the use of the different machines and help each other to a degree I have seldom witnessed.
- During Openlab, they offer their help to adult guests who are new to the lab.
- They interact and establish relationships with "regular students" in "Fablab Freetime."

It has been an interesting seven weeks.

A change of plans

I had first thought that I would have to do more instruction with our new students, but that changed after the first session. They simply had too many things they wanted to make to be bothered by my teaching — so that plan was abandoned. Of course, they needed a lot of guidance to start with, but most of them mastered the different machines (laser cutter, vinyl cutter, 3D-printer) rather quickly. They were very good at showing each other how to use the machines and learning what they needed to know when the need occurred.

I have a theory that a large part of the success we experienced came from mastering the fabrication technology that enabled them to make things. They are not just reproducing things but were intent on making and creating things for others. In a world where "special needs" is often looked upon as meaning "inadequate" it must be a boost to the self-esteem to be able to do something that not everyone (including their teachers) can do.

Creativity from the heart

Another thing that I noticed is how many ideas they have. They are really creative in many ways, much more than I experience with so-called "regular students," where it often is a bit of a process to get the ideas flowing.

The best thing to come out of this was the way that they took the lab to heart. Staying after school and late into the evening to make more stuff, helping the people who come to Openlab, but also hanging around, having fun, and establishing relationships with other kids.

We are soon going to start round two of this experiment and everyone has chosen to continue. We will add a few more students due to the high interest, and we will use some of the most experienced students as mentors. I am really looking forward to seeing what the next round will bring.

"Build something that dances" was the only project that I chose for them. In this image we can see Victor's build which he loved doing and is working on an iteration of the design that involves remote-controlling it with a micro:bit.[1] The prompt "Build something that dances" is inspired by the article "Exploring Circuits: Make Stuff Light Up and Move" by Tracy Rudzitis in the book *Meaningful Making: Projects and Inspiration for Fab Labs + Makerspaces (Volume 1)*.

Making changes

We have now been running the program for one and a half years. But some things have changed. The lab is more integrated in the normal day of the students. The class itself is smaller but with a handful of really dedicated students.

There is no doubt that the lab has made a big difference for the special needs students. Some of them had never been able to participate in the regular school day, and now they are helping other kids learn how to 3D model, use the 3D-printer, make vinyl cut stickers, and help with laser cutting. They make up their own projects and execute them. But most of all, they have changed a lot of people's perception of what it means to be "special needs." They continually surpass all expectations with their imagination, skill, and compassion for others.

Notes

1. Video of Build something that dances projects - youtu.be/UrEPllZVto4

Garotas STEM: A Project to Encourage Girls to Pursue STEM Careers

by Charles Pimentel
This text was written in collaboration with Nicolly Figueiredo, a student at Polo Educacional Sesc in Rio de Janeiro. Thanks Nicolly!

Nicolly Figueiredo

On March 9, 2019, a Saturday, I was in New York City attending the FabLearn Conference, and in one of the hallways of Teachers College at Columbia University a very polite lady asked me about the auditorium where the event was taking place.

We went together to the auditorium, sat in the upper balcony, and that morning Professor Paulo Blikstein announced that the 2020 FabLearn Lifetime Achievement Award would go to computer scientist Cynthia Solomon. Yes, the same very polite lady I escorted to the venue.

Cynthia is a pioneer in the field of Artificial Intelligence, Computer Science, and Educational Computing. In partnership with Seymour Papert and Wally Feurzeig, she co-created the Logo Programming Language[1] for children, in addition to countless other innovations involving technology in education.

But when I met her that Saturday in the hallway at Teachers College, I did not recognize her. I knew about Logo, but whenever I had heard about the impact of this language on education here in Brazil, the emphasis was given to the work of the mathematician Seymour Papert.

In fact, Papert has an undeniable and extremely important contribution in the field of education through technology, in the creation of constructionist theory and in the metaphor of a Mathland, which has mathematics education as its focus. His work, and these themes, were always present in the lectures I attended when it came to the creation of Logo programming language and educational technologies. But I had not heard of the importance of Cynthia's work.

It is a problem here in Brazil that many people don't even know the work of very famous women in technology areas like Ada Lovelace, Grace Hopper, and Dorothy Vaughan. This is something that must be fixed.

Returning to Brazil, I researched Solomon's biography, and I was impressed by the work of this important computer scientist. I realized that maybe I did not know Cynthia's work well because men have more visibility in society than women, especially in STEM areas.

Cynthia Solomon, co-creator of Logo and pioneer of technology in education

At that time, I was studying for a Masters in Computing at the Federal University of Rio de Janeiro (UFRJ), where there is a university extension (project for social impact) called Minervas Digitais.[2] Minervas Digitais is focused on diversity and female empowerment in science and carries out, among different initiatives, actions aimed at K–12 education. I realized that it would be an opportunity to bring the discussion about gender equity and female representation to the school where I work.

Thus, in November 2019, we decided to try a project at our school focused on female empowerment in the area of computing. I suggested that we start by inviting the Minervas Digitais project members to visit our school to talk to some of our students. The meeting was a success!

From that moment on I started to integrate this extension with the aim for more girls and women to enter STEM (Science, Technology, Engineering in Mathematics) areas.

The low female representation in these areas is an issue that has its origins in K-12 education. It is during this time that students generally make choices that will define their educational and professional lives.

The article "The ABC of Gender Equality in Education" from the Organization for Economic Co-operation and Development published the results of a survey carried out in 64 countries.[3] The work highlighted that parents were more likely to expect their sons, rather than their daughters, to work in science, technology, engineering or mathematics.

The study also showed that only 14% of women entering university for the first time chose science-related fields, including engineering, manufacturing and construction. In contrast, 39% of men entered university for the same fields. This is significant not only because women are severely underrepresented in STEM fields of study and occupations, but also because graduates in these fields are in high demand on the job market, with the highest salaries.

The Garotas STEM project

In 2022, with face-to-face classes returning after the start of vaccination against COVID-19, I wanted to resume our focus on K–12 computing and new technologies curriculum for our female students.

In our school, students have seven elective course opportunities in STEM areas, and we observed that the number of girls in them was significantly lower than the number of boys. To encourage the presence of more girls in these courses, we started a project called "Garotas STEM" meaning "STEM Girls" in Portuguese.

"Minervas Digitais" – First meeting in 2019

Garotas STEM" Project Meetings – 2022

An important survey

Nicolly Figueiredo, a student in the Gorotas STEM project, wanted to study exactly how many students were enrolled in these subjects and survey them to identify the reasons that led girls at school who chose STEM electives to do so.

Nicolly sent a survey to all the girls in the seven STEM classes asking them to report their relationship with technology, how they feel about participating in the subjects, and their desire to pursue a career in a STEM area.

The data showed that among the 105 registered in these STEM courses, 76 were boys and 29 were girls. However, it was observed that some students chose more than one subject in these areas.

Filtering out the duplicates, she found:
- Total individual enrolled in STEM subjects: 64
- Number of girls enrolled in STEM subjects: 22
- Number of boys enrolled in STEM subjects: 42

Next, a survey using the Likert Scale was given to the 22 girls who participated in these subjects. The form had the following answers: 1- I totally agree; 2-I agree; 3-I do not know; 4-I disagree; 5- I totally disagree.

The students responded to these 10 statements:

The research aims to draw conclusions about the participation of female students in STEM electives
S1. I feel safe getting my hands dirty in the classroom in the subject.
S2. I am one of the only girls in my class.
S3. Before, in the subject, I had never heard of Technology in Education.
S4. I am not adapted to the classes, I have difficulty getting used to the environment.
S5. My contact with robotics/programming predates our school.
S6. I already see a lot of change in how women are seen, particularly in areas of science and technology.
S7. I believe that my lack of interest in technology in elementary school is somewhat related to gender issues.
S8. I never thought about relating my choices to gender.
S9. Curiosity motivated me to take part in this course
S10. I want to pursue a career that directly involves technology.

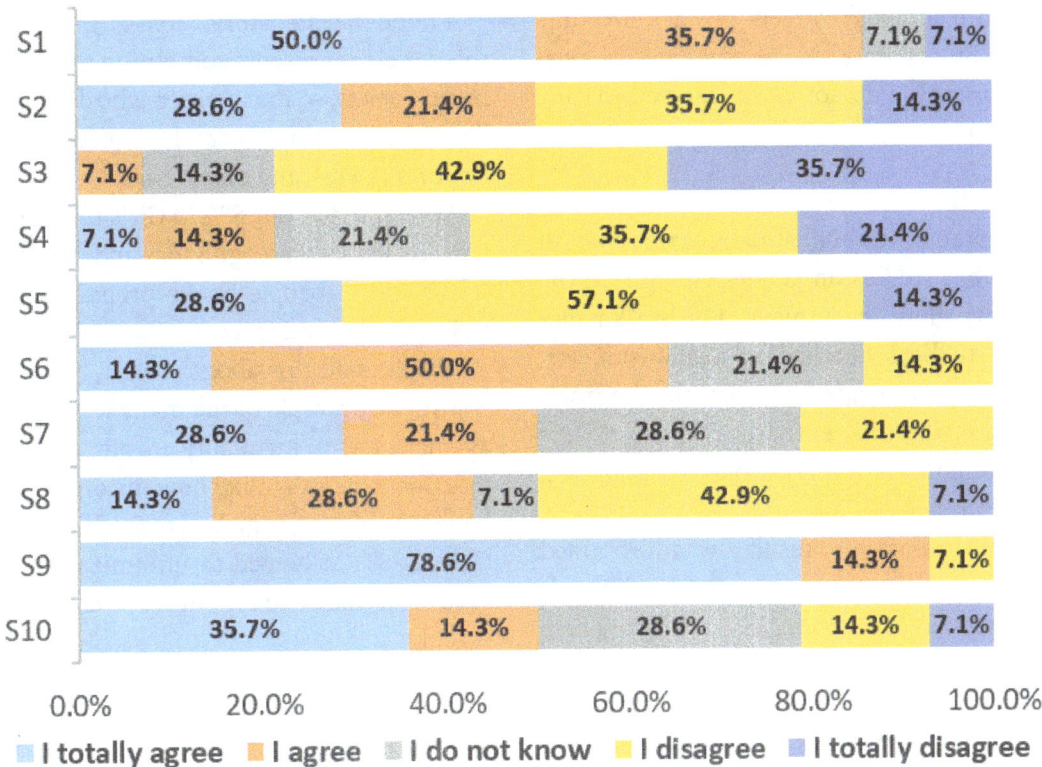

The table above presents the results obtained through the questionnaire.

When analyzing the data from S1, we observe that the respondents feel very safe when getting their hands dirty in the classroom. In relation to S2, we see that there is a division of the answers between agreement and disagreement, 50% each, confirming the imbalance in the number of girls in the class.

Regarding S3, it is worth mentioning that the term "Technology in Education" was not defined. This may have resulted in the large percentage (14.3%) who say they do not know, which may be simply a lack of knowledge of the term.

S4 responses show that more than 50% disagree or totally disagree with the statement about adaptation, which suggests good adaptation in the environment.

According to the data obtained in S5, it can be inferred that most of the respondents had no contact with robotics or programming in elementary school, given that our institution is only a high school.

The answers to S6 were mixed. Although half of the respondents agree with the statement, only 14.6% fully agree. It seems to convey a bit of optimism that no one fully disagreed, even though 21.4% answered "I do not know," which exceeds the number of responses to "I disagree".

S7 (I believe that my lack of interest in technology in elementary school is somewhat related to gender issues) highlights that half of the respondents say they agree or totally agree with the sentence presented, the majority being "I totally agree." It is notable that 28.6% of the respondents said they did not know their opinion on the sentence, which highlights the possible need for discussion in this area.

Analyzing the answers obtained in S8, we observe that there is a large percentage that claims to disagree with the statement and, therefore, at some point, made choices regarding participating in STEM subjects based on their gender.

In S9 there is a strong agreement that they chose a STEM course out of curiosity. From this data, it is possible to deduce that while the subject may be new, it did not stop them from taking a course about something they didn't know much about.

In statement S10, which highlights the willingness to get involved with a career directly associated with technology, half the students were in at least some agreement. This suggests they are open to technology careers but are not fully convinced. But at least the agreement and even those responding "I do not know" far exceeds any disagreement.

Conclusion

The data obtained through this research was in line with what studies on gender equality in the larger society show: the number of girls is smaller in relation to boys enrolled in STEM subjects. Currently, female students represent approximately 34% of the total enrolled, pointing to the continued importance of the Garotas STEM project for the institution.

Another important result was obtained through the questionnaire answered by the girls participating in these subjects. Their answers help us to understand the motivations that led them to participate, the challenges they faced, and how they see future possibilities. The results will help the project propose actions to increase the number of girls participating in activities aimed at STEM areas.

Promoting initiatives in K–12 education that provide students with an environment for reflection on the society in which they live is an important step so that in the future there can be more policies aimed at inclusion and equity, so that social justice can be developed.

In the future, these students will occupy roles in the job market and will be responsible for supporting the inclusion of future generations of students. Thus, awareness today is vitally important for the changes that are expected tomorrow.

I hope that the story I told at the beginning of this article represents something that is changing in our society, so that women who develop projects like Cynthia Solomon can be highlighted for their important work and discoveries.

We hope that our STEM Girls project is a small part of society recognizing and rewarding the talents of all people as we prepare students for STEM majors and careers.

Nicolly said this about project, "Garotas STEM is just one example of the many ways we can fight against gender inequality in our community. It took me time to realize how uncomfortable I was being one of the few girls in my technology courses. Garotas STEM helped to minimize the issue and gave me a chance to try out research skills."

Notes

1. Logo Programming Language – el.media.mit.edu/logo-foundation/what_is_logo/logo_programming.html
2. Minervas Digitais – facebook.com/minervasdigitaisUFRJ/
3. oecd.org/pisa/keyfindings/pisa-2012-results-gender-eng.pdf

Let's Think, Build, and Code!

by Michael Mumbo

In January 2022, EduTab Africa had a great opportunity to facilitate a robotics workshop during the 12th annual Think Young Coding Summer School in Nairobi, Kenya. This workshop was a collaboration between two Fablearn Fellows, me, Michael Mumbo, the co-founder of EduTab Africa, and Brenda Nyakoa from the International Rescue Committee. Our avid love for maker education brought us together to share best practices in student-centered learning to create an engaging, interactive, and fun workshop for the boot camp participants.

The participants were largely children from Kenyan primary schools and a handful of secondary schools from around Nairobi. The age of the participants was between 6 and 16 years. The boot camp was structured to run through two weekends and had sessions on Web and Game Development, Robotics, and Drones. Over the first weekend, we had two, three-hour introductory sessions which covered basic concepts of robotics, one in the morning and the other in the afternoon.

Since most of the learners were participating in a robotics session for the first time, we initiated conversations with them to understand what they thought robotics was all about. We used simple guided probing questions like:

"What comes to mind when you hear the word robot?"
"What can robots do?"
"Why do we need robots?"
"What does it take to make a robot?"
"Have you ever seen a robot?"

We observed that the participants started sharing their opinions and discussing them amongst themselves. We also watched a short video clip showing how Rwanda, a country in East Africa, used robots during the COVID-19 pandemic to reduce human contact between health care workers and patients by taking temperature measurements, checking the proper wearing of masks, and reporting to doctors about the condition of COVID-19 patients.

We then started the robot building process. Brenda gave an overview of the different components of the programmable Lego Spike Prime kit, including motors and sensors. With a little guidance, the learners were able to assemble these components and build a simple driving robot. The kit uses block-based programming called the Lego Spike Prime app which the participants easily learned.

Create and Code

By the end of the session, they could program the robots to perform simple actions like moving front and back, making turns at different angles, making sounds, and using different sensors like colors and motion sensors to control the motion.

We saw the kind of learning that Seymour Papert's talked about in his book, *The Children's Machine*. "Construction that takes place 'in the head' often happens especially felicitously when it is supported by the construction of a more public sort in the world."

On the second weekend, since most of the participants were familiar with the LEGO kits, instead of going through a guided process of building a robot and programming it, we gave them the freedom to explore different designs and build robots to their liking. We gave them a simple prompt: design a moving object that has wheels. While working in groups of about 6 students, they designed and created different wheeled vehicles. It was amazing to see the deep collaboration and creativity of the teams as they strategically divided themselves into smaller task forces within their groups as designers, engineers, and programmers to effectively complete the task.

In our last session with the learners, we had a moment of reflection to collect feedback to improve future workshops for different learners.

Here is what some of them had to say about their robotics experience.

"One of my favorite moments was when I was able to build up a robot from scratch because that's what engineers do"

"During the robotics session, I learned how to be open-minded and appreciate other people's decisions."

Some learners were able to showcase their robots in the closing ceremony where parents, caregivers, and other guests were invited. It was impressive how the teams were creative in so many different ways. For instance, one team used only color sensors to control their robot as it navigated the room. Another team used color sensors, motion sensors, and touch sensors to navigate. It was encouraging to see this organization be willing to support learners in their journey to creativity.

Maureen Mbaka, the Chief Administrative Secretary in the Kenyan Ministry of ICT, Innovation and Youth Affairs, who attended the showcase event said,

> "We are determined to facilitate universal access to ICT infrastructure and services for the youth through our programs."

This collaboration opened our eyes to what we can achieve in improving learning outcomes for students through global partnerships to share best practices and resources.

Game of Drones: The Beauty of Mistakes

by Lars Beck Johannsen

In the summer of 2021 we wanted to host a MakerCamp for 12–15 year old kids in their first week of the summer vacation. My initial idea was to run it as an open lab, but since many kids didn't really know what they could expect by turning up, we decided to make it a bit more directed than usual. We bought a classroom kit of 6 Air:bits[1] for building drones and gave it the theme "Game of Drones."

The invitation, translated from Danish, sounds something like this:

"Welcome to MakerCamp 2021. You will be working in a team of 4-5 kids, where each team gets an Air:bit drone to assemble. Your task is to improve the software, tweak the drone, and create an identity for your drone. At the end of the week, your drone will compete with the other drones on a field that we create together as well. During the MakerCamp there will be introduction workshops for 3D modeling in Fusion360 and micro:bit programming."

Even though we had good reasons for making these choices, I had some concerns:

1. Would making it into a contest be counterproductive towards the willingness to take risks in their designs?
2. I'm not a fan of kits in general. You could call it DIY but it is more DIBSEHADIFY (Do It Because Someone Else Has Already Done It For You) — a term I came up with during my first visit to the BETT conference in London back in 2015.
3. What about their own ideas? Would there be room for messing about with other stuff?

My concerns turned out to not be a problem, and there were several reasons for that. One of them was that the MakerCamp took a turn on day one that changed everything.

Crisis!

On the first day, after learning a bit about each other, we made our first models in Fusion360. The next step was to create teams, unpack the Air:bit kits, and get to work. But when I opened the box, there were no drone kits in it. My boss had accidentally ordered a classroom set of Hover:bits instead! Uh-oh was my first thought, but then again, the controller board was the same and the motors were almost what we needed in terms of having two clockwise and two counter clockwise motors for each drone. Plus, I had ordered a few spare motors prior to the camp, which was just about enough. But everything else we suddenly had to make on our own. It was a little crisis! And a crisis gives birth to authentic problems that need to be solved.

Not a crisis!

What happened was that the kids went head on in getting the missing parts made in the lab. The air was filled with determination and urgency in getting the job done. The newly achieved 3D modeling skills went into making the spacers needed for the drone to be set a bit above ground. The body of the drone was laser cut. We used the base that is provided as a resource from the Air:bit website, but they also made personal tweaks to it. Though the day took an unexpected turn, and a lot of extra time was needed for making the basic parts of the drone, it was a much more interesting and educational experience had it not happened this way.

MEANINGFUL MAKING 3

Finding screws from scrap materials

Laser cut parts

3D-printed spacer – and the screws fit!

Testing the design

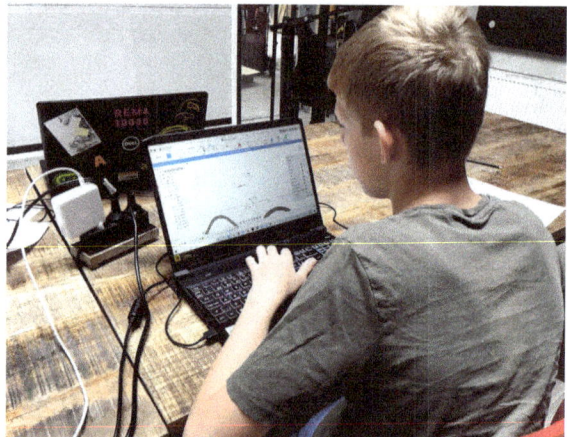

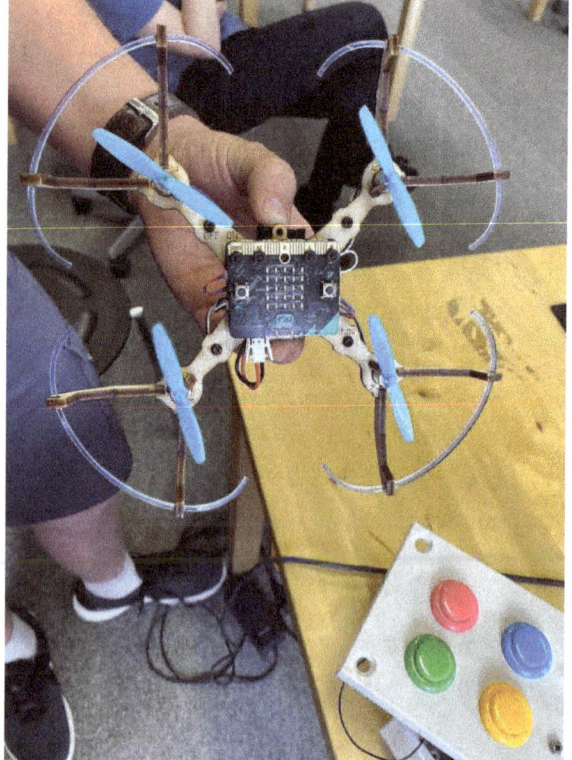
A completed racing drone

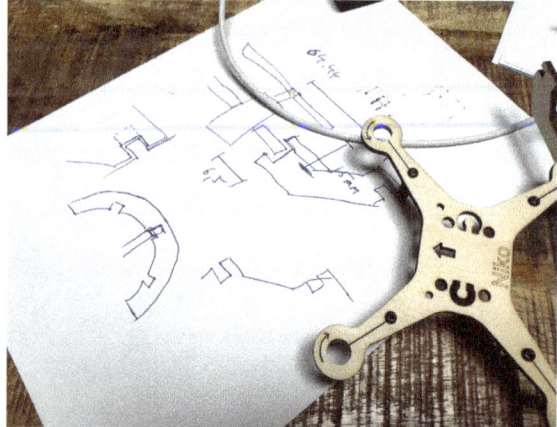
Designing protectors for the propellers

Lessons learned

The lesson here could be — buy the wrong kit or use kits another way than they were intended. On a more serious note, I would say just buy the controller board, battery, some motors and make the rest yourself.

As for the concerns about a competition, I believe the students were more engaged in making the drones fly and redesigning them to fly better, than in winning the race. Let me share the story of one of the most daring designs, built by a brilliant student, Mikkel.

On the first day of camp, Mikkel found a prototype of an arcade machine with an analog joystick and a few buttons. He wanted to use that as the controller for the drone. He ended up taking it home with him and worked on it the whole evening. He continued working through day two and succeeded in having it working smoothly on the final day. But he was the only one able to fly it properly, as the rest of his team had focused on the drone body, protectors, stabilizers, etc.

On race day, the first heat of the race went well and Mikkell's team had a lot of points. One of his teammates, one who contributed the least to the project, asked if he could fly the second heat. Mikkel handed him the controller just like that — go ahead he said. The other kid had no experience with that controller, and it was a disaster, but no one was angry with him. In fact, Mikkel had already won his own game. He had made it work the way he imagined and succeeded!

I will be doing this workshop again this summer but the next time I will frame it as "make something move." It could be a drone, hovercraft, boat, car, or maybe something completely different. And I think I will let it be up to them if they want to make a race.

Lesson learned: Embrace mistakes and allow them to take you in an unexpected direction.

Notes

1. MakeKit - Airbits and Hoverbits – makekit.no

The race field version 1. It was simplified in the end

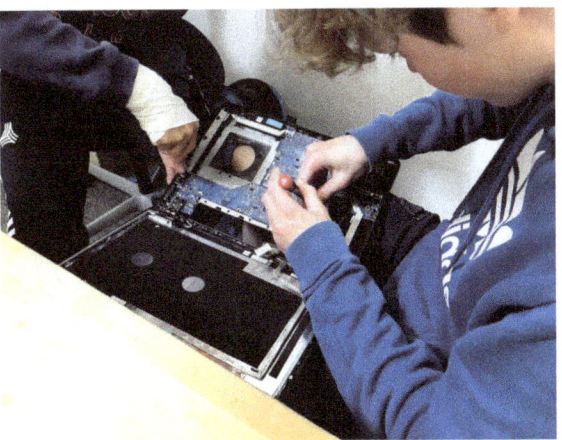

On the hunt for a neodymium magnet to make the drone pick up metal

Redesigning an arcade controller to fly a drone with a Raspberry Pi connected to a micro:bit.

SenFabLab: Our Robotics Workshop for Children

by Mouhamadou Ngom

SenFabLab is a space for creativity, learning, prototyping, and sharing. SenFabLab is located in Grand-Yoff, one of the most populated and low-income areas in Dakar, Senegal, with high unemployment for young people, lack of educational opportunities, and difficult conditions for people with disabilities. Women are an especially vulnerable segment of the population.

SenFabLab aims to spread digital technologies and promote learning and training through practice. Its main objective is to engage young people, women, craftsmen, and people with reduced mobility in the use of computers and digital technologies.

One of Senegal's SenFabLab programs is to offer robotics clubs and workshops, in partnership with the company Samarabot (My Robot), to welcome children ages 7 to 15 into robotics and computing. The objective is for all young people to have physical computing experiences to no matter where they live or how well-resourced their school is.

We use the free educational software for children called GCompris.[1] Young people start by using the keyboard and the mouse by playing games.

Then we introduce programming with Scratch, which is an easy-to-learn programming language using blocks. After mastering the Scratch interface,

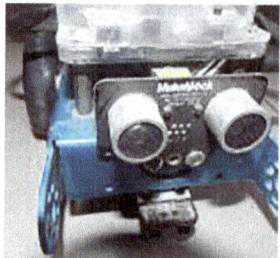
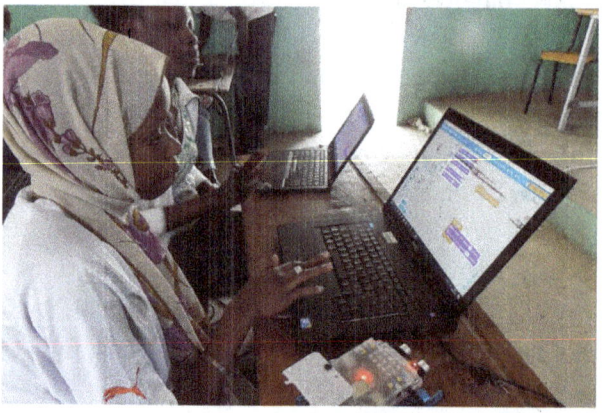

Kene, the teacher, asks them to imagine and then design a scenario they can program.

Introductory classes in the lab are led by Kene and Salma, who work with children every Wednesday between 4 and 6 pm. On Saturdays, a team goes to the schools with Bamba, to teach robotics.

Children who live in the neighborhood come to SenFabLab, but others come from as far as 20 km to take workshops and classes.

The children can stay for hours without even realizing it, because the classes are interesting for them. They learn by playing.

Currently we are setting up Lynx[2] which we discovered with the Fablearn Fellows and will be taught to the children next year.

Notes

1. gcompris.net
2. Lynx programming - lynxcoding.club

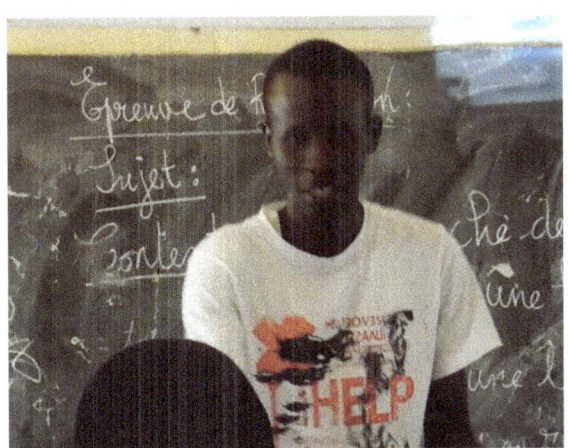
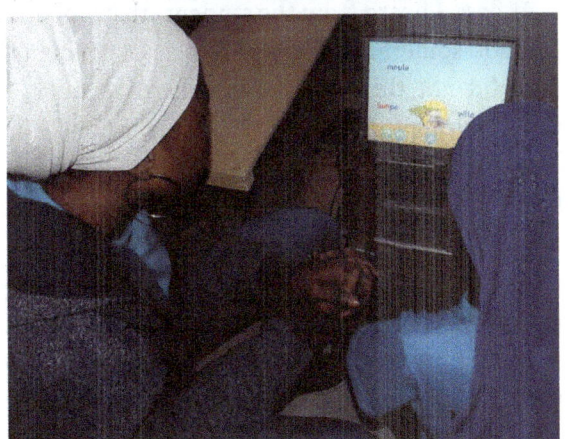

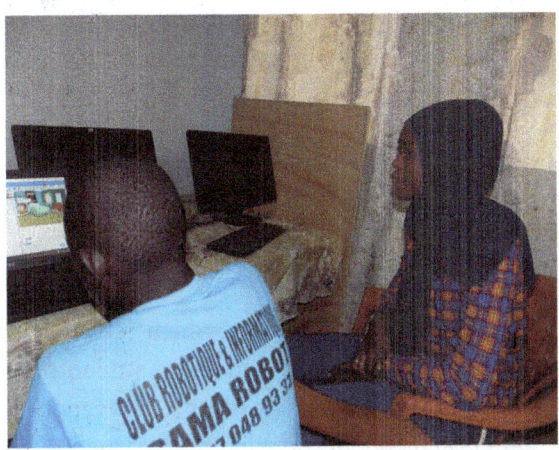

Reflecting on the Teachings of Gary Stager and My Work with Robotics with Scrap Materials

by Débora Garofalo

I have reflected a lot on what the PhD, educator, author, and speaker Gary Stager told us in a recent FabLearn Fellows webinar.

Dr. Stager, the founder of Constructing Modern Knowledge Summer Institute[1] for educators has helped students of all ages in six continents not only to embrace learning by making, but also "the power of computers as intellectual labs and vehicles for self-expression." In addition to that, he led professional development in the world's first laptop schools and has taught students from preschool to doctoral programs. Dr. Stager is currently the curator of the website *The Daily Papert*[2] which helps educators to understand the huge influence his colleague, Seymour Papert had in the field of education.

His relationship as well as his synergy with Dr. Papert's ideas bears on my own work, especially the ones about the learning theory, constructionism, which says that people learn better if they are working on projects that are meaningful to them, and when they are sharing their learning.

These ideas make me reflect on the importance of the scrap robotics project here in Brazil. Teaching robotics with scrap materials has demystified the teaching of programming and robotics here in Brazil. In doing so, we have dealt with many paradigm shifts in the process of designing student experiences that are challenging yet playful as a gateway to the maker movement and the teaching of programming and robotics.

The robotics work with scrap was conceived in 2015 at Escola Municipal de Ensino Fundamental (EMEF) Almirante Ary Parreiras, a public elementary school. The project was born of a need to imagine school in a new way, through technology teaching and working with the maker culture as a gateway to teaching programming and robotics.

Starting with the needs of students

We started with the questions and needs of the students. Of the more than 1,000 students in the Technology and Innovation classes from the 1st to 9th grade, 70% reported that garbage was a problem in the community. On rainy days it prevented them from coming to school, due to flooding, and also that the dirty water brought diseases such as dengue and leptospirosis.

In response to this overwhelming response, we initially proposed to have outdoor classes in order to understand the issue related to the garbage in the community and, during the walk in the community, to collect recyclable materials to develop the robotics work with scrap.

At first, I heard from the students that "robotics was not something for public school students." They did not think they could learn robotics, it was something only for rich private schools. The situation was solved with a lot of talking and dialogue and consistent encouragement to become the protagonists of their own learning.

To overcome the challenges, it was necessary to allow myself to learn from the process and to exercise active listening with the students. We worked together to build the project in steps:

- Public classes and community awareness about garbage and proper disposal
- Walking through the community to collect of recyclable and electronic materials
- Weighing and separating out materials that we could use
- Selling recyclable materials we could not use
- Constructing prototypes with creativity and critical thinking
- Holding a technology fair, which reconnected with the community and gave students the opportunity to be take a leading role by reporting about their robots and what they learned.

Dr. Stager said in the webinar that children deserve to learn about how the modern world works. I believe this goes beyond learning scientific facts. For them to really learn, we must help them solve real problems. It made me appreciate that our robotics from scrap project achieved that goal.

Seymour Papert invented a programming language for children not because he thought the math they were being taught was too hard, but because the math we teach in schools has no connection to their experiences in the real world. He said children need to be active agents and protagonists in their own learning.

I recall that many people said our robotics program would be too difficult to do. Even the children held the belief that robotics are for students from private schools. What I learned is that our children rose to the challenge and created something even more wonderful than anyone expected, which made learning meaningful for them.

Learning from meaningful experiences

We saw the idea of constructionism in the daily work of the students. They continually explored difficult concepts and displayed more complex levels of cognitive development in the search to solve real problems.

At the same time, teachers learned to take the role of creative facilitator by providing an environment capable of providing connections to big ideas and subject area knowledge by using innovative technology to solve a social problem.

To encourage the students' creativity and inventiveness and bring the maker universe to the classroom, the first scrap materials prototype built by a 6th grade class was a cart powered by a balloon. This hands-on experience amazed the students, and they discovered their own potential as makers and creators. It was so exciting that I had to repeat the experience with all my classes!

And I was sure I was on the right track when my 9th grade class interrupted a storyboarding lesson to ask me if they could make the cart too.

All the project's steps were built with the students, who had total freedom to create and build their prototypes from recyclable materials. Over three years there have been many prototypes and they have improved their projects and found additional solutions for the community.

I think the biggest lesson from both Gary Stager and Seymour Papert is allow the children to be protagonists of their own learning. They want to learn, they deserve to learn, and we must find ways to make this happen for everyone.

Notes

1. Constructing Modern Knowledge Summer Institute – constructingmodernknowlege.com
2. The Daily Papert – dailypapert.com

Curiosity Heals at the Repair Café

by Mathias Wunderlich

About 11 years ago I founded the first Repair Café in a German high school near Dusseldorf where we started to fix devices, repair chairs, and make broken and abandoned things work again. The kids volunteered to stay after school and learned to fix things.

The Repair Cafe is open about a dozen times per year here.

Once, a 12-year-old boy from my class came to the Repair Café with a big bag. The bag contained a complete automatic coffee machine including a water tank, the coffee and filter holder, and even a printed manual. He told us that he pulled it out of the garbage because he thought it was wrong to discard a machine that was only two years old. His mother told him it's out of order and she already ordered a new machine. He was a curious kid and wanted to know: what's the problem with this thing? So, he brought it to our repair appointment. Fortunately, he saved all the accessories for the machine, so we could fill the water tank, install the filter holder, and do a check.

After connecting the machine to electricity and switching it on, a tiny red light on the front appeared, and the machine did ... nothing. OK, what does this red light mean? For the boy's mother the light was telling her: "I'm done, throw me away." For us, a little gang of technically interested kids and two adults, the light said: "Hey, I have a problem, could you please care for me?" The kids around the table speculated: "What's inside this machine? How does it work exactly? Which parts do what? There's still life in it, so the cable must be OK, otherwise, there would be no red light." So, we instantly were sucked into a technical investigation. They searched for the screws that held the whole thing together and one of the boys got a screwdriver.

Sometimes we just open devices to investigate what's inside.

I would have let them open the machine and investigate what's inside and what could be wrong. However, my Repair Café colleague who was not a teacher, but a very skilled technician, stopped them. He explained that he would try to first find out what this tiny red light was trying to tell us before investing a lot of effort into opening the machine. And yes, we even had the manual! So, four or five boys huddled over this tiny booklet and searched for the meaning of the red light beneath the three push buttons on the front. After a while they found the German chapter and a description for the push buttons and the red light. The kids had to read carefully and exactly to decode the meaning of the text.

Eventually, they discovered that the light was saying that the machine needed to decalcify. What's that? My experienced colleague helped with a perfect short explanation of the chemistry of water and what chalky deposits, caused by water evaporation, can do inside the different parts of the machine. We needed a liquid for decalcification. Now! Instantly! We only had one small grocery store nearby, so we sent three kids out with some coins for a bottle of vinegar. When they came back, we made a diluted vinegar solution and filled the water tank. After that, the kids followed the instructions in the manual for the decalcification routine.

They all had a big surprise when they pushed two of the front buttons at the same time, as described in the manual, and the water pump inside came to life and made a deep humming sound. The routine worked exactly as described. They had to repeat the routine several times, at first with the vinegar solution, then with fresh water. And after running this routine properly – surprise! – the red light was off! The machine worked as it had on its very first day.

For some of the kids, that afternoon was an awakening. They didn't miss even one of our Repair Café meetings throughout the years! Later we found out a lot more about these kinds of machines — how to open them, and how to change fuses, water hoses, the boiler, or the water pump. We learned that most of the cases are connected simply to decalcification and the disability (or inability) of adult people to read and understand a manual.

For the boy with the big bag, it was a great triumph that day when he arrived home and presented the working machine and what he learned to his parents. And they also learned something! Not only that their son is a smart boy but also that it's worth it to think about our modern life and to reflect on what is waste and what things are of value.

For many of the students who have come to the Repair Café, it is more than just things that are healed. They heal themselves, as they learn that they are smart and have value in society.

There is a well-known German phrase that applies here, "*Alle sagten: 'Das geht nicht!' Dann kam jemand, der wusste das nicht und hat es einfach gemacht.*" It translates to English as "*Everyone said, 'That's not possible!' Then someone who didn't know that came along and just did it.*"

For our after-school-initiative, this story was one of the sparks and reasons why it succeeded. We were able to grow and open it up from the small school community to the wider public. At least one Repair Café per month was held over many years where hundreds of people got advice and help with their technical stuff.

A lot of communication and new connections developed between students and the community. Many elderly people who still understand the value

Students investigate a kitchen appliance. They know that electricity is dangerous, and they are careful with it If they are not sure what to do, they can ask. Otherwise we trust them to be responsible.

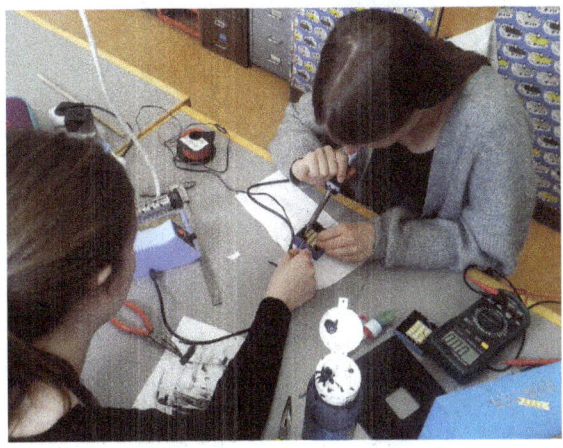

Soldering isn't an ability just for itself, it's a skill that kids can use to fix broken devices.

of repairing things were impressed when they met our smart and by then trained kids who knew how to deal with mechanical and electrical problems.

Parents have been very engaged in our project over the years in a variety of roles — as learners, as supporters, as our advocates in the community. I believe the Repair Café experience helped parents understand or maybe even to remember what they already knew, that education can and must be more than sitting six hours a day, five days a week in a room only to learn theory and facts.

Over the years, the Repair Café has proven time and time again that learning is best done in a community. The fact that a few appliances are fixed is secondary to the valuable experiences of a community coming together and learning about each other.

We see every year that lives are changed as young people see themselves as important, competent members of a community, and learn how smart and skilled their older counterparts are.

The older generation sees that young people are capable, caring, and compassionate, perhaps dispelling myths about how "kids today" are lazy and glued to video games.

The Repair Café may seem like a simple idea, one that could not possibly solve such a complex problem as healing communities. But even complex, difficult problems can be solved. It may not be easy, but has to be done anyway, so as we say in our Makerspace — *"Einfach machen!"* — *"Just make it!"*

Repairing things with kids is always fun, and always a gathering of young and old!

Encouraging Diversity in Computer Science

by David Malpica

I was a middle school teacher for three years before I confronted the reality that teaching public school and financial safety in the San Francisco Bay Area don't square up, especially with a baby on the way. I therefore quit my brief teaching career and enrolled in the most competitive coding bootcamp available.

This essay is a reflection as an educator and software engineering professional on what can be adapted to any enterprise seeking to improve outcomes of underrepresented minorities in the tech industry.

It's never too late to start, but public middle school is the key place and age group to build long term impact

My fellow students at the bootcamp were mostly young adults, male, and Asian or white. There was only a dozen or so of us who stood outside these demographics. And although efforts were made by the organization to attract minorities, it was clear the incoming demographics were not diverse enough.

Studies have shown that interest in STEM is either nourished or starved during the transition to adolescence.[1] By the time they reach high school, women and people of color have less interest in STEM subjects, largely due to a lack of exposure capable of competing with the myriad distractions of life as a female or minority youth.

Providing those opportunities and inspiration at the public middle school level should be an educational imperative. Any enterprise seeking to improve this situation needs to understand the right time and place to make a long-term difference — public middle school. There's only so much we can do at the high school level when interest has already dropped.

Be willing to train teachers and teach kids

Many vendors offer resources and materials, but more effort needs to be put into widening the curricular makeup of teacher preparation programs, which are short and lean enough already. For example, middle school math is a great place to introduce computing connections with 2D and 3D coordinate planes, which is fundamental to any future work in the field of building front-end applications (the visual components of websites) and a great place for entry level jobs in software. K–12 education can't just be about English and math anymore.

Industry should seek to collaborate with teacher prep programs and schools to increase the number of teachers (not just specialists, but all teachers) capable of computer science education.[2]

Industry should also partner with middle schools, high schools, and community colleges to run meaningful courses, workshops, and hackathons with effort, investment, real tools, and life-changing opportunities and rewards for both students and teachers.

Maintain a relationship with families and children

Low SES minority families struggle supporting their children's educational interests. Limited budgets for enrichment and math anxiety are just two of many roadblocks. Because this process needs to start early, any enterprise needs to acknowledge that a reasonable metric of success will follow the middle-school-through-college trajectory of beneficiaries. This means sustaining a close relationship through programs that culminate in scholarships, internships, and jobs. It also means providing life-changing resources to families. Often, families don't even have the means to secure internet access.[3]

To attract diversity, offer diversity. In time, narrow it down.

A heterogeneous population cannot be served by a homogeneous curriculum. Maxine Williams, Facebook's Diversity Chief, recently said, "What we look for are people who are very good in two specific subjects: data structures and algorithms."[4] For the middle school population, the relevance of "data structures and algorithms" might not be apparent. Therefore, a child's budding engineering identity would be well served by a series of scaffolded experiences that bridge their interest towards the hard skills.

Creative computing and collaboration are two solid starting points. At my bootcamp I learned about pair programming, SCRUM, and git (GitHub offers resources for education) which could be easily taught in middle school and above. Maker and STEAM projects are particularly well suited to attract a wide range of students with creative interests that can eventually evolve into more specific computer science knowledge.[5]

Projects that incorporate the Internet of Things, games, robotics, graphics, sound, and technology-based arts and crafts will attract an even wider audience. Variables and structured programming will follow but must build on a foundation of creative and collaborative projects. Eventually, students will be ready for data structures and algorithms, machine learning, AI, full stack concepts, frameworks, and more.

Even if students do not fully venture into computer science majors and jobs, an introduction to these big ideas of the 21st century will be useful to them no matter what their eventual interests are. We need all students, whether they become historians or artists or biologists to be at least acquainted with the power of the computer.

Notes

1. Planning Early for Careers in Science (2006) afterschoolalliance.org/documents/STEM/RHTai2006Science_PlanEarly.pdf
2. Universities aren't preparing enough computer science teachers (2017) codeorg.medium.com/universities-arent-preparing-enough-computer-science-teachers-dd5bc34a79aa
3. Innovation in East Oakland: The Realities of Keeping Up Outside of Silicon Valley's Bubble (2018) kqed.org/news/11665681/innovation-in-east-oakland-the-realities-of-keeping-up-outside-of-silicon-valleys-bubble
4. Facebook Diversity Chief: 'We Still Have More Work To Do' (2018) kqed.org/news/11679941/facebook-diversity-chief-we-still-have-more-work-to-do
5. Mitchel Resnick: Designing for Wide Walls (2016) mres.medium.com/designing-for-wide-walls-323bdb4e7277

Emancipatory Maker Practices in the Global South

by **Renato Russo**[1], **Leah Rosenbaum**[1], **Paulo Blikstein**[1], **Yipu Zheng**[1], **Anisa Bora**[1], **Yue Liu**[1], **Brenda Nyakoa**[2], **Ridhi Aggarwal**[3]

The paper was co-authored by individuals from the Transformative Learning Technology Lab (home of FabLearn) and several FabLearn Fellows. It was awarded the "Best Student Paper Award from the Learning Sciences SIG" at the 2023 American Educational Research Association's annual meeting.

Abstract

Maker education has been extensively documented in developed countries, and research points to benefits for learning and to pitfalls in efforts to democratize those benefits. There are, however, opportunities to investigate those factors in developing countries. In this paper, we examine maker practices in communities in two countries of the Global South. For data collection, we partnered with local maker educators who also work in grassroots organizations that offer programs focused on skill development. Our evidence points to emancipatory practices that parallel well-documented strategies found in literature both in the learning sciences and science and technology studies. This paper contributes to broadening the understanding of the importance of maker activities that bring local cultures front and center.

Introduction

Maker education has gained attention in the learning sciences and education research, and there is a considerable debate about its contribution to the development of competencies beyond STEM skills (e.g., Halverson & Sheridan, 2014). Research and critique have also focused on alternatives to normative, US-inspired views on making in educational settings, calling for expressive approaches that integrate students' lived experiences and cultures (Eisenberg, 2002; Buechley et al., 2013; Blikstein, 2008). Others have emphasized how makerspaces embody pervasive educational injustice and that practices from non-dominant groups could contribute to a more inclusive maker education (Vossoughi et al., 2016). Nevertheless, much of the critique's focus still remains on North American and Western European schools.

In this paper, we go beyond the Global North and look at maker practices in countries other than the US and Europe, marked by different histories and educational systems. We report on a global fellowship program that gathers maker educators from 12 countries across different levels of socio-economic development. We ground our work in the learning sciences and theoretical perspectives of design and science and technology studies (STS) to answer the following question: **How do maker practices connect with emancipatory education in underserved communities in the Global South?**

Theoretical framework

Maker education inherited a few assumptions from its parent trend, the broader-encompassing maker movement. One such assumption is that making is emancipatory — by making their own products, individuals can subvert the producer-consumer antagonism. Such a promise, however, has been criticized by researchers in different traditions of education research. Despite the potential of maker education to equalize access to the development of STEM skills, many programs fail to incorporate youth's social and cultural "funds of knowledge" into making activities (Barton et al., 2017), limiting the "democratizing effect" of maker education among underrepresented youth. In response, researchers have designed learning experiences that address the cultural practices of indigenous populations (Barajas-López & Bang, 2018) and urban groups of marginalized youth (Holbert, 2016), among other groups. However, much of that research is conducted in the Global North and fails to consider the intricacies that characterize under-resourced areas in developing countries.

Examples of emancipatory practices through making have been documented in settings not traditionally associated with formal education in the Global South. For instance, in discussing the repurposing of combustion engines in Thailand, Cavallo (2000) identified that people with little formal instruction were involved in a sophisticated culture of innovation that academia and the government did not acknowledge. Blikstein (2008) laid out the connection between making and emancipation through a robotics workshop in which students had the opportunity to address community issues through the development of projects that used scrap metal and old computer parts. And more than a decade later, hackerspaces and technology-driven community spaces in an underserved community in Brazil have been the stage for artistic expression by youth that question structures of power (Dalla Chiesa & Foletto, 2022).

Additionally, the subversion of ready-made products has been well documented in science and technology studies. de Certeau and Rendall (2011) argues that ascribing new meanings to products is associated with the struggle between individuals and powerful institutions. Ascribing such new purposes is a way of resisting oppression by balancing the power dynamics between the strong and the weak. Akrich (1994) similarly documents how designers define scripts within industrialized objects and that those scripts incorporate assumptions about those who employ those artifacts and in what contexts. These imagined uses, nonetheless, can be "de-scripted" by users who can technically manipulate those objects and, thus, reshuffle social relations in their milieu.

Those perspectives from the learning sciences and science and technology studies guide our analysis of making practices — specifically those that employ repurposing of materials as a vehicle for emancipatory maker education.

Methods and data

The research team first conducted five focus groups (N=18, total length: 5 hours) with maker educators from 12 countries on four continents. The research team (composed of 6 researchers) then transcribed the content of the focus groups and developed research memos. After an initial round of analysis, the team identified three emerging themes (Charmaz, 2006). Members of the research team then invited 3 of the participants of the focus groups for in-depth interviews (N=3, total length: 3 hours) in which they further discussed the practice of repurposing, motivated by work described in the theoretical framework. Two of those participants are co-authors of this manuscript.

Data for this paper comes mostly from the in-depth interviews, complemented by data from focus groups. The research team transcribed the content of interviews and developed research memos that were then reviewed in team meetings. Besides textual data, members of the research team also analyzed pictures and videos of projects implemented in the maker educators' communities.

Results

We present summaries of two case studies that illustrate connections between repurposing and emancipatory practices through making, one of the dimensions of *cultural making* (Blikstein, 2020). We focus on two main aspects of those connections: the appropriation of technology as an instrument to question the reality imposed by systems of oppression (de Certeau & Rendall, 2011); and how creative "de-scription" of objects (Akrich, 1994) empowered a group of youth in procuring materials for projects.

Emancipatory practices in rural India

R. is a maker educator who runs a makerspace in a rural Indian context whose challenges include lack of education amongst the population, poor infrastructure facilities, culturally rooted orthodoxies, social inequalities, and low recognition of local knowledge. Every two months, R's organization runs "open innovation days." Initially, educators gave decontextualized material (e.g. electronics or robotics kits) to students, and students built projects by mixing those components with locally sourced materials. For example, students combined wires and an LED with bamboo to make a pencil torch. In another example, the students collaborated with the village potter to devise a solar-enabled matka-cooler (earthen pot solar cooler).

As the children started applying local knowledge by repurposing locally available resources to problems identified in the community, they also began collaborating with community members. Upon reflection, R. and her team understand the effectiveness of exploring the community context and children's lived experiences in maker activities. In her interview, R. shared nine projects, 4 of which had features designed to address social issues raised by the community: a bicycle-powered fodder cutter, a bicycle-powered mechanical washing machine (Figure 1); a bike umbrella; and a solar mobile charger. Those artifacts express applied creativity and reflect the idea that makerspaces allow for technical workarounds to overcome socio-economic limitations (Dalla Chiesa & Foletto, 2022). R. described the washing machine, for example, as an engineering innovation to alleviate local girls' domestic duties, freeing more time for studying.

By designing a new artifact out of existing products, the youth in the village seem to move closer to the "tactical" role described by de Certeau and Rendall (2011): they appropriated technologies and made unexpected use of ready-made products. In the process, they found ways to reimagine power dynamics by exploring their freedom to experiment.

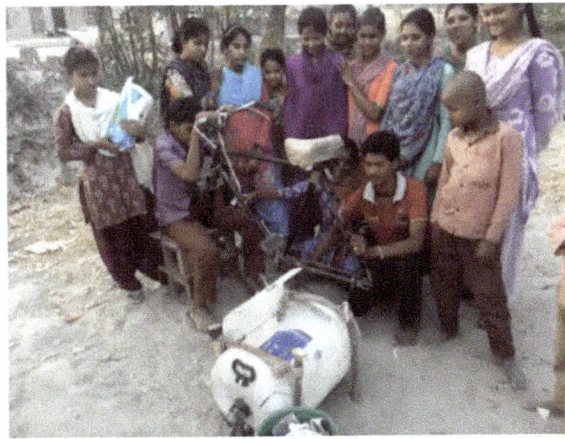

Figure 1. The bicycle-powered washing machine created by and for girls in a rural Indian village

Emancipatory practices in urban Kenya

B. runs a maker education program in Kenya serving high school youth or recent graduates in Nairobi, a densely populated urban area. The program in Nairobi exposes youth to events such as hackathons and innovation bootcamps and conducts guided visits to local tech industry facilities, like a factory producing 3D printers out of electronic waste. This program aims to ignite youths' interest in inventing locally, innovating, and problem-solving.

Similar to the work described above in the rural Indian village, much of the students' innovative work involves repurposing available materials. B.'s organization annually enrolls in an international robotics competition that supplies a kit of component parts. However, participants did not always use all parts in the kit, leaving several components — such as gears, wheels, metallic beans and rods, nuts and bolts, and chainlinks — available for repurposing. One group of students built a working prototype electric bike composed exclusively of parts leftover from the robotics kit (except for the paint). Program participants also built a prototype water filtration system using spare robotics parts as a frame. Participants are currently testing this prototype.

Remarkably, participants subverted the scripted use of the technology proposed to them, instead ascribing new meanings to those artifacts (Akrich, 1994). In her account about supply and demand mismatch, Akrich maintains that designers create objects with scripts that "predict" how the user will interact with those artifacts in their specific context of use. Still, the user (through their expertise or support from an expert) can reprogram those objects and de-script them.

Discussion

This paper considers maker practices in informal learning settings in two countries in the Global South. We collected data in partnership with educators committed to the development of those communities. Through two case studies, we show that activities developed by those maker educators involve youth in practices of making that employ locally sourced materials to address community needs. The first case study suggests a re-thinking of power dynamics through the appropriation of technology — a principle addressed in the learning sciences literature (for example, Holbert et al., 2020). Technology's role in emancipation resembles the role Freire assigned to literacy (1983): in a process initiated by the identification of local generative themes, devices created by the students in the village in India become their tools to affect change in their material reality. In this case, locally sourced materials mediate the appropriation of technology in a way that enables reimagining the stories of children in the village. Looking back on the program's achievements, R. proudly tells the story of an alumna who was the first girl in the community to enter college, pursuing a career in Chikankari (traditional embroidery) craft and design entrepreneurship.

The second case study offers a glimpse into practices of *de-scription* of artifacts in addressing community needs (water filter) and personal desires (electric bike). As proposed by Akrich (1994), participants in the Kenyan program "partially reconstruct" the usage script devised by the designers of the kits provided to them. In previous research in the learning sciences, Sheridan and Konopasky discuss how resourcefulness — "the ability to be aware of the potential around you" — is part of the ethos of the maker movement and has been adopted as a core value in some community makerspaces (2016). Our case study demonstrates how that ability is deployed in a setting with sharp differences from makerspaces depicted by most of the literature. Here, de-scription presents the chance to experiment with technologies and create artifacts that are otherwise far from reach. Without readily available electronic goods, we found examples of kids reimagining the affordances of components to construct their own devices.

The findings in this paper offer an opportunity to rethink the role of making in diverse communities. First, our data support the reasonable assumption that emancipation and agency mean different things in an urban US community compared to a rural Indian or a Kenyan city. In American urban settings, making might offer the chance for girls to connect with computing by producing e-textiles (Searle & Kafai, 2016). Conversely, emancipation in a developing country might mean the possibility for school-age kids to dedicate time to school instead. It is not our role as researchers to assign what types of emancipation are valid or not, which raises our second point. Based on the evidence presented, we propose that studying maker practices in the Global South can bring a different perspective to the debate, one that takes into account its benefits, more than its pitfalls, especially because maker education has been sometimes portrayed as legitimating larger, structural problems in society. That is not to say that makerspaces should be regarded as neutral environments with the inherited right to be complicit with those inequities. On the contrary, focusing on global communities might inspire the search for practices that bridge the Papertian "learn by doing and sharing" with a genuinely Freirean emancipatory education.

Notes:

1. Transformative Learning Technologies Lab, Teachers College, Columbia University, United States
2. International Rescue Committee, Kenya
3. Swatantra Talim, India

References

Akrich, M. (1994). The De-scription of technical objects. In W. E. Bijker, & J. Law. (Eds.). Shaping technology/building society: Studies in sociotechnical change (pp. 205–224). MIT press. Cambpartiridge, MA.

Barajas-López, F., & Bang, M. (2018). Indigenous making and sharing: Claywork in an Indigenous STEAM program. Equity & Excellence in Education, 51(1), 7-20.

Barton, A. C., Tan, E., & Greenberg, D. (2017). The makerspace movement: Sites of possibilities for equitable opportunities to engage underrepresented youth in STEM. Teachers College Record, 119(6), 1-44.

Blikstein, P. (2008). *Travels in Troy with Freire: Technology as an agent for emancipation*. In P. Noguera & C.A. Torres (Eds.), Social Justice Education for Teachers: Paulo Freire and the possible dream (pp. 205-244). Rotterdam, Netherlands: Sense.

Blikstein, P. (2020). "Cheesemaking emancipation: a critical theory of cultural making," in *Designing constructionist futures*. eds. N. Holbert, M. Berland, and Y. B. Kafai (Cambridge, MA: MIT Press), 105–114.

Buechley, L., Eisenberg, M., Catchen, J., & Crockett, A. (2008, April). The LilyPad Arduino: using computational textiles to investigate engagement, aesthetics, and diversity in computer science education. In Proceedings of the SIGCHI conference on Human factors in computing systems (pp. 423-432).

Cavallo, D. (2000). Emergent design and learning environments: Building on indigenous knowledge. IBM Systems Journal, 39(3.4), 768-781.

Charmaz, K. (2006). Constructing grounded theory: A practical guide through qualitative analysis. Sage.

de Certeau, M. & Rendall, S. (2011). *The practice of everyday life*. Berkeley: Univ. of California Press.

Dalla Chiesa, C., & Foletto, L. (2022). On Gambiarras. Global Debates in the Digital Humanities.

Eisenberg, M. (2002). Output devices, computation, and the future of mathematical crafts. International Journal of Computers for Mathematical Learning, 7(1), 1–43.

Freire, P. (1983). *Pedagogy of the oppressed* Seabury Press. New York.

Halverson, E. R., & Sheridan, K. M. (2014). The maker movement in education. Harvard Educational Review, 84(4), 495–504. doi.org/10.17763/haer.84.4.34j1g68140382063

Holbert, N. (2016). Leveraging cultural values and "ways of knowing" to increase diversity in maker activities. International Journal of Child-Computer Interaction, 9–10, 33–39. doi.org/10.1016/j.ijcci.2016.10.002

Holbert, N., Berland, M., & Kafai, Y. (2020). 50 Years of Constructionism. In N. Holbert, M. Berland, & Y. Kafai (Eds.), *Designing Constructionist Futures: The Art, Theory, and Practice of Learning Designs*. Cambridge, MA: MIT Press.

Searle, K. A., Fields, D. A., & Kafai, Y. B. (2016). Is Sewing a "Girl's Sport"? Addressing Gender Issues in Making with Electronic Textiles. In K. Peppler, E. Halverson, & Y. B. Kafai (Eds.), *Makeology: Makerspaces as Learning Environments* (pp. 207–222). Routledge.

Sheridan, K. M., & Konopasky, A. (2016). Designing for resourcefulness in a community-based makerspace. In *Makeology* (pp. 30-46). Routledge.

Vossoughi, S., Hooper, P. K., & Escudé, M. (2016). Making through the lens of culture and power: Toward transformative visions for educational equity. Harvard Educational Review, 86(2), 206-232.

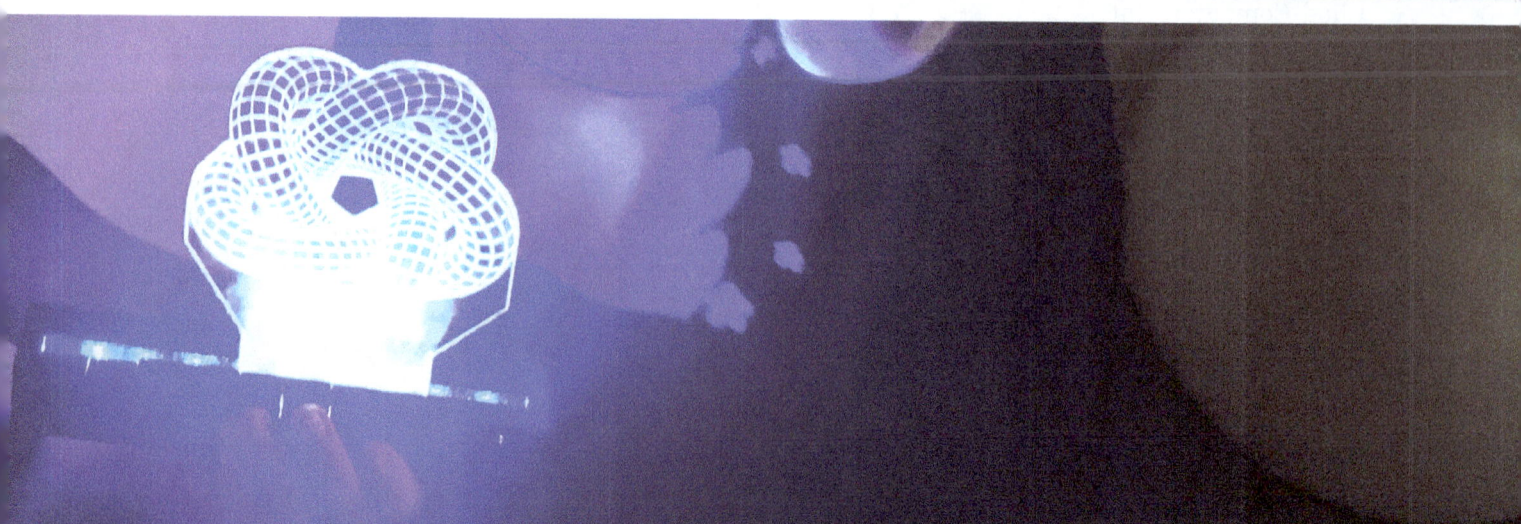

Change

Change. It's an old adage that everyone wants change, but no one wants TO change. We all want education to be "better," but what does that mean? And even if we could all simultaneously agree what it means, what will it take — money, time, new policy or law, or all of the above?

Sometimes the world seems to change in an instant. Easy to access Artificial Intelligence (AI) tools burst on the scene in 2022, and are sure to change education, but how? Will schools try to ban AI, embrace it, or ignore it? And is it new?

Nope – in 2002, Seymour Papert gave a lecture at MIT about how he missed the good old days of "big ideas" about the nature of knowledge and human learning.

"I have been through three movements that began on a galactic scale and were reduced and trivialized," Papert said. "The three movements — child development, artificial intelligence, and kid-friendly computer science — were especially vital and big in the early 1960s." (MIT News, July 9, 2002)

He went on to say that Piaget's brilliant insights about child development have been reduced to "little strategies for presenting math problems" instead of the powerful idea that children develop intellectually without being taught. And as the cofounder of the Artificial Intelligence Lab at MIT with Marvin Minsky, Papert said that the "cosmic question" of making a machine that rivals human intelligence had been forgotten in a race to improve bottom lines and create more efficient workflow. Hmmm, sound familiar?

Papert said many times in his career that educational systems are "idea averse." This certainly makes the idea of change difficult. If new ideas are rejected or trivialized, the same systems will be invented and reinvented again and again with new labels and acronyms, but no real change. But despite his critique of the system, Papert engaged in a lifelong effort to make schools better places to learn.

In these articles, the FabLearn Fellows offer their own ideas for change, both in their own schools and for education in general. Like Papert, we are optimists who never give up, even when things seem difficult.

How FabLearn Changed My Perspective Towards Technology in the Makerspace

by Ridhi Aggarwal

In our makerspace, the focus has been to use contextual and culturally relevant material that children can use to rebuild, iterate, and construct new knowledge. Some 3–4 years ago, the only technology commonly used were mobile phones and not every household had one. So, no-tech or low-tech was the basis of our philosophy to operate our makerspace in the village.

We also thought that introduction of technology generally brings in a lot of alienation among adolescents and youth. Research speaks to the ill-effects of technology as people get detached from their roots and lose connection with local context, ecology, and relationships. Technology was seen as only a tool for consumerism and not a tool for creation. All these combined to create apprehension and distrust of technology in educators like us. It was reinforced by our association with Krishnamurthi school of thought and democratic schooling, which values freedom of choice and expression, learning by doing, and making learners active and informed members of the civic society.

Being a part of the FabLearn Fellowship at Columbia University has given me new perspectives to reflect upon. On one hand I have been exposed to the exciting work of other maker educators from around the world and on the other hand leaning about the great thinker and educator Seymour Papert has opened up new horizons in our work.

Papert criticized the usual paradigm about the use of computers in education. For example, a common use of a computer is to automatically adjust the next problem being presented to the user based on how accurately one has answered the previous question. Papert views these programs as glorified worksheets that fail to capitalize on the unique power of computers. Papert deliberately sought not to build computer programs that aimed to get students to do something specific like solving math problems or repeatedly practice a particular concept. Rather, he viewed computers as tools that should empower children to explore topics meaningful to them. Papert believed computers could uniquely help students develop a deeper and a more intuitive understanding of mathematics.

Following this vision, he created the programming language Logo in which users create on-screen geometric patterns and simulations by giving programmed instructions to a "turtle" icon on the screen. This gives students concrete opportunities to practice usually abstract mathematical and problem-solving skills. This idea of using computers as a tool to enable children's

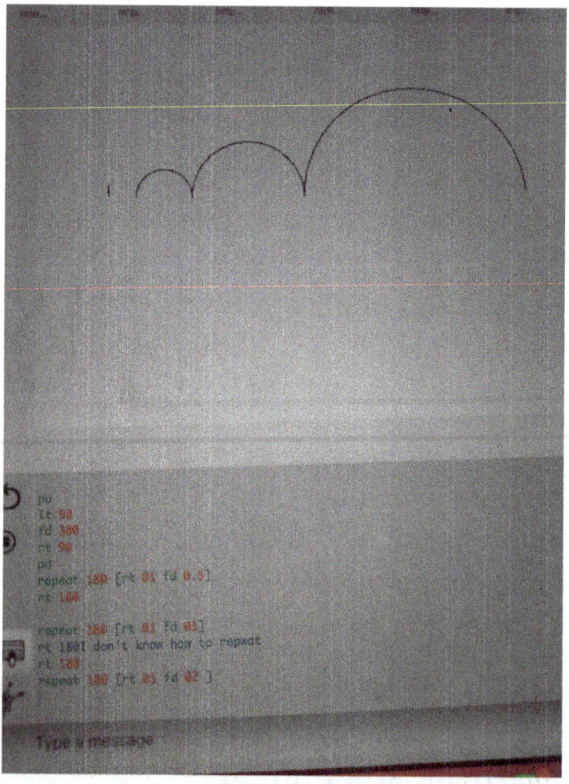

thinking and enhancing mathematics skills gave us the starting point to introduce computers in our makerspace. We just had to find a common ground from which to start.

The mathematics of patterns was that common ground. Our community's rich knowledge of chikan kaarigari embroidery patterns served as a link between contextual knowledge and Logo turtle. We had often used their embroidery as a base to introduce patterns to the children but this time we integrated that with the Logo turtle. We asked them to make some patterns, explore for themselves, and then make new patterns from their own exploration.

Constructionist learning focuses as much on the process of making as in the end result. Children not only tried out new patterns in Logo but they also translated them to their embroidery and showed it to their parents and community which gave their art a new dimension. This is how we started opening doors to introduce computers and technology into our maker space. And now slowly and steadily we have started taking small steps by introducing Arduino microcontrollers and other technology. Going further, as our community is rich in art and crafts, we started to think about how can we integrate technology in the makerspace to enhance these crafts.

At this stage another FabLearn webinar with James Rutter from Haystack Mountain School of Craft gave insight as to how a makerspace can be well integrated with art and crafts. An example that stayed with me was how in a jewelry designing workshop a person had to turn the coils many times to make a particular piece of jewelry and how that person thought of making a tool with the 3D printer to make the process easier. To me, this was a beautiful example of how the makerspace can be an integral part of an art and craft space.

These inputs from the FabLearn community gave our makerspace new vigor to integrate technology with the rich traditional art and craft while keeping our values intact.

Contemplating Education Reform

by Toni Marie Kaui

The purpose of education

The first free public school in America, Boston Latin School, opened in the town of Boston in 1635 (Lisa, 2021). While Boston Latin was open to any boy in Boston, we can speculate that only families with some wealth could send a boy to school rather than to work. With classrooms reserved for the males with some amount of privilege, it might be appropriate to question whether this was true public education, since this education prepared these sons to assume control of the family business; a task the home might no longer be equipped to provide, but hardly benefiting most Boston families. Free public schools were not the norm in America well into the 19th century.

Starting in 1837, Horace Mann radically changed education in the United States with his concept of free, public "common schools" as a means of standardizing public education, supported by "normal schools" to train professional teachers (Cremin, 2021).

Horace Mann advocated for public education for all Americans, regardless of race, ethnicity, or gender, through primary grades. His model which focused on six fundamental propositions: (1) an ignorant populace is unacceptable, (2) public education should be free, (3) diversity creates a better educational environment, (4) public education should not be based on or controlled by any religion, (5) democracy should prevail in classrooms, and (6) education must be provided by well-trained, professional teachers (Cremin, 2021, p. 4). Horace Mann's determined advocacy for public education as a means to create literate, educated citizens suited to participate in a democracy became widely accepted and adopted across the United States.

But even with the rise of public education, there was often a lack of standardized curriculum. Throughout the 1850s and 1860s, around the time Darwin published *On the Origin of Species* and Americans fought in the Civil War, "geographic location largely determined whether students learned biblical creation or evolution in class and whether slavery was taught as the central cause of the Civil War instead of states' rights and Northern aggression" (Lisa, 2021, p. 20).

We know all too well that political power and propaganda often propels change in education. Nearly a century later, when the Soviet Union was beating America in reaching outer space, education reform became a means to compete in the quest for domination of space and scientific prowess. At the turn of this century, as America loses its dominance in the global economy, education reform has again become the focus of calls to address perceived literacy and numeracy incompetence, as well its lack of vocational training.

However, have these efforts improved education and prepared students for their futures? The reasons behind why we educate our children drive the decisions regarding how we educate our children.

A personal perspective

My personal experience with the impact of global events on education began with another urgent call to regain America's position in the global technological competition. Science, technology, engineering, and math (STEM) competencies were declared insufficient.

"U.S. eighth graders continue to rank in the middle of advanced economies in international mathematics and science assessments … [and] foreign-born individuals account for a sizable share of U.S. S&E [science and engineering] employment, particularly among workers with graduate degrees" (Khan et al., 2020, p. 2), indicating the need to improve America's mathematics and science knowledge, skills, and experiences and increasing the number of Americans enrolling and completing graduate programs.

Our nation's response to this crisis was the Bush administration's "No Child Left Behind" legislation in 2001, holding schools accountable for students' performance on standardized tests, and essentially forcing teachers to "teach to the test." In 2009, the subsequent administration of President Obama passed "Race to the Top" and "Every Student Succeeds Act" legislation, both of which gave more control back to schools and school districts and allowed them to make administrative decisions that supported the learning needs of their students. The Obama legislation moved educational reform in the right direction and demonstrated a commitment to student learning by leaving the decisions in the hands of the people who work most closely with students.

But I found myself asking the question—should national needs drive our purpose for education and be used to navigate our educational landscape? Will responding to data and statistics bring the improvement envisioned?

Meaningful reform starts with student needs, not national needs

There is great potential for meaningful change when school district leaders and school administrators are allowed to make decisions. Given the power to decide who they serve, why they serve them, and how they serve them, schools and school districts can change their educational landscape. Although I work at a private school, when determining the purpose for education, asking these questions is critical. I serve the students who attend Nā Hunaahi and their families. I serve them because they chose to attend Nā Hunaahi, and these students and their families trust me to prepare them for their futures, whatever that might be. I prepare these students for their futures by including them in vital educational decision-making and allowing their goals to drive their curriculum. Based on these three tenets, my personal perspective on the purpose of education is to provide students with the necessary knowledge, skills, and experiences for them to achieve their goals through a culturally relevant and engaging curriculum.

Reforming curriculum

The reasons we educate our students drive the decisions we make as school administrators. The content and context of these decisions run wide and deep, and the repercussions of these decisions leave an indelible mark on the students we serve. Our purpose drives the decisions we make regarding student curricula.

I believe the purpose of education should be driven by students—who they are, what they want, where do they want to be — and this information should be used to identify how to best serve them.

For example, a Native Hawaiian student committed to restoring and revitalizing coastal fishponds interested in engineering and art deserves a curriculum and learning environment maximizing his/her commitments and interests. This means employing a variety of pedagogy and practice, including design-based learning (DBL), just-in-time instruction (JITI), and place-based learning (PBL). This student would have the opportunity to perpetuate his/her cultural practice, while simultaneously learning and experiencing professional practices of engineering and expressing his/her learning and achievement through art.

Individualized student learning plans pose an issue for many teachers for many reasons. One of those reasons includes not aligning with and/or containing content learning standards. Consequently, teachers view individualized or customized curricula as requiring too much work to make it feasible for a classroom of 20 to 30 students. Adding to the issue might be teachers' lack of knowledge and experience with content standards alignment to curricula.

When contemplating the standards issue, I began wondering about the importance and need for content standards in K–12 education. In a 2021 FabLearn Fellows webinar, Gary Stager reinforced this contemplation when he shared that Papert "always fought against terrible ideas like a national curriculum and the Common Core" (FabLearn, 2021 9:34), which emboldened me to dive into the idea of learning driven by student culture, goals, and interests.

A tradition of standards

In 2009, a group of state leaders led efforts to develop the Common Core State Standards (CCSS) with the release of the final English language arts and mathematics standards in mid-2010. By 2015, "42 states, the Department of Defense Education Activity, Washington, D.C., Guam, the Northern Mariana Islands, and the U.S. Virgin Islands have adopted the CCSS in ELA/literacy and math" (Council of Chief State School Officers, 2015). In the summer of 2011, the organization Achieve coordinated the development of the Next Generation Science Standards (NGSS), with the final document released in April 2013 (Achieve).

Teachers today are well versed in standards such as the Common Core. But this is not new. Standards have guided instruction throughout history. In the 17th century, religious concepts such as morality, family, and community, rather than academic pursuits, dominated the guiding principles of education, such as "Puritans ... required parents to teach their children to read and also required larger towns to have an elementary school, where children learned reading, writing, and religion" (University of Minnesota, 2016 ch 16). At the culmination of the Revolutionary War, the publishing of textbooks started as first attempts to standardize learning content, and could be considered a first use of content standards.

From an educational reform perspective, content standards have "...three purposes ... [1] publicly identifying what is important for schools to teach and for students to be able to demonstrate. ... guide ... instruction, curriculum, and assessment ... [2] providing a map of where the curriculum should go and ... [3] to fit the needs of diverse learners. Finally, ... they can guide the allocation of instructional resources" (National Research Council, 1997, p. 114). Unfortunately, a problem with content standards lies in the differing and varied content standards available for schools. While content standards tend to have similarities, they vary depending on the publishing institution/organization and specific state needs, which begs the question, what are content standards standardizing?

To understand the breadth of this issue, we can review the recent changes in content standards for mathematics. As the chair of the National Governors Association, former Arizona Governor Janet Napolitano created an initiative that focused on improving math and science education. This became the foundation for what would become the Common Core State Standards in math. However, not all states use these standards. Some states continue to use the National Council for Teachers of Mathematics content standards, while others use state-specific math content standards. Independent and parochial schools often claim their own modified and/or revised versions of a multitude of content standards possibilities. The variations found for mathematics can also be found for all other content disciplines, which might translate to not having a truly standardized content area.

A new tradition for content standards

Reigeluth (1997) believed that rather than using content standards "to help make students alike ... they can be used as tools ... to meet individual student needs" (1997, p. 203). The diversity of student abilities in learning supports his beliefs about how to use content standards, but how can this be implemented? I believe that the traditional education systems of Native and Indigenous peoples provide a model.

The education of Native and Indigenous peoples happened and continues to happen without the need for traditional Western education. The inherently incorrect idea that Caucasian male colonizers know what is best for the educational and academic advancement of Native and Indigenous peoples is an idea that needs to be squashed. Native and Indigenous peoples have been educating themselves and their youth for centuries before white colonization, and with this education, they built facilities that withstood natural disasters, attended to medical needs and issues, cultivated flourishing terrestrial and marine agriculture and aquaculture, and traveled vast distances over oceans without modern navigational tools; these accomplishments represent only a fraction of what Native and Indigenous nations are capable of attaining.

These achievements came without the need for a set of content standards. Native and Indigenous nations understood how to teach future generations the knowledge and skills necessary for any occupation without needing a written set of instructions. Through practical experiences and efforts, masters passed on their knowledge and skills to apprentices. An argument against this method of teaching and learning could be the limited number of apprentices masters could teach, which might have led to the need for large educational institutions teaching common knowledge and skills for a given profession.

Adding colleges to the conversation means thinking about how secondary educational institutions prepare students for success at the post-secondary level. However, can success in college be completely attributed to demonstrating proficiency in content standards? I posit that while it might offer some insight into the possible success of a student, it does not paint the whole picture of a student. Therefore, there might also be some room to revisit the need for content standards and looking at different options that allow schools the flexibility to prepare students for specific college and career pathways without adhering to a full list of content standards.

Innumerable possibilities

My school, Nā Hunaahi, "prepares students for their futures, whether it be to pursue further education or training, to assume adult roles in their families, careers, and/or communities, and/or to cultivate personal well-being," which means it is our responsibility to prepare students for a variety of future possibilities, which may or may not include traditional Western education. Consequently, as we work toward accreditation, we are responsible for offering educational and academic opportunities that address the needs of our students, not necessarily the needs of education as a system.

As we continue our journey of providing Native Hawaiian youth with an education they deserve, we continue to ponder and discuss these important issues with our peers and our ancestors. In the words of the great historian Herbert Kawainui Kane, "there must be another way, if only because there has to be."

References

Achieve. Developing the standards. nextgenscience.org/developing-standards/developing-standards

Council of Chief State School Officers. (2015). Development of the Common Core State Standards Initiative. corestandards.org/about-the-standards/development-process/

Cremin, L. A. (2021). Horace Mann. britannica.com/biography/Horace-Mann

FabLearn. (2021). FabLearn Fellow webinar with Gary Stager. fellows.fablearn.org/ffmedia/zoom/2021-04-20/zoom_0.mp4

Khan, B., Robbins, C., & Okrent, A. (2020). The state of U.S. science and engineering 2020. National Science Board.

Lisa, A. (2021). History of the American education system. msn.com/en-us/news/us/history-of-the-american-education-system/ss-BB1gz0NK

National Research Council. (1997). Educating one and all: Students with disabilities and standards-based reform. The National Academies Press.

Reigeluth, C. M. (1997). The Phi Delta Kappan. Educational standards: To standardize or to customize learning.

University of Minnesota. (2016). Sociology: Understanding and Changing the Social World. University of Minnesota. open.lib.umn.edu/sociology/chapter/16-1-a-brief-history-of-education-in-the-united-states/

Is ChatGPT a Threat to Education? For the Banking Model of Education, Yes

by Charles Pimentel

OpenAI's ChatGPT[1] is a newly developed Artificial Intelligence (AI) agent designed to perform high-level cognitive tasks and produce original text that is indistinguishable from human-generated text.

It is essential to highlight that AI only generates a synthesis of what humans have already created, in activities for which it was trained, but performs them with greater speed and (sometimes) greater accuracy than a human being.

Nonetheless, this draws a parallel to the traditional approach of education, wherein schools often mold students to replicate established rules and memorize concepts. This starkly underscores the antiquated nature of our current educational system.

For example, if a teacher proposes an activity in the classroom such as, "Write an essay about elections" the students will search for the information on the internet and by rewriting several texts found and trying to connect them in a consistent way, they will present an original essay. ChatGPT performs the exact same process.

However, it is important to emphasize that writing a text does not mean learning and internalizing issues related to the topic, but only demonstrates the ability to carry out searches on Google and write something that respects syntax and semantic rules. That's what OpenAI's application does... only faster.

Thus, when asking ChatGPT to write a paragraph about elections on two consecutive occasions, the platform presented two distinct responses. Both these responses were classified as originals on platforms that identify plagiarism.

Try #1

Elections are a fundamental aspect of democratic societies, as they allow citizens to participate in the selection of their leaders and the direction of their government. The process of holding an election is both complex and vital, as it must be fair, transparent, and representative of the will of the electorate.

Try #2

Elections are a process by which citizens of a country or members of a organization choose their leaders or representatives. This is typically done through a vote, in which eligible individuals cast their ballots for their preferred candidates or party. Elections can be held at different levels, such as national, state or local level, and are used to select leaders for government, political parties, and other organizations.

Is this a threat to education?

Schools that value traditional education, would give good grades to students who write texts like these, considering them prepared for society's demands, as they "write well." Paulo Freire (1977) called this the "banking" model education, where ideas and content are "deposited" into students and "withdrawn" when tested. But education for the 21st century, which needs critical thinking, creativity and real problem solving, seeks to develop student skills and competencies that go beyond formulaic writing, memorization, and test taking.

There are amazing, creative, critical, innovative, and sensitive students who might not write as well as ChatGPT. In fact, while writing skills and performing good internet searches are extremely important, they are not the only evidence that should be used to assess the student's academic development.

AI and its applications need to be seen as allies for a constructionist education based on the ideas of Seymour Papert and also for a transformative education based on the critical and reflective pedagogical practice of Paulo Freire.

Mathematics, language and humanities dialogue with each other when the school understands that the advancement of new technologies expands the opportunities for student-centered learning, promoting a multidisciplinary educational process, while seeking solutions for the real world.

Emerging technologies provide opportunities in the school context for an active and meaningful learning environment, provoking important reflections on what is expected from the 21st century school.

ChatGPT may be a threat to a traditional model of education, but our job is not to preserve old models of learning but to engage in an important discussion: *"Where should education for the New Millennium go?"*

Notes

1. openai.com/blog/chatgpt

References

Paulo Freire, Pedagogia do Oprimido, Editora Paz e Terra, Rio de Janeiro, 1977, 4ª ed., (N.E.).

Education in the Age of AI

by Lars Beck Johannsen

Some technologies are truly innovative, changing the way we live our lives. Recent development in the field of Artificial Intelligence (AI) is certainly in that category, some even compare it with the invention of electricity. In this article I would like to share both some of my experiences in education and share my thoughts and hopes for the future.

Five months prior to writing this article I wrote a blogpost about the subject and already in that short amount of time, a lot has changed. AI technology moves fast, really fast, and both businesses and the general public have adopted the technology to a high degree. I can not begin to fathom all the aspects of AI technology, but will focus on education.

In Denmark, the debate about ChatGPT as a tool for cheating with school assignments is ongoing. The debates range from banning the tools, restricting WiFi, and trying to detect AI generated work. Probably not a good approach. Others talk about changing the assignments and working together with AI instead. They suggest that students analyze the output that is generated, checking the facts and statements that is the AI´s output. Another suggestion is that students prompt ChatGPT to write about a topic that is well known to the student. Will they agree with what is being generated or is something that is obvious to them be missing?

A recent documentary series made by the Danish national television (DR) invited different experts and scientists to debate and explain AI. What is AI is already changing and what it might become in the future is uncertain. The experts shared a few perspectives on education and none of them looked good for teachers. But I would argue that it is the school system that is challenged, and that it needs to change the way education traditionally is being practiced.

One example is the teaching of a foreign language, where high school teachers right now struggle with extensive use of AI generated papers and translations. And yes, the students are cheating and not really learning much about the language. But what if the AI was a personal assistant that listened to your pronunciation and grammar and gave you corrections in a safe and personal space where you did not have to worry about classmates thinking that you sounded funny?

I think a lot of subjects and the way that students are being taught will change in the future. There is a lot that AI can assist us with, but also a lot that the technology cannot. AI is very bad at being human; it only mimics, and it only sees the world through the data it is given. It cannot replace the relationships between human beings.

In the Danish school system there has been a focus on working together in groups and how to deal with conflicts since the seventies. I think that in the future it will be even more important to learn how to be together physically in the same room as well as in virtual rooms. Another thing that comes to mind is the way that we learn, feel, and manufacture through our hands. There are crafts that are still a long way from being automated and still hold great value both as a learning experience and making tangible objects.

Constructionism could work well in cooperation with AI, since creating tangible objects in the real world is something that could benefit from AI. Enabling the ideas to become real would be much easier and nonetheless a learning experience, especially if it grows out of the world around you, your culture, interpersonal relations, wicked problems or even silly and useless stuff AI would never come up with.

I have been wondering about what I will do differently in the future. My work is all about creating and teaching how to create. Using AI is something I will encourage, not limit. There are two major new areas I will focus on: prompting as a new aspect of computational thinking and the discussion about ethics involved with AI.

Prompting is giving instructions to the AI and the more specific you can be, the better result the AI will generate. It is kind of a language of its own and something you can do on different skill levels. Computational thinking is a part of this and it will be interesting to develop ways to learn it. I am no expert in prompting but I am looking forward to go on the journey alongside with my students in the process of creating the projects that grow out of the classroom or the fablab.

You can not talk about AI without touching on the ethical part of the technology. I think that it is very important to have an open and free discussion about this not only in the classroom but on all levels of society.

I have already experienced different approaches by students in the use of AI. Some students cheat with AI. Some students "tease" the AI to make faulty outputs. Students use AI for generating code for their projects. Other students have a sense of responsibility in how they behave towards AI and are always polite in the conversation with the language model.

In many ways these examples show that the choices we make are fundamental to how we might use AI. AI can enhance what we do, both good and bad. It is very much up to us what we will allow it to do.

Of course there is also the intentionality from businesses that use AI in their products, that is another challenge for the generations to come. One recent example is Snapchat's AI which seems to be another tool to keep you on the app longer but also for getting more personal data from the user. This is not transparent and something that is the basis for a good discussion about personal data and ethics. On a larger scale AI is being discussed globally on all levels of government and business. Should it be open for all, regulated, or something else?

AI will change the future of education for sure, and I think it is good news for the constructionist approach and bad news for the more instructional education models. What else the future will bring to our local and global society is very much up to every individual and the choices we make in the use of AI. It is certainly an interesting time in history to be experiencing and I am sure that there is a lot of potential to prosper as humanity as long as we remember to be human along the way.

Technology is a New Kind of Trojan Horse: Reflections on a Text by Professor Paulo Blikstein

by Charles Pimentel

Is the ideal school possible? What is the role of technology towards this purpose? How can teachers promote a meaningful learning atmosphere? This article shares an experience in a high school in Brazil after reading and reflecting on the article by professor Paulo Blikstein, *Travels in Troy with Freire: Technology as an Agent of Emancipation*.

The ideas of Paulo Freire and Seymour Papert are the fuel for this discussion, and the Maker Movement, through new technologies, is the engine that can lead us to a school where teaching and learning might become significantly improved.

Ideally, the implementation of maker education in schools would be well planned, with very clear objectives. Here, the Cheshire Cat in *Alice's Adventures in Wonderland* offers a warning, "If you do not know where you are going, any road will take you there."

Although we find different social and educational realities in the world, I find that Paulo Freire's pedagogy has the power to address all learning contexts. Among his contributions, "Generative Themes" are well known (Freire, 1970). That is a pedagogical methodology that aims at making students perceive themselves as agents of change — that their own ideas, hopes, and vision for the future are valuable. Generative Themes can be a good start to implement actions that result in meaningful learning.

Providing students with an atmosphere of belonging, sharing, innovation, and meaning are principles shared by Lev Vygostsky and Seymour Papert. When students collaboratively develop a project with a common goal, exchanging experiences, debating on best practices, agreeing on some points and disagreeing on others, their collective and significant construction generates active learning and stimulates the quest for new knowledge. In this sense, new technologies that facilitate any of these things are important tools for an emancipatory education.

> "Another means is for individuals to design devices, systems, or solutions, using knowledge from science and technology, and then use language to improve these devices through critical interaction with fellow designers." (Blikstein, 2016)

At Polo Educacional Sesc, a project was developed in our makerspace to encourage the use of available technological tools to develop and carry out activities in alignment with the school curriculum. The project proposed the following reflection to students: *How can digital fabrication resources available at our school space support the development of low-cost learning objects for science teaching?*

Polo Educacional Sesc

Polo Educacional Sesc is a private high school in Rio de Janeiro, Brazil, offering free-of-charge, top-level transformative global education to low-income students from Rio de Janeiro. Unfortunately, before going through this life-changing educational program, many of these students were in schools that lacked educational and technological resources, laboratories and often, teachers.

It didn't take long for the students to detect a problem: many resources for experimental science teaching are very expensive, which makes them quite inaccessible to many schools. So, they thought they could use the prototyping supplies from the makerspace at the school to contribute towards the cause of low-cost science resources.

As they researched, an experiment similar to a Linear Air Rail was identified by the students as a potential project to be developed. A Linear Air Rail is a perforated rail connected to an air blower. This device can be used to study and experiment with important concepts in kinematics, such as speed and acceleration. It is an aid to the teaching of physics and mathematics. In Brazil, this experiment costs around US$ 1,000, which makes it impossible for many schools to acquire.

With these thoughts in mind, the students decided to develop a track with sensors that would measure the speed of a Mousetrap Car, thus generating performance tables and graphs. They developed this track so that other students from their own institution or from other educational spaces with few resources would be able to create these cars. The only source of energy for the prototypes is a mousetrap, and the cars can have different designs. Thus, by placing their model on the track and activating the trap, students can measure the performance of their creation.

Although the Sensor Track is different from the Air Rail, mainly because it has friction between the car and the track, the students still needed to use concepts of math, physics, basic electronics, and C ++ programming skills to develop the project.

With an Arduino Mega microcontroller, 9 LED arrays, 8 ultrasonic sensors, a 16X2 LCD screen, wires, MDF wood, creativity and the help of a laser cutter, students produced a solution for less than $ 100.

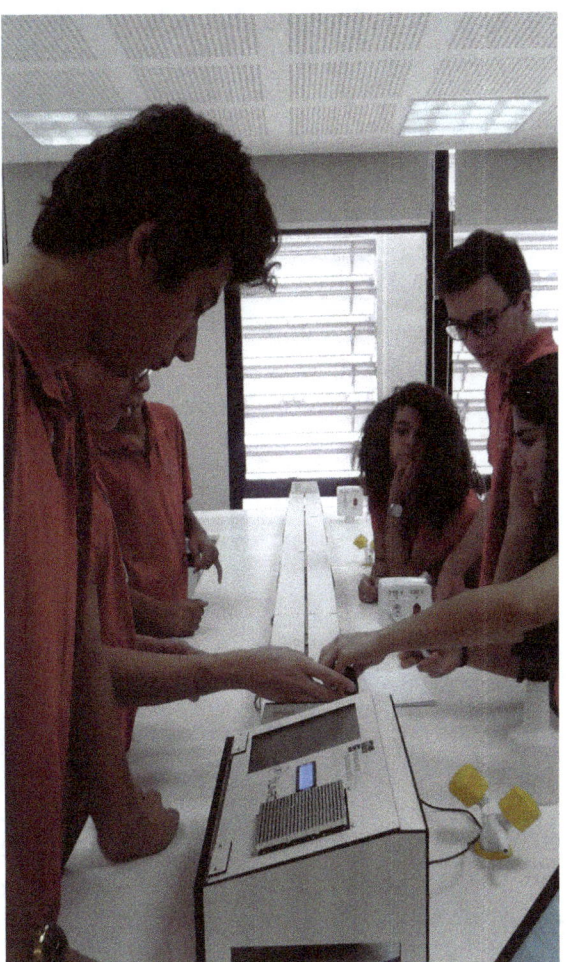

Track with sensors for Mousetrap Cars

Reinventing an existing technological experiment to reduce its cost dramatically was the path taken by the group of students who participated in the project. They knew that many schools, like the ones they came from and studied in previous years did not carry out experiments with their students due to a sheer lack of resources. Empathy was an important mobilizing agent of transformation.

Mousetrap Car modeling workshop

"Freire's focus on humanism and Papert's emphasis on the creation of personally meaningful artifacts are highly complementary" (Blikstein, 2016)

As Blikstein points out, an authentic Generative Theme has the power to provide engagement and "true emancipatory knowledge must make people feel like agents of action and change in the world".

The Sensor Track project showed that when students had the opportunity to engage in an action that could promote change, they identified a problem (which was part of the academic life of some of them) and then, developed a solution for it.

This is what is expected of education: that it changes students' lives but also that students in a privileged situation can commit to promoting changes in other spaces that have fewer resources and possibilities. Education has that power. Science, Technology, Engineering and Mathematics are the mechanisms and students are the agents.

"Students appropriate the Trojan technology as authentic means to liberate themselves from the incarceration of traditional pedagogy. Once deschooled, students shake off the dust and engage in authentic inquiry and construction." (Blikstein, 2016)

Blikstein's image of technology as a Trojan horse in the school is spectacular. The technology may be delivered in the horse, but the Trojan horsepower is that it allows students to marvel at the awareness that they are also an agents of change in society.

Special Acknowledgment: I would like to thank Paulo Ceotto, specialist at Sesc's International Advisory Office for his invaluable contribution in the translation and adaptation of this article.

References

Freire, P. (1970). *Pedagogy of the Oppressed*. New York: Herder and Herder

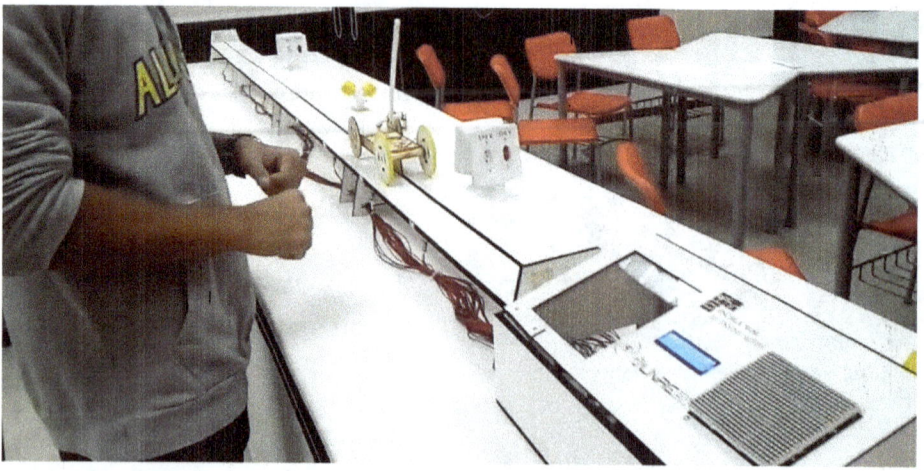

Having Financial Resources Does Not Guarantee Learning

by Débora Garofalo

I recently visited Recife, the capital of a northeastern state in Brazil and their Municipal Department of Education to find out what they have been doing in the field of teaching programming and robotics.

In conversation with several teachers in person, after nearly two years of social distancing and COVID-19, I got to know about their work and anxieties.

One of their anxieties is that although they have cutting-edge resources, such as humanoid robots and LEGO kits with which they have won several national and international championships, the greatest difficulty was in promoting learning that was meaningful and real, such as solving real problems with those devices.

I showed them how to start the work of the Robotics with Scrap project, introducing maker culture without having so many resources. They were interested in finding out more, and how children and young people turned it into a teaching methodology for 3.5 million students.

At that moment, I remembered Papert's teachings and his pedagogical and epistemological concerns he documented in his books. These concerns arose when classes remained essentially the same after the introduction of technology. Decades later, we are still struggling with the same issues. Technology does not guarantee learning. We must allow creativity and critical thinking in the education process.

It is not just a matter of bringing expensive technology and robotics to school to achieve improvements in the quality of education. The innovative use of technology on a daily basis, by students and teachers, can radically change the focus of the teacher's practice. But the technology must be used by students to develop their own ideas. With creative uses of technology, students become responsible for their own development and, therefore, responsible for their own education.

Papert's learning theory of constructionism says that people acquire knowledge through the construction of artifacts, which is what I saw when students constructed robots with scrap materials. These constructionist ideas were based on the work of Piaget, his mentor in the years he worked with him in Switzerland, but actually date back to his childhood, when mechanical components and gears became mental models that he could use in his understanding of the world, of mathematics, and of learning.

Papert's interest in gears shapes his constructivist view of learning — what an individual can learn, and how they learn, depends on the models they have.

Papert and Freire both defend and advocate for the role of mediator in the social aspect of learning. For Freire, the use of technology in education should embody technological praxis, since all use of technology is influenced by ideology. It is necessary to identify the underlying principles of technological practices as we search for genuine justifications for their use.

For Freire, technology needs to be used with an awareness of the potential for political-ideological manipulation which permeates technological environments and mediums. But Freire still asserts that a full understanding of technology humanizes people and makes them capable of transforming the world.

Both Papert and Freire demonstrate that the scientific and technological moment in which we find ourselves affects education. A fresh approach to educational practices, seen through an epistemological lens, can generate autonomy for both learners and teachers. The development of a new education system should take advantage of new technology not only to guarantee access to information and content, but also to allow students to be discoverers and researchers. There are all kinds of technologies, including inexpensive ones, that can enable the learners to explore and be creative.

References

Freire, Paulo. Pedagogia do oprimido. Rio de Janeiro: Paz e Terra, 1979.

Freire, Paulo. Pedagogia da Esperança: Um reencontro com a pedagogia do oprimido. Rio de Janeiro: Paz e Terra, 1993.

Freire, Paulo. Pedagogia da autonomia. 9. ed. Rio de Janeiro: Paz e Terra, 1998.

O Futuro da Escola: Seymour Papert e Paulo Freire – uma conversa sobre informática, ensino e aprendizagem. Produção da Pontifícia Universidade Católica de São Paulo – TV PUC. São Paulo: PUC-SP, 1995. Vídeo na Internet (60 min.), Formato MP4, son., color. Disponível em 177.11.48.108:8080/xmlui/handle/7891/395 >. 10 de out. 2021.

Papert, S. Mindstorms: Children, computers and powerful ideas. Brighton: Harvester Press, 1980.

Papert, Seymour. A máquina das crianças: repensando a escola na era da informática. 2. ed. Porto Alegre: Artes Médicas, 1994.

Quilts: Collaboration, Coding, & Culture

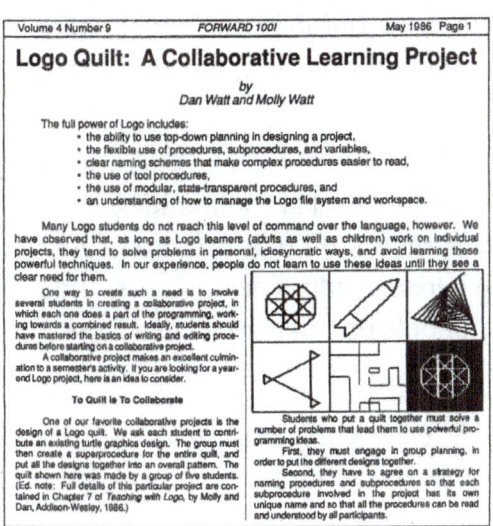

Midway through the FabLearn Fellow Cohort 3, we embarked on a project that is well known to the Logo community — to collaboratively build a quilt out of individual patches designed in the Logo programming language.

At the time, the world was still deep into the COVID-19 pandemic, so this project modeled constructivist distance learning. People could work on their small piece on their own, but still be part of a larger construction.

In the 1960s, Seymour Papert, Cynthia Solomon, Wally Feurzeig and others invented Logo, the first programming language for children. The "big idea" was to not just give computers to children, but as a way for children to grapple with deep mathematical ideas.

By giving directions to a friendly turtle, the turtle moves and draws. The original turtles of the 1960s were floor robots with a pen attached. As computer graphics became more sophisticated, the turtle took its place on the screen and "turtle graphics" was born.

While modern incarnations of Logo like Scratch and Turtle Art are very popular, for this project we used a variation called Lynx from LCSI, a company Seymour Papert co-founded. It runs in the browser, but is text-based, like earlier versions of Logo. Gary Stager provided us with a handout to introduce the language and how to get started with the quilt project.[1]

As the popularity of Logo grew in the 1980s, some educators who were early adopters became evangelists. Perhaps the most famous were Dan and Molly Lynn-Watt who wrote fun and accessible books and articles to teach teachers about Logo.

They shared the idea of making a quilt using Logo in an article in the magazine *The Logo Exchange*, in May 1986,[2] excerpted here.

To quilt is to collaborate

One of our favorite collaborative projects is the design of a Logo quilt. We ask each student to contribute an existing turtle graphics design. Students who put a quilt together must solve a number of problems that lead them to use powerful programming ideas.

> The full power of Logo includes:
> - The ability to use top down planning in designing a project
> - The flexible use of procedures, subprocedures, and variables
> - Clear naming schemes that make complex procedures easier to read
> - The use of tool procedures
> - The use of modular, state-transparent procedures
>
> Many Logo students do not reach· this level of command over the language, however. We have observed that, as long as Logo learners (adults as well as children) work on individual projects, they tend to solve problems in personal, idiosyncratic ways, and avoid learning these powerful techniques. In our experience, people do not learn to use these ideas until see a clear need for them.
>
> One way to create such a need is to involve several students in creating a collaborative project, in which each one does a part of the programming, working towards a combined result.

Dan and Molly describe valuable aspects of this project, including:
- "Group agreement on naming procedures
- Understanding the computer science concept of "state transparency." The turtle must begin and end at the same position and heading, or else the next person's procedure will not draw correctly.
- Everyone can contribute at their level of expertise. The designs can be simple or complex. Programming techniques are shared and can be appreciated.
- Some programmers may find they need to use variables to adjust the sizes of their drawings."

Constructionism and culture

The Fellows who undertook the quilt challenge came to these conclusions naturally as they worked to make patches that fit together. This is an often misunderstood aspect of constructionism, that there is no intentionality in the lessons that are learned. Dan and Molly show their deep understanding of how to teach computer science principles not by lecturing about them, but by creating projects with criteria, constraints, and challenges that are guranteed to push students into new understandings.

Dan and Molly also mention the respect for culture that this project shows. Around the world, the concept of a quilt is valued. Not only are quilts useful and beautiful, but they tell stories and are created by many hands.

"We also like the fact that quilt-making is a traditional art form, with techniques and aesthetics that make use of different materials and technologies. This shows that computer activities do not have to take place in a high-tech vacuum, but can incorporate ideas from other ages and cultures."

The reflections by the FabLearn Fellows in this section show the power of this collaborative project has not diminished over the years.

Notes

1. Cooperative quilt instructions in Lynx and Turtle Art by Gary Stager. constructingmodernknowledge.com/quilt/
2. Logo Quilt article el.media.mit.edu/logo-foundation/resources/nlx/v4/Vol4No9.pdf
   Full archive of Logo Exchange magazine el.media.mit.edu/logo-foundation/resources/nlx/

Digital Quilting Around the World

by Greg Houghton

The ability for teachers and learners to contribute, learn from each other, and remix work is a powerful shared experience for all involved. The process provides opportunities for individual interpretation and expression of ideas. Through the introduction of the Lynx patchwork quilt project, the FabLearn Fellows were given just this opportunity and tasked with designing at least one tile or patch using the lynxcoding.club software.

Too often creative activities are delivered through meticulous step by step instruction resulting in whole class facsimiles of the same product, this not only stifles creative expression but limits the potential to explore individual ideas.

The project allowed for individual expression yet the end product was the result of everyone's contribution. As the Fellows shared the code used to make their patches we were able to overcome challenges by learning from each other's discoveries and move forward with our creations.

More often than not the computer is utilized in the classroom in an attempt to "program the child" as Seymour Papert would say. This approach is very much an opportunity for the child to program the computer. The visual feedback provides a fun and accessible way to try out code, and the ability to copy commands into procedures was an intuitive way to build complex patterns.

When using the software I sometimes found that the code I had created generated unpredictable results encouraging me to go back to the procedures and try and debug where the issue was. Sometimes I even found myself turning my head or body to simulate the movement of the turtle.

Although the contribution of ideas to create a collaborative piece of work is a technique I have employed in creative activities in the past, the use of Lynx provides a new context to the approach. The ability to utilize, combine, and modify each other's code created a scenario that emulates a developers use of repositories such as GitHub.

This modular approach to projects provides the opportunity for everyone to contribute to a bigger idea or finished product, while all can be involved in creating a rich environment for collaboration and the cross pollination of ideas. To hear that Lars Beck Johannsen's students in Denmark had utilized some of my initial code was a great feeling and demonstrates the community aspect of this approach.

The variety of interpretations of the brief was enriched by the Fellows introducing cultural elements, such as traditional tile designs and patchwork quilt production methods. This introduced us to cultural elements and provided insight into each other's heritage.

Teaching Collaborative Programming: A Creative Adventure Using Lynx

by Débora Garofalo

It is important that teachers and students understand that they can contribute to the effective use of technological innovations, as well as new ways of using them in activities and projects in the classroom. Making the teaching of programming possible through playful resources can be a key to learning to think, figuring out new possibilities, persisting, and developing 21st century skills.

Adventures in creativity can happen in many ways and one of them is using Lynx! Lynx is a new web-based Logo dialect and I had not tried this tool before but was challenged to do so with my FabLearn Fellows Cohort 3 to build a collaborative quilt, programmed in Logo and drawn by the turtle.

I believe programming is a great lever in the teaching-learning process, as it goes beyond understanding how the computer and programming commands work. Programming activates logical thinking to promote new learning connections, especially when students analyze their hypotheses and debug their programs.

The purpose of the activity was to recreate patchwork quilts, using mathematics in its everyday form, not in the formal way math is usually presented in teaching materials. Requiring every person to create a uniform patch, and putting them together to create elaborate geometric patterns, connects programming and constructionism, through the Logo language, and also honors quilting traditions that can be found in cultures all over the world.

The project challenged us to create at least one patch and share our patch with our peers. We could then take some of those patches and make a quilt from them.

In this sense, we went beyond a programming activity that an individual could complete, towards fostering engagement and effective participation from the whole group. This is a new way of thinking and solving problems, rethinking the learning process not as an end, but as a process under construction.

It is no longer possible to imagine a society in which people do not need basic computer knowledge, it must be considered important for contemporary living, alongside basic knowledge of mathematics, philosophy, physics, and other sciences (Resnick, 2017).

The activity reminded us that Papert and his constructionist approach to learning aims to promote the construction of knowledge by the young person who tells the computer what must be done, through the programming language.

Logo is not just a language, but also a philosophy about the nature of learning using technology (Papert, 1996), which provides students with conditions to explore their intellectual potential.

One of the powerful ideas of Logo is that once you figure out how to do something, you can "teach the turtle" a new word that will remember this sequence of instructions. These new words are called procedures. Procedures behave just like *primitives* (the built-in commands of a language), except that they are unique to a particular project.

For Papert, the goal of education is to create an appropriate context so that learning can be developed in a natural way. What is intended with the Logo language is to create an opportunity for a creative environment that makes it easy to solve problems. By proposing significant challenges like this one, related to topics relevant to student learning, we can create contexts where students are the ones seeking innovative solutions and representing their own ideas using Logo.

One of the main lessons learned in this type of activity is to allow students to solve problems through immediate feedback on their actions. Thus, they can compare their initial ideas with the result obtained, analyze their successes or errors, ask questions, make new attempts, check their results, and continue to build new concepts from this process.

There are many benefits of teaching programming in the classroom, and reflecting on this challenge allowed me to think about teacher practice using technology in the construction of knowledge and worlds of creativity!

References

Papert, S. (1996). *The Connected Family: Bridging the Digital Generation Gap*. Longstreet.

Resnick, M. (2017). *Lifelong Kindergarten: Cultivating Creativity Through Projects, Passion, Peers, and Play*. MIT Press.

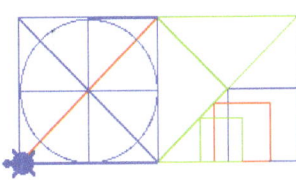

My quilt

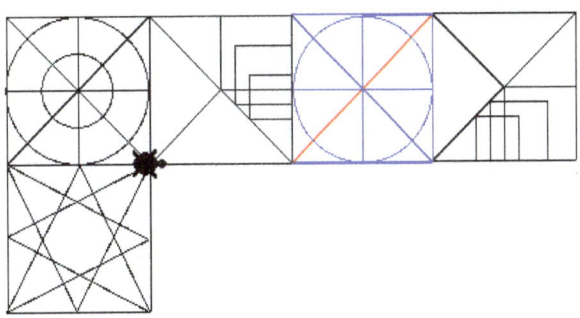

My quilt using the patches produced by my peers

Create a Quilt That Wraps the World

by Lina Cannone

A particularly interesting aspect of being part of the Fablearn Fellows group is to have first-hand experiences of activities that we could offer to our children.

Last month's project was to make a collaborative quilt, in which each component must use one or more frames, each frame becoming a patch in the quilt. The design of each frame was to be written in Lynx, a cloud-based programming environment derived from Logo. I had never used this software before and I did not know the syntax. The programming space at first approach was quite spartan but over time I was able to discover its potential and I really appreciated it.

When I start learning new software or a new language, I always prefer to use already made code from which to start and that I can modify. This allows me to understand the syntax rules and to find out which part of the code does what by analyzing different outputs depending on the changes I make.

For this reason, when I introduce a new project in the classroom, I always try to propose to kids some inspiration projects whether it is software, such as Scratch projects that can be modified or used only as inspiration, or construction projects. I noticed that initially, the students rely a lot on the suggested products but once they become familiar with the software or material, they tend to discard the prototype and build something completely different and that better reflects their tastes and abilities.

This approach was also useful on this occasion, I started from a piece of code created by another fellow. I modified it gradually to create my frame.

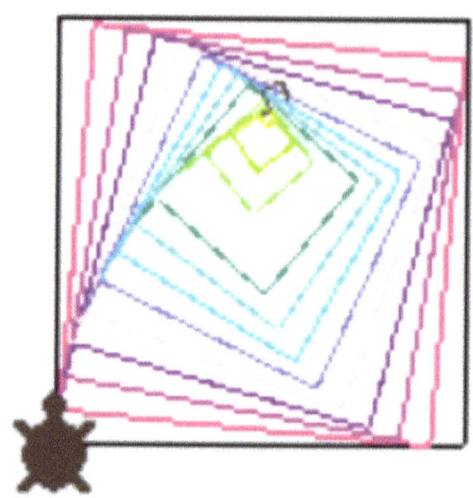

The next step was to join the different frames and create a quilt. I particularly like this aspect because even if at a distance, distributed all over the world, we were able to create something together. I felt part of a community — inspired by a project that unites us. It is a very topical issue, that of remote collaboration, which teachers have been trying to incorporate due to the pandemic. I believe that projects of this type can involve and engage students in a collaboration even if they are not physically close.

During the activity, cooperation between peers occurred spontaneously. There were several times that someone shared their code and asked for support to find an error that they could not identify, and the group supported them, thus avoiding the frustration of failing. I analyzed a peer's code, and that gave me a greater knowledge of the tool and led me to reflect on how different people built codes with very different characteristics to do very similar things.

The work of others inspired further ideas for other frames, and I believe that this "idea contamination" is very positive because even if someone initially does not feel able to design or build their own project, thanks to the projects of their companions they can find their own way forward. Often, when we work face to face, I find it very useful to let students pass between the tables to find opportunities or to help those in difficulty.

The final step is to show your work to the group, which has two important benefits: First, sharing generates greater self-confidence and leads to reflection and finding inspiration from the work of others. Second, to tell what happened and how, to activate the metacognitive functions that lead to a greater awareness of self, revealing the logical and creative processes that are triggered. Mitch Resnick inserts sharing as one of the phases of the creative learning spiral followed by the reflection phase (Resnick, 2017).

Just like my students, I had an initial phase of disorientation in which I did not know the software and had no ideas of what to do. There was a period of latency, of searching for inspiration, and then I started to build something. The comparison of my own work to the work of the other Fellows was fundamental to be able to finish my project.

References

Resnick, M. (2017). *Lifelong Kindergarten: Cultivating Creativity Through Projects, Passion, Peers, and Play*. MIT Press.

Experiencing a Powerful Mathematical Idea

by Ridhi Aggarwal

> "The universe cannot be read until we learn the language in which it is written. It is written in mathematics, and the letters are triangles, circles and other geometrical figures, without which it is humanly impossible to understand a single word."
>
> — Galileo Galilei

The universe is a source of basic geometric shapes, we discover them through the observation of nature. This understanding of basic shapes and their functions have taught us to mark time and space in a variety of ways which has inspired mathematics, technology, language, and ever evolving civilization.

As geometry is inspired by nature, children should also understand its elements by discovering the world of shapes around them. The Logo turtle is one such tool that I experienced, which would help children discover the concepts by exploring on their own.

My experiences

I remember when I was first introduced to Logo turtle, I was so excited to try it despite lacking any technical or coding background. I was even more excited to see the turtle move according to my wish on my computer screen. I could make it move up and down, right and left, and experiment with its movements.

Spending time exploring the different commands gave me the confidence to experiment more. Initially I was confused by the right and left command as I thought that the turtle would simply start to move in that direction, but when I understood it better, I realized that all the possible angles could be explored. I loved exploring reflection and transformation concepts and bringing them alive in the form of the art my turtle could make.

Math talk

As a teacher, while exploring Logo and the turtle, I was thinking that this tool would give children so much space to explore and learn while talking about mathematics. This interaction and conversation is often missing in mathematical learning. Reuben Hersh in his book *What Is Mathematics, Really?* says mathematics "… is learnt by computing, by solving problems and by conversing more than by reading and listening."

This important element of mathematics can come alive as the teacher can start a discussion on angles, directions, and movement of the Logo turtle with questions like – *What happens when you enter 45? What about 180?* Some prompts like – *Can you try making a shape using what you all have learned or explored till now?*

Talking about their learning and thinking in a mathematics class through the actions of the turtle would help children construct many learning dimensions. Even if some students might struggle putting these pieces together, combining actual physical movement, concrete experiences, or walking like the Logo turtle, along with verbalizing, would help them to conceptualize the geometry they are learning.

Constructivist curriculum

A constructivist curriculum focuses on students actively experiencing and building ideas to solve personally meaningful problems along with taking ownership and being self-motivated. The traditional geometry curriculum often starts from the concept and then asks the child to solve a problem which may be out of context. However, if we teach geometry through the movements of the Logo turtle, children explore on their own and come to the concepts after having a concrete contextual experience. This would mean that children would be inventing basic concepts in mathematics on their own, thereby learning to be mathematicians. There are numerous reports that students fail to learn basic geometric concepts, especially geometric problem solving due to lack of geometric intuition. The children do not have enough examples to experience conceptual and procedural understanding of topics to be studied in higher classes like vectors, coordinates, transformations, and trigonometry.

Intuitive geometry

The whole process for me started with exploring concepts intuitively on the Lynx coding platform, which uses a text-based form of the Logo programming language. While making geometric shapes and complex patterns, I started to think that Logo turtle is a powerful tool for intuitive learning.

Seymour Papert in his book *Mindstorms* said,

> "I take from Jean Piaget a model of children as builders of their own intellectual structures. Children seem to be innately gifted learners, acquiring long before they go to school a vast quantity of knowledge by a process I call 'Piagetian learning' or 'learning without being taught.'"

As an educator who believes in the principle that children learn a lot intuitively, I have experienced the same when I observe toddlers playing with loose parts, making shapes or patterns, using things in symmetry while making a pattern or balancing things, and making decisions intuitively.

This process of children experimenting on their own makes me further reflect on Papert's "objects to think with," as a powerful concept that keeps the learner at the center of the learning process. The best part is that the child does not have to think about creating these objects, but as they use it naturally, they create and discover on their own. This is constructive learning as it means that learners construct the mental models to understand the world around them.

The Logo turtle creates that space for intuitive learning, while also serving as an object to think with, which I need to explore myself with children to understand it further.

It can be said that physical actions on concrete objects are necessary to help students construct geometric ideas, such as through concrete manipulatives like geometry rods, blocks, geo-board, isometric papers, and many others. Using manipulatives facilitates the learning process and it is equally important to see whether the children are able to establish a link between the action of the manipulative to describe the action. Thus, students must internalize such physical actions and abstract the corresponding geometric notions.

Learning geometric ideas can be seen in the use of the Logo turtle as the children will invent basic concepts which will help them progress to higher levels of thinking in mathematics. Van Hiele proposes a model of geometric thinking levels in which the students move from one level of thinking to the next.[1]

If a teacher plans the lesson combining concrete manipulatives, experience from the real world, as well as the Logo turtle to teach geometry, I strongly believe that students would not only progress into higher levels of thinking but also would build stronger conceptual understanding of geometry which they would be able to use in other situations to solve other problems. They would thus be learning geometry relationally.

Reflections and implementation

The quilt project with the FabLearn Fellows came at a time when we were exploring revolution as a theme with children in our organization. The community has been doing embroidery and thread work on things around cloth. So, we were exploring ideas about how cloth, and specifically quilting, has been used as a tool for revolution. The children created quilts and did thread work around revolution. I am excited to give them the exposure to turtle geometry through Lynx where they can explore more making digital quilt patterns and then making those quilts physically.

It has been an enriching experience for me to explore the concepts of Logo and turtle geometry and reflect on how it challenged my own comfort zone, and made me wonder how technology can be integrated with children's hands-on-contextual experiences. One of the aims of our organization is to give students ownership of their learning. This mission sometimes comes with frustration on their part, but putting them in charge and giving them freedom often pushes them through roadblocks, from which they emerge with an eagerness to continue learning.

This experience of working on the Logo quilt project with other Fellows has given me the push to think about how, up to now, concrete hand-on-contextual experiences of making have been the key to my work with children. But this experience has given me many points to ponder and enhanced my own learning as an educator. This has been a powerful idea for me to explore further.

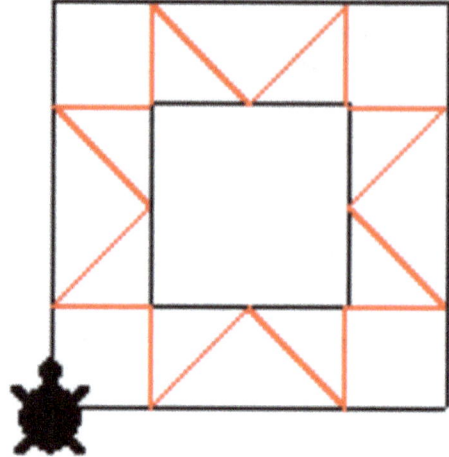

Note

1. Van Hiele model of geometric thinking en.wikipedia.org/wiki/Van_Hiele_model

Quilting the Young Coders

by Michael Mumbo

The word programming is misunderstood. It is a fallacy that it is disconnected from other subjects, that this "language of computers" is foreign and hard to read, and takes years to learn. Maybe this is because some "experts" use abstract terms while introducing young people to programming.

According to Seymour Papert, "Construction that takes place 'in the head' often happens especially felicitously when it is supported by the construction of a more public sort in the world" (1993). Shouldn't the children program and create ideas that can be examined, shown, probed, and even admired by not only themselves but also others?

During one of our virtual programming sessions with 8-year-olds, I met a student who made me think hard about my perception about teaching programming to kids. In Kenya, the Grade 3 curriculum does not allow them to dive deeply into concepts like geometry. When you mention angles and geometry to a Grade 3, some of them might think that you are asking them about their "favorite tree" (Geometry).

We were using a programming application called "Little Quilt." The learners need to have a basic understanding of geometry principles to proceed with some of the programming stages. Needless to say, the little girl proceeded to change the angles and the bearings to program a bird to pick a worm. This young girl was fully aware that making the birds turn at 15 units will not make it pick the worm but when changed to 10 units it picks the worm. We progressively changed the values 15 units at a time, 0,15,30,45,60,75,90. We agreed that it can only pick the worm when the units are between 0-10. But wait, what are we talking about here? ANGLES of course!

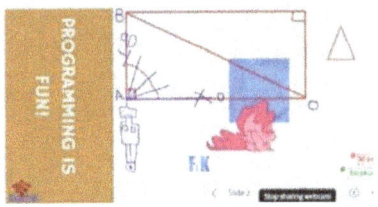

The little one seemed to be aware of something she called a "right-angled triangle." Perhaps she heard someone mention it somewhere. Having all these tiny pieces of information, I decided to put programming on hold and walk her through some math concepts about triangles.

We drew a rectangle, which I then diagonally cut. The little programmer agreed that one of them was a right-angled triangle, but was not sure that the other upside-down half was also a right-angled triangle. It made me think for a moment that perhaps she had only seen right-angled triangles drawn one way.

After this, we got back to programming, where I introduced the concept of loops and conditions. This too often is introduced as an abstract concept. But when you think of it as crossing the road, you usually look left, right, then left, and if the road is clear you cross, else you wait. I find this to be a powerful way to introduce if and else commands in programming to the young programmers.

Reference

Papert, S. (1993). The Children's Machine: Rethinking School in the Age of the Computer. Basic Books.

Cultures of Reuse & Recyling

This section is about reuse and recycling as a way of approaching the world, and how this mindset can be turned into learning opportunities. It starts with an article in both Portuguese and English about a project that has spread across Brazil called "Robotics with Scrap." The project started with students identifying a problem in their community and solving it with ingenuity and technical skills. Other articles in this section approach recycling and reuse from other angles, but all with the point of view that students can be recognized as citizens of the future with rights to a clean, safe, environment, and a say in determining this future.

Also included in this section are three interviews with Fellows about student projects focused on reusing and recycling. These interviews followed a series of protocol questions that were also part of the process of writing the AERA award-winning paper, "Emancipatory Maker Practices in the Global South" found on page 87. These extended interviews offer insight into ways that students and teachers interact with materials and technology, and how local culture plays a part in the decisions and practices described.

Robótica com Sucata: Por uma educação criativa para todos

by Débora Garofalo

> "Precisamos contribuir para criar a escola que é aventura, que marcha, que não tem medo do risco. A escola em que se pensa, em que se cria, em que se fala, em que se adivinha, a escola que apaixonadamente diz sim a vida."
>
> —Paulo Freire

Você já pensou em transformar um problema dos estudantes e ou do território educativo em currículo?

Essa é a história por detrás do trabalho de robótica com Sucata, que atualmente é uma política pública estadual de São Paulo, presente em mais de 5.400 escolas e eternizadas em obras e relatos de experiência, recebendo diversos prêmios, entre eles, Professores do Brasil 2018, Desafio de Aprendizagem Criativa do MIT 2019 e considerada uma das 10 melhores Professoras do Mundo pelo Global Teacher Prize 2019.

Bastidores do trabalho de Robótica com Sucata

Quando cheguei a escola municipal EMEF Almirante Ary Parreiras em 2015 me deparei com uma das realidades mais difíceis como professora durante a minha carreira docente. Os estudantes estavam expostos ao alto índice de violência trazida de fora do ambiente escolar e ao tráfico de drogas.

Outro problema latente da comunidade escolar era a ausência do saneamento básico e estrutura precárias das casas. Foi nessa realidade que decidi sair da minha zona de conforto como professora de algumas turmas e me candidatar para a vaga de professora de Tecnologias. Com o objetivo muito claro de **transformar a vida de crianças e jovens através do uso das tecnologias**, ao ressignificar a aprendizagem através do uso de tendências digitais como o ensino do pensamento computacional, através da cultura maker, programação e de robótica como propulsoras a essa transformação.

No entanto, como em muitas outras realidades que adentram o Brasil, a escola não possuía os materiais adequados para ensinar robótica aos estudantes e a solução para minha angústia veio de um problema social relatados pelos estudantes: "o lixo". Olhar para esse problema social que impedia os discentes de irem à escola em dias de chuva e que trazia doenças como dengue e leptospirose, foi a solução para ressignificar o ensino e desta maneira nasce o trabalho de robótica com sucata impactando os estudantes do 1º ao 9º em aulas regulares.

Para se inspirar na sala de aula

Para que você possa replicar o trabalho em sua aula, conheça alguns passos e como foi concebido a partir das vozes dos estudantes e passos:

Aula pública – de sensibilização da comunidade sobre a importância do lixo e descarte de maneira adequado. Assim, foram realizadas saídas pela comunidade com trajeto definido em sala de aula por cada turma e série com o objetivo de sensibilizar a comunidade local sobre a questão do descarte do lixo e sustentabilidade 5R´s (reciclar, recusar, reutilizar, reduzir e repensar) e no percurso recolhendo o lixo eletrônico e materiais recicláveis.

Recolhimento de materiais – Recolhimento de materiais recicláveis e lixo eletrônico pelas ruas da comunidade.

Separação dos materiais – Separação e pesagem dos materiais do que seria usado em sala de aula e do que poderia ser vendido através de parcerias com ongs, tornando o trabalho sustentável e podendo adquirir itens como placas programáveis, fios, leds, entre outros materiais.

Mão na massa – Aguçar a aprendizagem para criatividade e experiências, como construção de diferentes protótipos e envolvimento das áreas do conhecimento, cultura maker, programação e robótica.

Pensamento computacional – idealização do trabalho através de mapas mentais e pesquisas com a programação realizada no scratch, software livre educativo e interativo, que funciona por blocos lógicos que dentro possui a programação.

Robótica com sucata – Exercício da criatividade, da inventividade, pesquisa e o desenvolvimento do pensamento científico, com a construção de protótipos com funcionalidades específicas dos anseios pessoais dos estudantes unindo o lixo reciclável e o lixo eletrônico. Entre os trabalhos realizados estão carros, aviões, barcos, robôs como Wall-e, casas, entre outros.

Compartilhando ideias – Exercício do protagonismo juvenil através da feira de tecnologias, um momento para os alunos demostrarem os seus trabalhos a comunidade e enfatizar a importância da sustentabilidade.

Feira de tecnologias – Por fim, um segundo momento com a comunidade através da feira de tecnologias. Um momento para que os estudantes fossem protagonistas ao apresentar os seus trabalhos, mas que pudessem ser multiplicadores de informações ao mostrar a comunidade o que haviam produzido com o lixo.

O trabalho deu – se em aulas regulares e incorporou diferentes conteúdos aprendidos a elementos da cultura maker, da programação e da robótica. O mais importante: aguçou a curiosidade dos estudantes para buscarem novas informações, despertando-os para o processo autoral e de autoconstrução do conhecimento.

Resultados

Com uma boa dose de criatividade na educação, foi possível oportunizar aos alunos da periferia da zona sul da cidade de São Paulo o acesso ao ensino do pensamento computacional e da robótica com sucata, mais do que isso, oportunizar que fossem protagonistas da sua história, ter sonhos, devolvendo a autoestima e possibilitando que os estudantes fossem multiplicadores de conhecimento ao intervir na comunidade.

Esse projeto, ao longo de três anos, contribuiu para a melhoria do Ideb da escola, que passou de 4,2 para 5,2 nos anos finais, em 2019, além de auxiliar na redução do trabalho infantil e da evasão escolar, através da identificação de potenciais estudantes em risco de deixar os estudos. Estes passaram a atuar como alunos-monitores, permanecendo em período integral, e me auxiliando na execução das atividades junto às demais séries. Houve também a retirada de mais de uma tonelada de lixo das ruas de São Paulo, que ao longo do trabalho foi recolhido, separado e pesado.

Além disso, foi importante também para a ressignificação do território educativo, impactando na autoestima dos estudantes e possibilitando novos caminhos de aprendizagem ao inserir na rotina escolar o pensamento computacional e as metodologias ativas aliadas ao currículo.

Por uma educação Criativa para todos

Ao unir a criatividade a um problema social, os estudantes puderam trabalhar de maneira interdisciplinar ao usar as áreas do conhecimento como matemática, história, geografia, língua portuguesa, ciências, artes, ressignificando a escola e maneiras de ensinar e aprender.

E este foi apenas o começo para trabalhar com temas essenciais como a inclusão. Tive muitos estudantes que possuíam deficiências e que o trabalho de robótica com sucata, inseriu os estudantes nas aulas e sua participação, através de experiências e de troca com o outro, fazendo que os estudantes pudessem trabalhar com habilidades cognitivas, motoras e sociais para a criação e execução dos projetos.

Durante as aulas os estudantes interagiam com os demais estudantes e materiais e pensava em problemas para resolver questões do cotidiano, como a criação de sensores para cadeiras de rodas e semáforos inteligentes para estudantes cegos.

Assim, os estudantes foram submetidos ao desenvolvimento de conhecimentos e habilidades relacionadas à solução de problemas complexos, ao raciocínio lógico, liderança e autonomia.

O ensino de robótica com sucata é uma abordagem integrativa, que reúne e mobiliza as áreas do conhecimento e uma maneira eficaz de trabalhar habilidades com estudantes especiais, promovendo a inclusão e ressaltando que as pessoas são o centro do processo de aprendizagem!

Note

1. Para conhecer mais acesse: youtube.com/watch?v=5rMZtqwcsKI

Robotics with Scrap: Creative Education for All

by Débora Garofalo

"We need to contribute to create a school that is adventurous, that marches, that is not afraid of risk. The school in which one thinks, in which one creates, in which one speaks, in which one guesses, the school that passionately says yes to life."

—Paulo Freire

Have you ever thought about transforming students' problems and/or educational interests into a curriculum?

This is the story behind "Robotics with Scrap." This project is currently public policy in São Paulo, Brazil, found in more than 5,400 schools, and documented in many articles and reports. The project has also received several awards, among them, Teacher's Brazil 2018, MIT Creative Learning Challenge 2019, and for my role in creating the project, I was named one of the Top 10 Teachers in the World, by the Global Teacher Prize 2019.[1]

Behind the scenes of Robotics with Scrap

When I arrived at the Municipal School Almirante Ary Parreiras in 2015, I came across one of the most difficult scenarios of my teaching career. Students were exposed to a high level of violence and drug trafficking brought from the school surroundings.

Another associated problem of the school community was the lack of basic sanitation and the precarious structure of the houses. It was at this time that I decided to leave my comfort zone as a classroom teacher and apply for the position of Technologies teacher. I did that having in mind a very clear goal of transforming the lives of children and young people using technologies, by reimagining learning using digital trends such as the teaching of computational thinking and through maker culture, with programming and robotics as propellants to this transformation.

However, as often happens in Brazil, the school did not have the appropriate materials to teach robotics to students. But the solution to this came from a local problem reported by students — the garbage. Garbage prevented students from going to school on rainy days. It spread diseases such as dengue and leptospirosis. Yet the problem was also the solution to our lack of materials and ended up giving new meaning to the work. Robotics with Scrap was started and grew to involve students from the 1st to the 9th grade in regular classes.

Inspiration for your classes

If you would like to replicate Robotics with Scrap with your own students, here are some steps from conception to implementation. As always, this is going to vary based on the students' needs and local conditions.

Public classes – Increase community awareness about the importance of garbage and its proper disposal. Groups of students (different classes and grades) created paths to be followed in tours of the surrounding areas of the school with the objective of raising awareness in the local community about the issue of garbage disposal and the 5R's of sustainability (recycle, refuse, reuse, reduce, and rethink). Along the way, students collected electronic waste and recyclable materials.

Recyclable materials collection – Recyclable materials and electronic waste were collected from the community.

Materials separation – Collected materials were weighed and separated into what could be used in the classroom and what could be sold via partnerships with NGOs, making the work sustainable. The money raised made it possible to purchase items such as programmable boards, wires, LED lights, and other materials.

Hands on process – To enhance creativity and hands-on experiences, students built different prototypes and involved different areas of knowledge, maker culture, programming, and robotics.

Computational thinking – Ideation of the process through research and mental maps programed in Scratch, free educational software.

Robots built with scrap – An exercise of creativity, inventiveness, research, and the development of scientific thinking, with the construction of prototypes using recyclables and electronic waste. These robots were designed by students based on their individual ideas and desires. Among the projects were cars, planes, boats, robots such as Wall-e, houses, and many others.

Sharing ideas – Students planned and ran their own technology fair, a time for students to show their work to the community and to emphasize the importance of sustainability.

Technology fair – An important aspect of the technology fair is the opportunity for students to be the protagonists when presenting their work. They could show that they were working to improve a community problem with real solutions to the problem of garbage and waste disposal.

The Robotics with Scrap project work took place in regular classes and incorporated different skills learned from elements of maker culture, programming, and robotics. Most importantly, it has sharpened students' curiosity to seek new information, awakening them to the design process and knowledge creation.

Creative education for all

By uniting creativity with a social problem to be solved, students were able to work in an interdisciplinary way using areas of knowledge of mathematics, history, geography, Portuguese language, science, and the arts, giving new meaning to school and its ways of teaching and learning.

Robotics with Scrap also served as a platform for essential themes such as inclusion. I had many students who had disabilities and the robotics projects made it possible for those students to participate, through experiences and exchanges with others, improving their cognitive, motor, and social skills in the creation and execution of projects.

During classes, students interacted with other students and materials and thought of many solutions to everyday problems, such as creating sensors for wheelchairs and smart traffic lights for blind students.

Thus, students were exposed to the development of knowledge and skills related to complex problem solving, logical reasoning, leadership, and autonomy.

The teaching of robotics with scrap is an integrative approach, which brings together and mobilizes different areas of knowledge, and is an effective way to work with special students, promoting inclusion, and emphasizing that people are the center of the learning process!

Note

1. Tackling waste with robots | Debora Garofalo, Brazil | Global Teacher Prize. To learn more, visit: youtube.com/watch?v=5rMZtqwcsKI.

Recycling 3D Printing Plastics

by Lars Beck Johannsen

I have for a long time searched for ways to recycle the failed 3D prints in our Fablab. Since I started the lab I have been collecting all the PLA filament based prints in a bag just waiting for the right technique.

Last year I tested a process where I baked the prints in an aluminum can at 200 degrees Celsius for about 20 minutes, which resulted in a fine solid that could be milled by a CNC. But young kids and CNC don't mix well. It is also a long process that is more suitable for high school students who might learn more about the material science involved.

Later, I stumbled upon a 3D print recycling workshop from Fablab Spinderihallerne that I thought might be worth looking into.

I also found students who would take on the assignment. They were a group of Ukrainian kids who have fled the war and go to school here in Denmark. Part of that is learning the language as well and this turned out to be a nice project for that. They had to learn the names of the colors and the tools we used. It wasn't the focus of the project but was a good secondary outcome.

We started by piling a bag of prints on the floor and sorting it into similar colors. Each group took their color and smashed them with a hammer into smaller pieces. Then they were put in a blender and processed until they became granulated. The blender died in the process when it had to deal with too large chunks of plastic, but that is a lesson learned as well, and soon we had enough granulate to continue.

We then used the heat press normally used for transferring vinyl stickers onto T-shirts, putting the granulates between sheets of heat-resistant material for baking. We experimented with different temperatures and time until we got a decent new flat piece of plastic that wasn't too brittle.

At the end of the session, they were asked to think of things to do with the material the following week, where we would laser cut shapes from the plastic sheets. I also tried to use it for vacuum forming, which didn't turn out well because it was too thick.

When the students returned the next week, we had them draw the shapes they wanted by hand, vectorize it with the Adobe capture app, and cut them on the laser cutter. They came up with objects like pendants, earrings, guitar picks, and nametags.

This process of reusing PLA from 3D prints is easy and shows students one of the good abilities that plastic has. It can be reused and given new shapes many times over. One thing the students really liked was the way they could mix colors when they were making plates. The lesson here is also part of learning about the properties of different materials.

I am happy with the way it turned out, as it is an important step in the process of making the Fablab more sustainable.

Note: Do not try this with any non-PLA filament or PLA filament with additives.

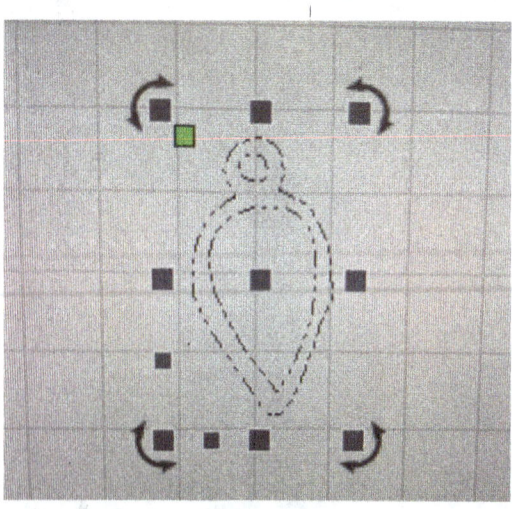

Interview: Coffee Grounds to Bioplastic

Interviewee: Lina Cannone.
Interviewer: Sylvia Martinez

Lina is a teacher at Istituto Comprensivo Orazio, a primary school near Rome, Italy. She teaches third to fifth graders in her makerspace, seeing them once a week for an hour.

Sylvia: In your makerspace, do you notice times when your students recycle or repurpose something into something else?

Lina: Yes. We use often recycled materials like cardboard and wood. We use a lot of these kinds of materials because they are not expensive and we have access to a lot of packaging. We use the recycled materials all the time to make new things.

We use also use organic materials, like coffee grounds from the teachers' break room. We create bioplastics from the coffee grounds, and then mix that with cardboard, wood, and hot glue to create shapes. The children decide on the different shapes to make every time we do this. And we use the shapes in other construction.

Sylvia: So bioplastics, that seems very futuristic. How did you come up with this project?

Lina: This project came from research that I did about two years ago. I tried to understand how to use products that have low impact on the environment in our makerspace. I also I wanted to use products that are from our roots, our culture. I saw many websites with recipes using shells, avocados, or other fruits and products that we don't have in Italy. So, I focused on what we have and that is coffee, and so we have a lot of coffee grounds.

Sylvia: Yes. Very good coffee! So you focused on the coffee grounds. Was that your first choice or the only choice? Have you tried other things and this worked out the best or how did that happen?

Lina: First I tried sodium alginate and calcium that is from algae. But it's only a product that I bought and not something that I could recycle.

Sylvia: Some cultures use that in food, but it's something you had to purchase, so it wasn't exactly right. And so how did you come up with coffee grounds?

Lina: I researched it on materialsproject.org. That is a website that has a lot of recipes. The first time we mixed the product, we tried it with the exact weight and we used a balance. Now we just mix it until it feels right — do we need it to be harder, more gummy, or more flexible?

Sylvia: And when you introduced it to the students, do you think they understood what the purpose of this material was? That it was about reuse and recycling?

Lina: Yes. The first thing was to get the coffee grounds out of the coffee machine. So we have to open it and dry it. And then we start the process. So, they know it's something from the trash bin and it's a recycling process.

Sylvia: So when you dry it and you have the dry grounds, do you process it further to make it a solid material? And what do the students use that for?

Lina: We boil it, dry it, add glycerin and cook it with the grounds. There are many recipes on the internet. We use gloves, safety glasses and we learn how to cook the material.

Then we create shapes. Some make shapes like bowls or cups and they need to figure out how to create a mold. For example to make a bowl, they have to press it into a bowl and then add a little bowl inside to make the shape, things like that. It's a process to understand how to create what we need because it's a gummy product until it dries.

Sylvia: And how long does that take?

Lina: One week.

Sylvia: A week? So that's the next time you see the students, when they unmold what they've made and be surprised in a good or bad way!

Lina: Yes.

Sylvia: So what are some interesting things that students have made out of the coffee grounds material?

Lina: The first time we tried to do a simple flat shape, but we didn't have the recipe perfected, and it cracked like a biscuit. But we got better at the recipe and have made pots that we were able to use to plant and grow lettuce for salad.

And now I'm trying again to do something more creative, maybe make things that can be used in projects like cardboard automata, or decorative things to be used in anywhere.

Sylvia: Did the students like it? Did they have a good time with this project?

Lina: Yes, they like when they create the molds, but sometimes there is a frustration when something goes wrong and the mixture doesn't dry and just remains a little bit like mud.

Sylvia: That's frustrating. So have kids ever come up with a second idea where they want to try again and do other things?

Lina: Yes. They tried to create more resilience in the material by trying other ways to create, adjust the recipe, and to try new ideas. Or they helped someone who had a good result in making other things with the final product. So we try for two weeks and then we use what we created. If something goes wrong, we have to restart. And that takes a lot of time.

Sylvia: It's hard when things take a long time. I guess it teaches patience and that not everything happens immediately too. Do you think this project helped students think of trash in a different way? Do you think it helped them understand recycling?

Lina: I don't know that. I don't think they really felt any different about recycling. But I noticed that they are careful to use just a little bit of the product because they know how hard it is to make and how much time they needed to create it.

Sylvia: So they value it more because they know how hard it was to create.

Lina: Yes.

Sylvia: Interesting. In their everyday lives they are asked to recycle plastics and bottles? Is that important to them?

Lina: Not so much. I think there is still a lot of work to do to help them understand these ideas.

Sylvia: You don't think they really understand the connection with saving the planet and all of that?

Lina: No.

Sylvia: We talked a little bit about building with cardboard. Do you think the cardboard reuse is easier for them to understand because it can be transformed into big things? Do you think that's easier for them to understand than the coffee grounds?

Lina: Yes. It's more immediately available in their lives. They can find it at home and everywhere, and use it whenever they want. It's more common in our culture to use cardboard to make something. I am sure they know if someone at home wants to create something, it's easy to do something creative with cardboard.

Sylvia: It's a good prototyping material that's cheap and easy to find. Whereas the coffee grounds, you have to spend a lot of time making it into a usable building material. Do you think that repurposing the cardboard gave them a sense that they were recycling and doing a good thing?

Lina: Yes. They love cardboard. Sometimes they come at school with a lot of cardboard boxes to give us to create something during our hours in the makerspace.

Sylvia: Do you think that's in the culture? Do you think that their families — the mothers, the grandmothers, the grandfathers recycle and repurpose and reuse a lot?

Lina: No, I think not. We have to recycle, but that gets taken away in the recycling bin.

Sylvia: That's interesting. You think of older people being very thrifty and fixing things instead of throwing them away. But you don't think that's part of the culture that your kids experience at home?

Lina: No. I think that for my kids now, they prefer to buy something new than to fix what they have.

Sylvia: Do you think that's cultural? You've told me you work with kids whose families have moved to Italy, mostly from Eastern Europe.

Lina: I think the improvement in their economic status is the bigger influence than culture. When they come to Italy, some find good ways to live and they enjoy the economic benefits. They focus on buying things, like clothes, video games, toys, things like that.

Sylvia: I guess you can understand it, the things you were deprived of, the things that seem like, "This is a mark of me being part of this new society, that I have money so I can spend it. Why should I fix things when I can buy them?" And they didn't have that opportunity before.

Lina: Yes. Just that.

Sylvia: Are you planning to use any other recycled or repurposed materials in any other projects?

Lina: I am going to try two new things this year. One is using eggshells to create other bioplastics. And another one is to have students bring old toys to school, and to create something new. Things like motors in toy cars, or the speakers in talking toys or dolls.

Sylvia: Any other thoughts you want to share about the bioplastic project?

Lina: I should say that it's difficult. We have to stay with kids and pay close attention because when we make bioplastics it's a careful process. We have to be very organized and take a lot of care with safety and using the equipment correctly. The other problem is that it's not perfect and it doesn't work the same way every time.

Sylvia: Did you feel that there was any difference in the way that certain students approached this project versus other projects? Were some students more interested who hadn't been interested before?

Lina: Yes. Some love to create a project when they use cardboard because it's quick and easy to put something together, to create masks, create objects, and artifacts. But others like the bioplastic project because it's a process that needs attention, patience.

Sylvia: Do you typically try and connect their projects in the makerspace to things that they're learning in the subject areas?

Lina: Yes, we try to. Maybe not in this specific way with bioplastics, because the actual material science is a bit difficult, but with the other activities, we try every time to connect with the curriculum. So if we do a Scratch project, it's connected to the storytelling, or if we do a tinkering activity, like light play, we try to connect with science curriculum, the function of the eye and how it sees light.

Sylvia: Is there anything else you want to share?

Lina: I would like to do more, but I only have an hour a week for everyone.

Interview: Repurposing Projects at Nā Hunaahi

Interviewee: Toni Marie Kaui
Interviewer: Renato Russo

Toni is the Founder and Head of School, at Nā Hunaahi, an independent competency-based high school in East Hawai'i.

Renato: I want to ask you if repurposing, meaning finding new purposes for items or objects, is something common or usual in your community?

Toni: Yes. My school does not have a lot of funding, so we have to, by our nature, repurpose and reuse and recycle things. It's something that we do quite often. With regards to our community, like other community organizations, we do a lot of recycling, but I can't honestly talk about repurposing, if there's a lot of that happening. When I say recycling, it's just your standard type of recycling.

Renato: Okay, so that's in the community?

Toni: Yes, but my school does a lot of repurposing.

Renato: Can you please describe the project that you are going to share with us?

Toni: Yes. We found a project proposed by a student from the University of Sussex, and we built on that. It's basically a floating garden that you just toss out into the ocean, and it would become a self-contained vegetable garden that people can harvest food from. It would just float wherever it floated, and anyone who came into contact with it would be free to harvest whatever was in there. Because all of the work that the students do is around a native Hawaiian coastal fish pond, we decided to try and see if we could adapt the project to work for us using the materials that we have available to us.

Initial design studies

Renato: What materials were available to you?

Toni: The most important thing was to find the thing that we could use as the floating piece, because we don't have, again, a lot of resources. We already had these floating circles. I don't know what else to call them. You can see them in the photos. They were originally used to try and see if anything can grow on them, but nothing was working, so they were just floating out in the fish pond. We have a fish pond built specifically to raise fish.

Because they were just floating out there, we decided to try and see if we could use one to create one of these floating islands that could grow things.

Renato: Who is involved in making this project?

Toni: My students are the ones working on it. They started with just those circular pieces, and we found some netting to serve as a surface to put the planters on. Because that's all they had, they had to figure out how they were going to make it work. We didn't have the same resources or materials that this student from the University of Sussex had developed, so they had to design the entire project themselves. They started off with smaller studies using floral foam, making floral foam rings.

Luckily, since we don't have money to buy things, when we went to florists and asked if we could just have floral foam, they gave it to the students. They did a small study using, a 16-inch piece of floral foam to see if their idea would work. Then they revised it based on the data they collected, and observations that they made with those smaller ones. Now, based on that project, one of my students is actually building a full scale one now.

Toni: We have to try and find things that are available, or that we can ask people if they're no longer using, in order for them to build it. The entire process, because it's their design and their research going into it, is entirely student-driven.

Full size design

Renato: How many students are working on this?

Toni: There were three of them who did the initial studies, but only one student's design was successful, so she's the only one that's carrying on and building it full size. My other two students are working on a new project now.

Renato: How often do they work on this?

Toni: They work every day on this.

Renato: How old are the kids?

Toni: Seventeen. They'll be eighteen next year.

Renato: You mentioned the need-based decision to repurpose materials. Were there other reasons you selected this project?

Toni: Well, the project worked out because we had the big pieces, those floating rings. But it is also because as a landlocked community and with land being very scarce, especially land that can be used for farming, it served a real purpose to try and see if we could get it to work. If these designs can be used to help feed the community, like a free vegetable garden that people can come and harvest, that would be a real benefit to the community. Those were our two driving forces behind choosing to do this project.

Renato: Okay. Is this material used in other educational projects for you, or this is only for this one?

Toni: No, no one else had been using it. Those rings have been just sitting around doing nothing for a couple of years.

Once we decided that that was the project that they were going to work on, getting the other materials that the students needed was dependent on their design, so it was kind of a just-in-time type of collection of resources. And so, we had to problem-solve in order to figure out how we were going to get those resources with very little money.

Renato: Besides that specific material, do you see other materials that are used more frequently?

Toni: Well, no one else is doing a project like this, so I can't say much about that.

Renato: For example, we saw in a community where people had lots of old bicycles lying around, so many of their projects employed used bicycles. So in your case, it's not necessarily bicycles, but do you see any other materials being used more frequently?

Toni: Yes, we use a lot of invasive plants as material. So plants that don't belong here, when we cut them down, we use those a lot.

Renato: Can you give me an example of that?

Toni: We have a plant called Waiwi. Honestly, I don't know what the English name is for that, but it's an invasive species that grows rapidly and then takes up a lot of land. We use the Waiwi to build things a lot, and then to make things out of those. None of my students have decided to use any Waiwi on this project, but it is a resource that we use. We try to use as many invasive things as possible. If we can get it from nature, then we'll get it, especially those invasive species.

Renato: You mentioned the community practices of repurposing, which is different from what you do at school, right?

Toni: Yes. I mean, if the community is repurposing, I'm not aware of it. The only thing I know is that, of course, the community does a lot of recycling, but standard recycling of cans and plastics. I'm not aware of any other repurposing.

Renato: Do you think this is because of lack of value attributed to repurposing or to recycling? Do people avoid repurposing, or is it just not part of the culture?

Toni: I think it's just not part of the culture. I mean, I guess you could consider our use of invasive species repurposing, because we do cut down a lot of that to make other things. Repurposing things is not really, I think, part of the culture. Everything that is part of our culture has a specific use. A lot of our cultural practices involve the use of native plants and animals.

And so, since those are not in high abundance, we don't tend to choose to repurpose those things, because we don't have a lot of those resources in the first place. Versus repurposing things that aren't originally from here and are invasive to Hawaii, I guess. We cut them down and use those non-native materials to do other things that we need to have done, like building gates, building buildings, framing out stuff. I would say, I guess, that would be repurposing. Now that we're talking about it and I'm thinking about it.

Renato: Maybe it happens with natural materials, but not with manufactured materials? In the broader community?

Cultures of Reuse & Recycling

Toni: I mean, I don't see a whole lot of things just lying around. I can't think of an example where we have old bicycles not being used and lying around.

Renato: Very interesting. You think this happens often in your community, using invasive plants to build things?

Toni: Yes, we don't want them here. So we try to find a different use for it. For example, we have a lot of Albizia trees here, which grow far too rapidly. We found that, in our environment, those Albizia trees produce a lot of nitrogen as they're breaking down, so they make excellent mulch. Once we cut them down or get rid of them, we figure out ways.

Same thing with invasive fish. We turn them into fish emulsion to use for fertilizer. Invasive marine plants, same thing. We turn them into fertilizer.

Renato: Oh, this is interesting. If I understand correctly, you first remove them from the environment, and then find a use. Is that what you're saying?

Toni: Exactly.

Renato: This is what happened with the Waiwi trees, too?

Toni: Yes.

Renato: So in your community, popular materials for repurposing are more natural than ones made by man?

Toni: I don't see a whole lot of manmade things that we repurpose.

Renato: You also mentioned fish, but fish, at least some fish, you can eat. But instead, you use them for mulch?

Toni: There are aquarium fish that can't be eaten, but have somehow escaped into the wild. Those fish, we fish out. We use them as fish emulsion for

Repurposed invasives

fertilizer. But some we eat, for example, Tilapia, which is an invasive species. The fish we can't eat, we usually turn into a fish emulsion that we can use to help with plant growth as fertilizer.

Renato: Is this a practice that happens only within a small group of people or is it widespread?

Toni: Well, it happens for sure amongst the people living on the coast, people who do a lot of fishing, so we're aware of basic stuff. The mountain people, they probably do different things than we do. Plus, they don't have access to fish.

Renato: But they might do the same with the vegetables? The invasive plants and all that?

Toni: Maybe.

Renato: So perhaps it's safe to say that it's widespread, but with some variations according to materials available?

Toni: Right.

Renato: In some places or cultures, recycled or repurposed items are seen as lesser or less valuable. Whereas in other cultures, it's the opposite, you're being clever by repurposing something. How do you feel it is seen in your community?

Toni: Well, at least in our schools, there's not a whole lot of that going on, and so I would say that's more like a one in a million type of thing. Maybe I'm just not aware of those things, but I don't see that much here in our community. But if someone does build those types of things, we do consider them to be very clever and creative.

Renato: Okay, interesting. Sometimes, it varies, too. Between kids and grownups. Kids might see that as clever and grownups as just some workarounds. Do you see any difference on that?

Toni: Well, I don't work a lot with adults, so I can't really speak to that.

Renato: In terms of the choice to use new or repurposed materials, you mentioned that it is need-based.

Toni: Yes, it's completely financial.

If you don't have the money to buy it new, you better figure out a way to make something work for you.

Renato: Okay, let me ask you a question about the floating garden project. Do you think that would be a better project if you could use new materials, or materials that you bought specifically for that purpose?

Toni: Well, if we had new materials, then we definitely wouldn't have the issues and the struggles and challenges that my students had, because we could buy exactly what we needed from the very beginning. But I don't see any value or learning in that, because then they're just rebuilding what somebody else did versus trying to see if they can create it based on the materials that they have available and resources that they have available to them, and so I guess that I would prefer them to do it this way versus buying everything that they need.

Renato: So you think there is some learning, some educational value, in the repurposing?

Toni: There's nothing better, in my opinion, than kids having to figure out and solve a problem when they don't have access to something that they really want.

Renato: Do you think that they see it the same way?

Toni: Well, I don't think they see it initially, but I think after they've solved the problem and got it to work, they do see the value in it.

Toni: I think, at the very beginning, they just think it's me making it harder for them.

Renato: Do they verbally express that? Do they explicitly say that, or this is your impression?

Toni: It's just my impression.

Renato: Well, this has been super interesting. It's beautiful where you are, surrounded by nature, it seems. Thank you so much for your time.

Toni: My pleasure. Thank you

Interview: Upcycling an LED Racing Game

Interviewee: Federica Selleri
Interviewer: Sylvia Martinez

Federica is a Learning Designer at FabLab Valsamoggia and Astranoto srl, and a PhD candidate at the University of Foggia

Sylvia: Please tell us about yourself.

Federica: I am a Learning Designer and right now, a PhD candidate of learning sciences and digital technologies in a university here in Italy. And I'm also the co-owner of Fab Lab Valsamoggia, which is a local Fab Lab and makerspace in the hills between Bologna and Modena, my hometown. And I'm also running a tech startup, called Astronauto, where I design and develop courses and activities in local schools for both children and adults.

Sylvia: Wow, you're busy.

Federica: Yeah, maybe too much.

Sylvia: So in your various roles, do you notice times when people in your spaces recycle or repurpose something into something else?

Federica: Yes. At the Fab Lab, we developed a project called LED Racer. It's a race car track, but instead of using small toy cars, it is based on an LED strip, where the lights run along the strip by pressing a button as fast as possible. So, the faster you press the button, the faster the light will run on the strip, and win the race. It can handle four players at a time. It was made by using a lot of objects that were available at the lab, 3D printed stuff, wooden pieces, fake green grass, and a metal shelf as a container.

Sylvia: Could you describe the background of the makers? How old were they? Where did they come from? Did they have a lot of experience?

Federica: The two makers of the LED Racer are young adults, one of them is an electrical engineer, the other one is a mechanical designer. So, both of them have really strong technical backgrounds. It's similar to the technical background of the other members of the FabLab, which is a small FabLab but with a lot of people from the engineering and physics world.

Sylvia: Why did you choose to share this project with us? Is this kind of project common in your Fab Lab?

Federica: I've chosen this particular project because it perfectly merges two particular aspects of the FabLab movement: the reuse of technological tools and the do-it-yourself, DIY ability of trying to use what we have at the FabLab as much as possible instead of buying new. So, it was similar of other projects in the way that we usually reuse stuff at the FabLab.

Sylvia: Was it one among many similar projects, or was it more unusual?

Federica: FabLab's members always create personal projects in a very DIY way, using what they have

at hand and occasionally buying additional parts. A lot of people bring in their old computers, electronic devices, and scavenge parts to reuse. We also promote the reuse of older tools, maybe with a new purpose or just by using some of their parts.

But this particular project was the very first one fully related to the world of play.

Sylvia: Why do you think they repurposed those materials? Was it by choice or need?

Federica: It was a combination of both choice and need. They wanted to create a prototype by using stuff found in the lab, keeping it cheap and affordable. Also, as a prototype, it has been modified over the years, adding other objects found within the lab. But it was working, so a lot of people played it, and it was really fun, actually. So, it's pretty unique!

Sylvia: Do you notice these same materials used in other projects, too?

Frederica: Not really. The fake green grass was used to decorate the lounge area outside the lab, and the 3D printed objects were samples and prototypes of old projects. But I think that 3D printed objects could be easily reused in other projects, even in a funny way, to show that plastics (even if it is made from corn, like PLA) is not always so bad.

Sylvia: Are projects usually more serious, more utilitarian?

Federica: Yes, usually at the FabLab most projects are serious because of the way that people come to the FabLab. They come because they need something and they need help to build it, or they need other people to create a project together.

For example, one of our associates created a radio-controlled submarine. So, it was serious and purposeful. He needed a working submarine because he wanted to explore a lake. The LED Racer was made just for fun, to create a project that was available for all the people that come to the FabLab to play.

Sylvia: And did they use materials that were available there for other projects? Is it typical that people use recycled materials like that?

Federica: Yeah, it is quite usual, especially for technical stuff. I mean, as I said before, people usually reuse a lot of electronic cables, lamps, boards, circuits, and so on. Even old wooden pieces from the laser cutter from the CNC machine, people always try to put them in projects. Almost always people look around the Fab Lab before buying something new.

Sylvia: Are there certain values in your community that align with reuse and recycling?

Federica: Sure, the Fab Lab movement stands for recycling and reusing. We also organize periodical Repair Cafés, public events where we help people repair broken objects and small devices.

In the wider community, meaning the local area of our FabLab and even throughout all of Italy, I think that this is a common practice, especially among older people who reuse old stuff in their do-it-yourself projects. I know for many retired people it is also a matter of economics, because maybe they cannot afford to buy a lot of new expensive materials. But I also think that it is a matter of their past experiences, for example, if they were young during the World War, where there was a lack of resources. So, they have this kind of routine to always try to collect as much material as possible.

Sylvia: Right, because you had to.

Federica: Yes, because you were forced to. So it's a sort of a habit that they have maintained across the years.

Sylvia: And do you think that younger people see reuse as something that's virtuous, that is connected with saving the world? Or are they just saving money?

Federica: I think that young people think that older people do that just for saving money, not for saving the world.

But younger people think of themselves as saving the world by collecting stuff, old stuff. And I think also that younger people try to collect wider variety of materials, where maybe older people try to collect specific type of materials. So I have an example. My grandfather always used to collect a lot, a lot of electronic stuff, like a lot of cables, a huge number of cables, just to reuse at home, just for repairing stuff, and so on. In my personal example, I also am a huge fan of collecting things like used paper. I have a large collection of many types of used paper. But I would prefer to collect different type of materials, not only paper, or only cables, or so on. I want to expand my horizons.

Sylvia: And do you have any younger students, school-aged students come to your Fab Lab?

Federica: We have some of them, but it's really rare, because our Fab Lab is not near the city, so it requires a car to get there. Younger people do not have cars, so they can't come here, with a few exceptions. This summer I had a young high school student as an apprentice. She was 16 years old. Every morning for the whole period of the apprenticeship, I would pick up her in the city and we would commute to the Fab Lab together.

I really would like to have more younger students, but right now, because of the location of the Fab Lab, it is not possible. So, we are thinking about moving closer to the city or even into the city.

Sylvia: From the younger makers you've worked with, do you think they see recycling and repurposing as important and good, or just cheap and free?

Federica: I think that depends on two factors. One is the age of the children. And the other one is the context in which they live.

I think that with younger ages, up to about 10 years old, it's easier to introduce recycled materials without too many questions from them, because it's just another material. And they always try to play with all the materials they have around. With older ages, so from about 12 years old and on, it requires more reasoning. They have to think more about what they are doing, and what they are using.

I think that it is possible for them to see the bigger purpose of reusing materials, but you need to help them think about it more.

It is also based on the context, because it depends if their teachers or parents normally use repurposed or recycled materials. If they do, it becomes normal. The example of REMIDA in Reggio Emilia is fundamental, because they always try to show the beauty of recycling by simply providing a lot of different materials and trying to explore them from different points of view. And in this way, children from the very young age become comfortable with using unusual materials and things that are not made purposely as educational materials.

Sylvia: So as you say, REMIDA in Reggio Emilia is very intentional about bringing recycled materials in. So am I hearing you right? You think it's to increase the number and variety of materials and give people access to more and different things, or is there more?

Federica: If you are able to show how reused or repurposed materials can have meaning, can have an importance, even in a simple project, then people will understand the importance of recycling and repurposing. REMIDA is especially interesting, because they also have a particular eye on beauty, on harmony, this kind of thing. So you can see that some reused materials or recycling materials are even more beautiful than new ones. And I think that it's not always a matter of variety or quantities. I mean, you can also have a significant experience even with really few recycling materials.

Sylvia: So you are saying that in using recycled materials, you're helping people develop an eye that can look at something and see something different? It's an actual skill, it's an actual talent that you can teach people to see the world in a different way?

Federica: Yes, I think that repurposing is educational, because it helps children (and adults) build their imaginations and break past traditional meanings. Just have an idea, and anything can become something else, even the strangest tool or material.

Sylvia: Do you have a sense of how people react to projects made with recycled materials?

Frederica: I think that depends a lot on how the projects are developed and documented: a certain eye and sensibility are required to make reused materials capable of expressing their potential and beauty. Everything that has been used at least once has a hidden story to tell.

Sylvia: Are there other ways it is different from using new materials?

Frederica: In some cases, new materials could be safer to use than reused materials, especially within really complex and high-tech projects. But within the educational world, I think that reused materials are easier to use than new ones. There would be different motivations for different projects, of course, for example if it requires stability and safety or if it is just a prototype, or the people involved already had experience with a particular material.

I think by understanding that you can use even an old piece of wood instead a new one, you gain a lot of skill in how you can plan a project. You have more options. You have to make intentional choices. You don't always immediately think it is better to use a brand new light or a brand new whatever. You can create marvelous stuff, marvelous projects, even by reusing things that have been used at least once.

Sylvia: It also seems like there's a difference between recycling something just because it's a material and rethinking the form or function. If you take a plastic bottle and grind it up, and turn it into another plastic bottle, that is a very different project than taking a plastic bottle and making a bird feeder out of it. Those seem to be very different ways to think about recycling.

Federica: Yes, because in the first case you mentioned, the bottle remains a bottle. If you can reuse a plastic bottle for water or whatever, you can even fill that with soil, and you can make a plant grow in it. But you can also cut the bottle, and then you will have some materials, which is no longer a bottle. It will be something else. So I think that it's proper to call that repurposing.

You create a new object. You give a new meaning to an object, in a new way.

Sylvia: And do you think that the participants in the LED Racer project saw it in that way, in that kind of depth? Or was it just, here's some stuff, we're going to reuse it?

Federica: I think they just needed those materials. They choose the fake green grass because we had a lot of it.

I think that that kind of consciousness and in-depth reasoning comes later. It comes from a lot of experience working with reused materials. Not just occasionally, because you need something and you just grab it.

Sylvia: They weren't making a commentary on the artificiality of outdoor spaces or something profound.

Federica: No.

Sylvia: They were, "Here's some grass, let's use it."

Federica: Yeah, it was just to make it was nicer.

Sylvia: Do you think there's any difference in the types of people who tend to use recycled materials or not use recycled materials?

Federica: In my experience, older people use more of the used materials.

I think that younger people tend to buy new things more often than older people. I don't know why. Maybe younger people have less experience than the older people, so do not have a lot of examples that they can use.

Maybe they don't have the ability to search for recycled materials, because they don't know how to use recycled materials, or they perceive new materials as safer more stable, or if materials are specifically designed for the project they might be easier to use.

Sylvia: You might have to test a used wire, because it might be broken or burnt inside, but a new wire you might not have to worry about that. But if you learn to test things, it would work out for new or used parts.

Federica: That's why I think that in a place like the Fab Lab it's really important that younger people and older people work together on projects. Everyone can share their experiences. It's what normally happens in our Fab Lab. You might see someone with vast experience in mechanics or engineering, but they are not capable of turning on a computer. Maybe they are able to create complex metal and wooden structures. And the younger makers always say, "Oh, how do you do that? Please show me. I can show you how to use your computer in exchange."

It's a virtuous cycle.

Sylvia: So is there anything that you think is important to share about this project that we didn't touch on?

Federica: It's not really related to recycling or repurposing, but one reason I chose to share the LED Racer project is because this summer a young girl from high school apprenticed at the Fab Lab and redesigned the LED Racer. She decided to redesign it by 3D modeling new objects, and reusing materials as well. And she decided to give a Super Mario World aspect to the whole project. So right now, we have a Super Mario LED Racer.

Sylvia: Interesting! Why do you think she chose to redo that project?

Federica: She actually didn't really choose to redo it. It was a proposal made by me and her teacher. In Italy, there is an apprenticeship project that happens in high schools. Her teacher and I tried to think of a project that would be more interesting for her. The teacher said that she's really, really keen on 3D modeling, 3D printing, and doing things with her hands.

We needed to redesign and fix the LED Racer, because over the years it has been used a lot. People in the Fab Lab like to play with it! But pieces were broken, and the cables were not okay anymore. So she redesigned the whole project by adding new stuff, fixing the cables, reprogramming the board. So although she didn't really choose the project, she was very satisfied.

Sylvia: What kinds of things do you think she learned?

Federica: She learned how to deal with a complex project. She was completely free to update and fix it in any way she wanted. She had to make a lot of decisions — how many pieces to model, where to place them, the position of the LED strip, the colors, the identity, whatever she wanted. And then of course, she learned the technical skills — how to 3D model a complex object, how to do the 3D printing, how to use a CNC machine. She also learned how to present that, because she created a website for her project. There was a lot to it.

Sylvia: Do you think her teacher was satisfied?

Federica: They played together, so I think that they were satisfied. And the girl won, so she was happy.

Sylvia: This was like an internship at the FabLab?

Federica: Yeah. It's a free internship, because in Italy, there is a law that in high school there is a mandatory internship in a local factory, an association, or a company.

Sylvia: Do you think that she was able to transfer the success of that project back to her schoolwork?

Federica: I hope so. I mean, that internship lasted two months, June and July. But I don't know if she said something to her classmates, or how is she doing in her classwork. I do know that she worked steadily for eight hours a day. She was very motivated.

Sylvia: A lot of people wonder if kids can learn academic kinds of things from hands-on experiences.

Federica: It was really hands-on. She 3D modeled, 3D printed, she colored all the pieces by hand, and glued them on the board. It was really, hands-on. And she was also a girl with some cognitive issues, she has a sort of a dyslexia. I think that she had to learn a lot of things with this project. I don't know how to quantify what she learned, but I think so.

She was also really curious about all the mechanical stuff, and was able to figure out the instructions and processes.

Sylvia: Hopefully, she'll be able to take some of that success back to school and other projects she works on.

Federica: I hope so as well.

Maker and Makerspace Culture

The culture of making and makerspaces is often mentioned when people talk about what makes "making" special and important in an educational setting. Makerspaces are more than a place where we keep high tech tools, they represent educational freedom, where ideas become reality in a supportive community. They are a place where exploration is allowed, without the finality of correct answers. This is unlike the traditional way school is depicted, especially in media and popular culture, where learning is about memorizing and tests, and school culture often is reduced to caricatures of jocks and mean girls, with teachers who are either bullies or saviors.

Instead, in the following pages, the Fellows explore ways that ensure that making and makerspaces are responsive to student needs and ideas. The role of teacher is reimagined as one who facilitates this culture of respect and supports individuality and agency.

But what about curriculum, some would ask? We do not seek to "throw the baby out with the bathwater" and just let students "discover" whatever they feel like. What we seek is to reform the curriculum with real and relevant topics and projects that excite, challenge, and yes, teach.

Seymour Papert saw the Logo programming language in this light, as a microworld where mathematics was the language spoken. Thus, when kids "spoke" the computer in mathematical terms, they would learn math as easily as a child in France learns to speak French. The curriculum needs reform, yes, but we also need the processes and environments where learning takes place naturally, and educators who can create these learning spaces and places for all.

Children's Lived Experiences: An Integral Part of the Makerspace

by Ridhi Aggarwal

People are the driving force of a makerspace in a traditional rural community. Thus, what we do and how we do both need to incorporate the cultural and contextual aspect of the community. This was the starting point of a recent set of activities that were driving our curriculum at Ramdwari Khojshala (makerspace). In the words of a parent, the makerspace was a place where children go and fix, repair, and break, and make things of use to the community. This motivated us to ask community members to make a list of things which needed repairing in the community. We wanted to include maker culture and traditional knowledge that already existed in the community and build upon it. When we compiled the lists, we saw a few things that appeared on all the lists were a bicycle, a hand pump, and an umbrella.

This was the starting point of our object-based maker learning. People throughout history and across cultures have been designing and making objects for everyday use, from hand fans to telescopes. Objects can be practical or decorative, simple or complex. Some are crafted by hand while others are manufactured by machine. Some can be made in a few minutes while others can be built across generations. Usually, objects are made for particular purposes although their use often extends beyond their makers' original intentions. Even the simplest objects reflect the culture and more importantly the context (social and physical) in which they were created as well as the contexts in which they continue to be used. A close observation of these everyday objects not only sparks students' curiosity but leads to increasingly complex thinking.

We started with a bicycle that children used every day. They have seen the people around them repair it as well. The first step was to encourage

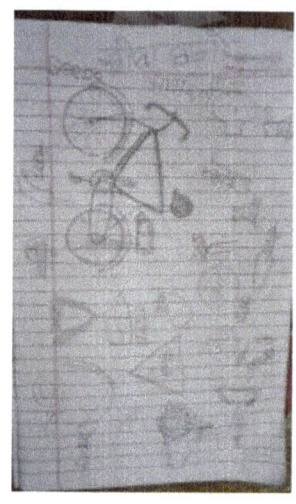
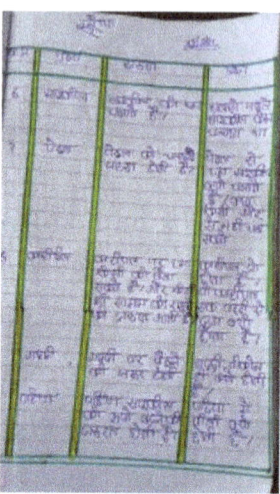

students to make careful observations of the bicycle to stimulate curiosity and set the stage for inquiry. To draw the picture, they needed to look closely at its parts like nuts, bolts, rods, etc. After drawing the picture, they discussed what they observed and wrote about the parts, their purpose, and the complexities of all of them coming together.

Observation led to exploration of the mechanism of the wheels and pedals and the children tried making it with paper and cardboard to explore how the movement happens. It intrigued them

as to how the parts were installed together so that they move together as the bicycle moves. Children had many questions about this, so it gave us the opportunity to include one more task which we had not planned, which was to completely take apart the bicycle and re-build it. They experienced some real comprehension when they compared what they thought a part did with what it could actually do when they were re-assembling the parts.

As we were trying to include the context of making culture, we shared some fun and empowering stories about bicycles. The first story was about cycling as a social movement for rural women in the Pudukkottai district of Tamil Nadu, and the next was about an amphibious bicycle (a bicycle turning into a boat).

These two stories sparked a good discussion amongst students. One said in her reflection that, "if we could break various objects and understand their working, and then combine different parts of different objects we might be able to make things which we can't afford, or make things we need but don't exist." This reflection was the turning point for other students talking about what they wanted to make with the parts of the cycle, and a new beginning for the class. The next day the class went around the village looking for things which were *jugaad* (a term used in India for things which are repurposed or hacked, like an object used as a quick fix) and they made a list of objects to fix and problems to solve.

Two weeks into the makerspace session there were eight student projects using the bicycle in ways that would be useful for the community.

Student Projects

1. One problem was riding the bicycle at night with no lights on the village roads. Jasmeen thought if she could attach a light which would glow when someone peddles the bicycle, this would solve the problem. She made a prototype where she attached a motor, a bulb, and some wires to the bicycle. The motor is attached with the crank and when the force is applied to the pedal, the chain wheel moves and in turn the motor moves which gives energy to the bulb.

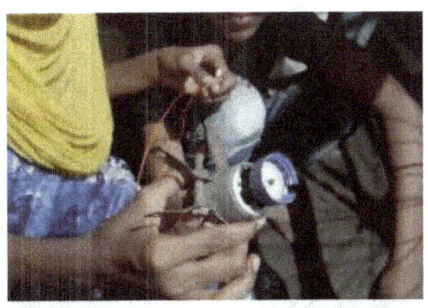

2. It is always a problem to cut grass or weeds on agricultural fields. Nazia thought if she could attach a sharp blade to the front hub of the bicycle, then she and others can easily cut the small to medium size grass and weeds by steering the bicycle towards them. This would take less time and effort and would cut the grass from the roots easily.

3. Rabia made a model to cut the grass with a fan attached to a rod and the rod attached to the front part of the bicycle. The same fan-like structure is available already, but it runs on electricity, and since there is an erratic supply of electricity in the village, Rabia thought of making a design which can work with bicycle. The grass is fodder, which after cutting can be given to livestock as food.

Student Projects (cont.)

4. Lakshmi, Jaid, and Raja made a bicycle-enabled pesticide spraying machine. When you peddle the wheel the pesticide from the tank comes out through a sprinkler attached to the front part of the bicycle. Through this attachment, one can save lot of time and effort. There are pesticide spraying machines available which run on batteries but buying and maintaining them is a costly affair, so this solution is cost-effective.

5. One of our students attached a wiper through the front part of the wheel. During rains when the drains overflow, it becomes very difficult to ride a bicycle on swampy roads. With this invention, when you are riding the bicycle the sludge and the mud on the road could be moved to the sides of the road allowing freer movement of the bicycle. This could also prevent accidents due to balancing issues.

6. Noor, Jahan, and Shabana attached a fan with gears and levers to a bicycle. The attachment could help get water for irrigation or drinking purposes. There are engines already available that do this, but they run on petrol or diesel which is costly and also adds pollution to the environment.

7. Aafia and Sana thought of cleaning the village drains with an accumulator and tank behind the bicycle. When it rains, drains often clog with debris which leads to the overflow of water and mud on the road, making roads extremely slippery and highly prone to accidents. With this innovation, the mud and sludge could be collected in the collector and discharged into open spaces, helping to clean the drains.

8. Naseem and Alisha made a bicycle-enabled water pump. Instead of a handle, the pump rod is attached to the crank of the bicycle. When one peddles, the crank moves which moves the piston rod. When the piston rod moves up and down it moves water more easily than turning the handle by hand.

In addition to making these prototypes, the students did a survey of the number of bicycles in the village and how many girls have a bicycle. They found that very few girls knew how to ride a bicycle so they decided to start a bicycle club where girls would learn to ride and they could rent a bicycle for purposes of mobility and emergencies.

Things often do not go the way we plan them. As a teacher I admit that there were moments in this project when my patience was put to the test, and I wanted to get into the discussion and make a point to students. But after all these years as a teacher I understand that it's not necessary that things go perfectly to plan. If the general framework is going as you planned then whatever way it goes is OK.

When things take their own path, especially if the path is guided by children, then the content is owned by them and the learning will be deep. As teachers we come to our classrooms day after day with our burden of knowledge tucked under our arms or carried in our heads, but if we make this our identity then the atmosphere of the classroom would be defined largely by our authority. We need to see and face our own limitations and biases.

When a teacher says, "I don't know... I am also learning" — that is when students respond freely, and knowledge or the lack of it is no longer a threat to personal selfhood. Only when students and teachers are in a relationship of learning together is there a release of creative energy. This was the essence of this lesson which resulted in student agency and ownership of their learning.

The bicycle as an object offered a tactile experience for students, which challenged them to carefully observe and conceptualize their thinking. While the teacher facilitates the session, the students construct meaning for themselves through their interactions with each other centered around the object (Hannan et al., 2013). It represents a social constructivist approach therefore in which the students develop their knowledge and understanding though interaction with objects based on a prior understanding (Chatterjee & Hannan, 2016).

This approach enables the student to explore ideas, processes and events related to the object and further gives them an opportunity to build upon their ideas. Communities making culture and inputs along with student interactions were the key focus of the session. So, we can say that the extent to which students are provided opportunities to interact and explore about disciplinary ideas as well as to build on others' ideas and have others build on theirs provides a big opportunity for student empowerment. Further, we can say that the object not only focused on learning concepts or exploring ways of making and fabrication, it also was a way that could contribute to children's development of agency (the willingness to engage), their ownership over the content, and the development of positive identities as thinkers and learners.

References

Chatterjee, H. J., & Hannan, L. (2016). Engaging the Senses: Object-Based Learning in Higher Education. Routledge.

Hannan, L., Duhs, R., & Chatterjee, H. (2013). Object-Based Learning: A Powerful Pedagogy for Higher Education. In A. Boddington, J. Boys, & C. Speight (Eds.), Museums and higher education working together: challenges and opportunities (pp. 159-168). Routledge.

Bicycle fodder cutting machine

Why Teach Maker Education?

by Lars Beck Johannsen

If you have been teaching in a maker-based setting you probably know that it is a good learning experience for both students AND teachers. You also know that there are a wide variety of challenges that both the teacher and the students meet on their journey into making. If you haven't started yet, I strongly urge you to take this journey!

I think there are two main outcomes from taking on the challenge of maker education.

1. Maker education allows the students to have a deeper learning experience.
2. Maker education allows the teacher to learn along with their students.

Let's talk about the second one first because it is important to look at your own role as a teacher. As a maker teacher you will be instructing students to use the software, tools, and machines that are used in a makerspace. This role is familiar to teachers. On the other hand, the students will follow their own ideas and bring them to life, which makes it a meaningful project to the student, but challenges teachers because they are not in control of the outcome. The role is more one of facilitating and guiding the student through their learning experience.

Some teachers might want to assign projects that are more limited in the number of possible outcomes, thereby controlling what they would need to learn in order to succeed. But this is far less engaging and motivating for students than following their own ideas for a project. On the way from idea to object there are a lot of challenges they will meet, especially when they lack experience.

If students are assigned a narrow, limited project, they often have a feeling that, "This is too difficult for me." If it is their own project idea or at least have a high degree of influence on what the project will be, it is more often a feeling of, "I need to get this to work!" Often the students have a way of surprising you and exceeding your expectations.

So, it turns out that changing your role as teacher results in both outcomes: **You give your students a deeper learning experience, and you learn something along the way as well.**

Here are some thoughts and observations I have made along the way. This is not a complete list, but just some points for reflecting on your own practice (and a few tips).

Student observations

Students are used to getting assignments that have a correct answer. Making open-ended assignments that are more complex and do not have one correct answer is far more interesting, but also frustrates students because they cannot rely on the teacher having the solution. The world is not like a textbook, and in that sense it prepares the student to be a part of the world outside of school.

- When you do projects in "the real world" they automatically get complex.
- Building something from scratch will give you a lot of challenges along the way.
- Prompts that are ambiguous will let the student be creative with their solution.

Students will not all be learning the exact same thing. Every project has its own challenges that calls for different knowledge from a variety of traditional school subjects. It could be mathematical tools that help them in their work, knowledge about the materials they have chosen, rules from physics, challenges in coding a microcontroller, etc. The list could go on forever. I have met a lot of teachers who believe that students should all learn the same things in order to pass their tests. I believe that the knowledge acquired or constructed through a personal meaningful project is better internalized and sticks in the memory. And I also think that students will be able to fill in the gaps they might have missed about a fact or two.

I have seen students that don't do well in a traditional class flourish with maker projects. In my line of work, I often lead workshops or one day events with groups of students unknown to me. Usually, their regular teacher informs me beforehand that one or more students might not behave well or do much work. Often, these students actually do the opposite, and surprise the teacher in a positive sense. They are the doers — they get things done, and they often have the most creative and funny ideas.

Reflections from my own practice

Minimize instruction. In a makerspace you will need to instruct in the use of the machines or learn how to use CAD software to build something. My experience is that minimal instruction, meaning "show don't tell" combined with student peer-to-peer learning is a good approach. Let us take the vinyl cutter as an example.

I start by quickly cutting a sticker and weeding out the extra pieces, and put the sticker on something in the lab. This can be done in a minute. And now they know what the output and process of the machines is. I have seldom met anyone that understood it before they saw it. Just telling what it does does not help.

The next step is to draw something that will become a sticker in whatever CAD software you are using (Inkscape is a great open source tool). Students work at different tempos, and as soon as a few are finished with a design, I show them how to set up the machine and cut. When the next little group is ready to do their design I will point to the group before them, letting them show their fellow students how to do it. In this way they consolidate their knowledge by teaching it to their peers and it frees the teacher up from being the bottleneck of the process.

Allow sufficient time. Time is one of the main challenges in working with projects in a makerspace. It simply takes a lot of time — and it should be allowed to take time.

Build agency. Prior to making larger projects I usually let the students do some simpler projects to learn the basics of coding, CAD design, or using the machines (CAM). It often gives birth to new and more personal ideas that the student wants to make, which could turn into a bigger and more complex project.

This is where you loosen the control and let the class go in different directions alone or in small groups. If they have sufficient experience, they can use what they have learned to follow their own ideas. To take control of your own learning process is a powerful lesson that will benefit the student in numerous ways.

Try faded guidance. Whether it is students or adults I teach, I use faded guidance. I try to provide only the necessary help, ideally just enough to keep the project in flow. Over time, the help provided by me is lessened as the students' knowledge grows.

Relationships matter. An important part of this is to establish a relationship with the student. Knowing when to push and when to hug.

Encouraging them to just try to do what they think is the right way, when they are uncertain, otherwise they will tend to seek confirmation from you even though they are 90% sure of what to do.

This may be an obvious approach but, I still sometimes fall in the trap and help too much, especially if it is something I can fix in a second. But I try to stay aware of it. Ongoing reflection of your own practice will help you become a better guide.

This is not a complete list but gives a few reasons why you should implement maker education in your life as a teacher. On a closing note, I would like to point out some things I don't think should be your focus.

Maker education is not meant to evolve every student idea into a startup company or raise money with a Kickstarter campaign. It's fine if that happens, but I don't see it as our goal as a school.

My mission is one of enlightenment or *Bildung* as we say in Denmark. Understanding the technology that surrounds us and being creative with it is also a way of learning about the world, learning about STEAM subjects in a hands-on way, and practicing the art of wondering and asking questions.

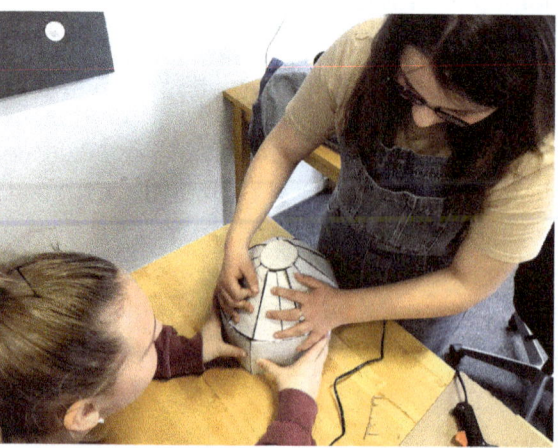

Culture and Making: A Strong and Powerful Connection

by Federica Selleri

During conversations between FabLearn Fellows, the question often arises as to what is actually meant by the term cultural making? Is it an action linked to the culture of origin or is it centered in the human need to belong to something? Personally, I'm becoming more convinced that it is an innate characteristic of human beings to build something linked to a need or an idea. The following two anecdotes reveal small demonstrations of this idea.

In October 2021 I started a new professional path as a digital atelierista, supporting the use of technology for teachers in children's hospitals. We began to experiment with new uses of technological tools, which allow children to escape the reality of their hospital rooms, simply using a tablet, sheets of paper, colors, and creativity. With the five-year-old children and their teacher we proposed a project based on transformations of the natural environment, so that they could build worlds different from their daily hospital experience.

The project started with the children and teacher looking at some examples of natural transformations related to both the plant and animal worlds. The children chose to focus on the world of insects, especially ants, and they drew the anthill, the meadow, and the sky on sheets of paper. They then photographed their drawings with the tablet. Then, on another sheet of paper, they drew some ants, photographed them and used an app to cut out the photos, crop the ants, resize them and insert them into the anthill they had drawn. This became a playspace, using their fingers they made the images of the ants move along the anthill, telling their story.

This is a valuable example of how, using simple tools such as a tablet, paper, and colors you can build worlds in which to play and learn, even in a difficult context like the hospital, where it is not always possible to have many tools and spaces with which to experiment.

Another example happened at a workshop I led for the Fab Lab where I work. We designed a creative coding activity for a group of university students from different courses based on the idea of a *wunderkammer*, or "cabinet of curiosities." Each small group could freely decide what to put in their box, building small objects and animating them with lights and code, using Arduino microcontrollers, LEDs, motors, and recycled materials.

After a brief introduction on programming the Arduinos, each group decided on an idea, and assigned roles for the members. Some were mainly concerned with the construction and design part of the object, while others were involved in programming and assembling the circuits. While most of the groups decided to make a Christmas-themed box (despite the fact that Christmas was more than a month away), one group decided to make a miniature '80s disco, complete with lights, music, and moving objects.

Here, in my opinion, the unconventional cultural component of making emerges. The students were inspired by something close to them, something that is part of their culture and their lives, and they naturally used digital and other tools to make it. The idea of building something from scratch, starting from a cardboard box, didn't scare them, it was an opportunity to experiment in a practical way.

Culture is not defined by what others think, but what each person thinks. To allow people to think their own thoughts, the project must be open enough to ensure maximum freedom of exploration and experimentation. To me, this kind of cultural making expands our thinking about what culture really means and what making really means as well.

Maker Culture: An Ally in Education and Curriculum Reform

by Débora Garofalo

I have seen the power of maker culture to transform education first-hand, both as a teacher in public schools in Brazil and in my work at the Department of Education on teacher training policy for the country.

I have always regarded maker culture as a broad framework that fosters innovation by encompassing various activities such as embroidery, sewing, programming, robotics, artificial intelligence, IoT (Internet of Things), and more. It facilitates hands-on learning, interdisciplinary connections, active methodologies, and investigative approaches like STEAM.

The beauty of the maker culture lies in its ability to shift students from a passive role to becoming the central protagonists of their learning journey. Over my seventeen years as a teacher, particularly during the last six years as a technology educator, I have witnessed this transformation firsthand. It has not only revolutionized teaching within schools but has also had a profound impact on the broader communities these schools are a part of.

By introducing real-world problems to be solved, such as transforming waste products into useful objects, students are engaged and empowered.

Through this approach, I have observed formerly disengaged students rediscovering their passion for learning, overcoming challenges related to race and ethnicity, and developing a newfound appreciation for reading and writing.

In Brazil, the work I have been involved in has become a public policy, providing students from diverse social and economic backgrounds access to robotics using scrap and recycled materials. Today, this movement is present in over 5,100 schools in the State of São Paulo, promoting creativity and everyday problem-solving while teaching important lessons about electronics.

However, I still grapple with significant questions about how to ensure that maker culture reaches all students, particularly those attending public schools in Brazil. These schools often face challenges such as lack of trained teachers, inadequate infrastructure, and limited

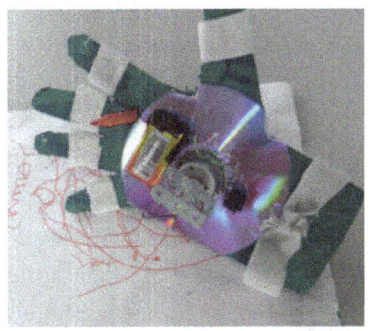
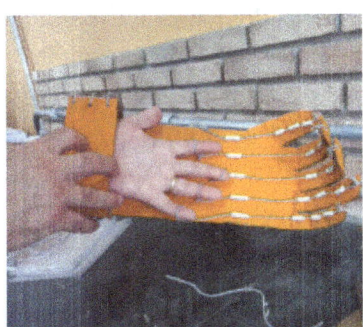

connectivity. Of approximately 180,000 schools in the country, 45% lack basic sanitation, and these schools represent 81% of Brazilian students. It is crucial to extend the benefits of the maker culture to these students where it can make a substantial difference in their educational experiences, motivating them to become critical thinkers and creative learners. Such an approach entails comprehensive education that involves solving real-world problems within the school and in the broader community.

While advanced technological resources are valuable, it is imperative for us, as teachers, to take the initial steps toward an education that is relevant to the world we live in. We must focus on developing skills and abilities and prioritize the needs of our students and fellow educators.

Maker culture as a gateway to creativity

Teachers often have questions about how to incorporate the maker movement into their practice. I believe the culture of the maker movement serves as a gateway to innovation, inviting both students and educators to learn through hands-on experimentation. It fosters youth empowerment by stimulating creativity, logical thinking, and problem-solving skills. By working with the maker universe, we can create a school environment that encourages active participation and enables students to tackle real-world challenges. However, this requires school curriculum to be more flexible.

To engage with the maker culture, it is not always necessary to have a dedicated makerspace. Simple reorganization of furniture and the creation of stations with materials and tools might be enough to encourage creativity. However, it is worth noting that some schools do have designated spaces equipped with tools such as 3D printers, laser cutters, and robotics supplies. These may be augmented with activities such as sewing, embroidery, woodworking, animation, 3D modeling with clay, and other crafts.

Being a maker is more than just having access to tools and equipment; it is about fostering a attitude that thrives in the collaborative learning environment within the classroom. Engaging in activities and experiential learning helps to create a nurturing space and may transform into more complex activities like computational thinking. Recently, I conducted a training session with teachers who created a low-cost mechanical hand. I was delighted by one particular teacher who went back to his primary classroom and asked all the children to create mechanical hands, which they did with great success. Witnessing such transformations is nothing short of magical.

Reimagining curriculum

Maker culture does not seek to replace the school curriculum; rather, it encourages us to reimagine it. For instance, in a history class focusing on Egypt, history lessons can combine with storytelling and computer science while creating games in the Scratch programming language. In a science lesson addressing environmental issues, talking about recycling can serve as a starting point, bridging other areas of knowledge such as material science, ecology, or the time it takes for materials to decompose and adding the potential to solve real problems in the community.

By embracing maker culture as an ally, we can make the school curriculum more engaging and meaningful for students. It enables us to bridge theory and practice, ensuring a practical and immersive learning experience. By experiencing learning in a diverse and collaborative manner, we foster true scientific thinking.

The benefits of incorporating the maker culture into the school curriculum are plentiful, including the opportunity to revolutionize education, promote youth protagonism, and provide a meaningful education for all!

Makerland: Exploring the Connections Between Makerspaces and Seymour Papert's Mathland

by Charles Pimentel

Introduction

Studies show that different factors may cause students to have poor performance in mathematics. But one accepted reason is a lack of connection between the subject covered at school and the real world (Ziegler & Loos, 2017).

This article seeks to relate the use of mathematics in the makerspace with the metaphor of "mathland" as presented by Seymour Papert in his book *Mindstorms: Children, Computers, and Powerful Ideas* (1980), in which the author compares learning math with the way a person learns French when growing up in France. A mathland would be a place where learning and using math naturally would be as easy as learning French when growing up in France.

Thus, inspired by the term coined by Papert, this work presents the "makerland" metaphor, combining the ways math is naturally used in a makerspace while the students develop their projects.

When educators proposed projects to support the mathematics curriculum, there tends to be two very different approaches. The first is the development of projects that aim to teach an explicit mathematics concept that meets curriculum objectives. The second type of project is one that expects and requires students to use mathematics to design and build something, however the "something" may not be directly related to a curricular goal.

In some cases, a project might have both explicit and implicit objectives for the use of mathematics such as in this high school project called Polygonal Jewelry.

Polygonal jewelry project

The objective of this project was to carry out a study on polygons in a concrete way. Students modeled their objects using paper, pencil, ruler, compass, and protractor. These sketches were transferred to the Adobe Illustrator vector graphics software. The final objective was the fabrication of the jewelry using a laser cutter. Students created their unique jewelry with varied combinations of polygons, which is squarely within the scope of the Plane Geometry curriculum.

Polygonal jewelry

However, for the final fabrication, the students did not need to understand the mathematics concepts that were used when transferring the project to the laser cutter control software, nor the mathematical concepts that the laser cutter uses to control the final fabrication.

This is a normal part of using fabrication devices in the makerspace. The software and the device do the math for you. The question is: does the student learn some mathematical concepts in the use of makerspace resources during the modeling and production process or is it just an empirical use of mathematics in order to be able to carry out his or her project?

When using a laser cutter, for example, the relationship between the speed of the equipment while cutting a resource and the laser power to perform this cut, the definition of perimeter and area to be cut, the time to perform the cut, symmetry relationships, relationships between variables and Cartesian coordinates, are usually applied automatically in the software.

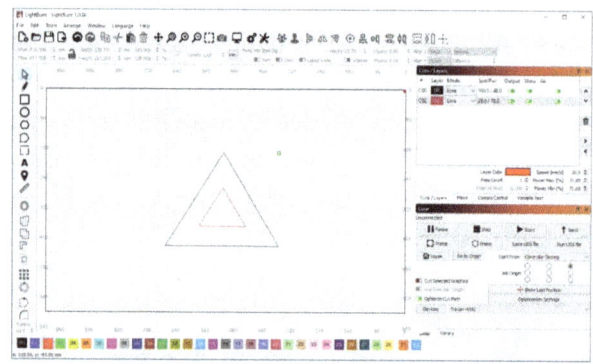

Mathematics in the control panel of the laser cutter software

This type of implicit mathematics use might be dismissed as unimportant to the mathematics curriculum. However, I'd like to dispute that and link this idea of implicit mathematics use and learning in the makerspace to the concept of learning without being taught that Papert proposes as a key component to his concept of mathland.

Theoretical foundation

Seymour Papert's mathland is connected to his theory of learning called constructionism. The theory is built on Piaget's theory of learning called constructivism. Constructionism posits that the educational process happens more effectively when students are co-authors of their own knowledge and share it with their peers (Blikstein, 2008). Considering the great advance of new information and communication technologies, constructionism is a true learning theory for today's world and today's youth.

In his book *The Children's Machine: Rethinking School in the Age of the Computer*, Papert states that:

> "One of my central mathetic tenets is that the construction that takes place 'in the head' often happens especially felicitously when it is supported by construction of a more public sort 'in the world' [...]. Part of what I mean by 'in the world' is that the product can be shown, discussed, examined, probed, and admired. It is out there." (Papert, 1993, p. 142)

Papert also argues that technology is not merely a means to improve traditional education, but a powerful resource to promote emancipatory learning, making it possible to meet different learning styles.

Niss and colleagues (2017) point out that the widely recognized need for mathematics courses to connect to the real-world has been the basis of educational reforms in some countries. Constructionism offers a framework to understand a way to teach mathematics concepts through technology projects and create pathways to needed reforms in mathematics curriculum.

Thus, as the Logo language was created by Papert's research group as a math microworld where students and educators are learners and everyone learns from their mistakes (Papert, 2020), the makerspace's prototyping resources provide a different kind of microworld for learning mathematics.

Maker-based learning teaches the student how to deal with challenges and face unexpected problems for which there is no pre-established explanation, thus acquiring the necessary skills to participate in the construction of new skills (Gavassa, 2020). However, it is important to consider that if integration of makerspaces into the school curricula can be accomplished, it should provide authentic and meaningful learning experiences (Fernandez et al., 2021).

When it comes to mathematics education, Brazil has undergone significant reforms. In 2018, the Brazilian Ministry of Education approved the Common National Curricula Base (BNCC in Portuguese), a document that defines the essential knowledge that all students have the right to learn.

In the field of Mathematics and its technologies, the BNCC describes the discipline as:

> "Human science, the result of the needs and concerns of different cultures [...] and a living science, which contributes to solving scientific

and technological problems and to underpin discoveries and constructions, including impacts on the world of work". (Brasil, 2018, p. 267)

In Brazilian reality, the discipline of mathematics is organized into five Thematic Units (TU). They are:

- **Numbers**: Developing skills related to numerical thinking and the meaning of operations.
- **Algebraic Thinking**: Identifying the dependency relationship between two quantities and solving problems through equations and inequations.
- **Geometric Thinking**: Interpreting and moving a figure on the Cartesian plane, and identifying isometric transformations and producing enlargement and reduction of figures.
- **Quantities and Measures**: Building and expanding the notion of measure by studying different quantities, in addition to obtaining means for calculating areas of plane surfaces and the volume of some geometric solids.
- **Probability and Statistics**: Building sample space for equiprobable events, in addition to planning and carrying out sample research.

In addition, the BNCC includes Computational Thinking in the scope of mathematics. Computational Thinking is an approach towards the formulation of problems and their solutions in a way that is similar to programming, yet can be applied in areas of knowledge that go beyond Computer Science (Wing, 2011).

Methods

While it is one thing to theorize about how mathematical ideas might be formed in the process of completing makerspace projects, another part of investigating this idea is to ask students themselves if they are connecting their indirect exposure to mathematical ideas to the mathematics curriculum.

In short, do the students recognize the mathematics of "makerland"?

To carry out this work, an exploratory study was conducted with 21 students in a high school makerspace in Brazil. The goal was to clarify how students perceive mathematics concepts in the use of equipment during the preparation of their projects. A questionnaire was designed for this study by observing the routine of students when modeling and producing their projects in the makerspace.

The first questions in the questionnaire asked how the students perceived the use of mathematics concepts in the makerspace, and at which stage of project development their use was noticed. In addition, it sought to identify which equipment was the most important to students.

The remaining questions were related to a preliminary study, which identified the main mathematics subjects used in the makerspace. These subjects were organized by Thematic Units (except for Probability and Statistics, which was removed from the scope of this work because their use was not observed in a significant way).

The makerspace resources were the laser cutter, 3D Printer, and robotics and automation materials. The low-tech resources consisted of tools such as drills, scissors, and cutters, plus glue and other supplies.

Collected data and discussion

The responses collected revealed important insights into the perception of students in the makerspace about mathematical concepts.

A large majority, 57.1%, indicated that the most important equipment for their projects was the laser cutter, followed by low-tech resources, 3D printer, and finally robotics and automation. This result aligns with what is observed in the makerspace.

An even larger majority, 76.1% said that they used mathematics in their projects very frequently or frequently. The rest stated that it is occasional or that they do not notice the use of mathematics at all.

The students responded to questions about mathematics use in the project stages: modeling and production. They noted the greatest use of mathematics use in modeling and production, 61.9% of respondents said that for them math is used in both stages, while 38.1% said that mathematics is used only during modeling stage.

The following table shows which math concepts students perceived being explored while using makerspace resources. It is important to note that these questions were asked about the Thematic

Thematic Unit	Laser Cutter	3D Printer	Robotics & Automation	Low Tech Resources
Numbers	6.8%	5.7%	6.7%	3.7%
Algebraic Thinking	23.8%	19.7%	15.6%	6.2%
Geometric Thinking	16.0%	13.9%	15.6%	19.8%
Quantities and Measures	31.6%	37.7%	28.9%	40.7%
Computational Thinking	21.8%	23.0%	33.3%	26.9%

Math concepts that students perceive being explored in the makerspace

Units (TU) from the Brazilian scope of the mathematics discipline, but they can be adapted to the educational realities of other countries.

From these results, it can be seen that students understand that Quantities and Measures are the most often used TU in makerspace projects. This result points to the perception of the importance of this TU when dealing with material resources, which require calculations related to measurement units, figure areas, and solid volumes. Computational Thinking and Algebraic Thinking were identified by the students as the next most often used mathematical areas. The manipulation of variables and methodologies to break down problems were themes highlighted by the students.

It was surprising that the Numbers Unit had such a low indication since the use of elements and operations with rational numbers is the foundation for carrying out the projects. Perhaps the students thought that the concept of numbers is more of an abstraction, whereas measurement is real and practical. Or perhaps students felt that number manipulation is so basic as to not really be thought of as math. Whatever the reason, there is much to think about in these survey results.

Conclusions

First, the study sought to analyze the resources available in makerspace, from equipment to software, and correlate the mathematics subjects that students perceive are used. This is one of the contributions of this research.

Subsequently, the application and analysis of the questionnaire pointed to the relationship between the mathland metaphor and the proposal of a makerland where resources used in the makerspace are microworlds and issues related to mathematics are naturally explored.

One indication that the application of mathematical concepts is implicitly and naturally explored is reflected in the projects created. Whether the project is successfully carried out or not, it provides valuable feedback to the student regarding the utilization of mathematical concepts. Mathematics serves as a fundamental element for executing the proposed activities, encompassing both modeling and the setup of software and machines for production.

The questionnaire provided some insight into student perceptions of mathematics in the makerspace. Observations provide other conclusions. In the makerspace, it was often observed that the work creates natural opportunities to use mathematics vocabulary when students work on projects. We see students using mathematics terms without being formally taught, thus connecting with the idea of a makerland where students use the tools and materials and connect to mathematics as naturally as when learning to speak French while living in France.

Further research might ask if the formal disciplines and units of mathematics are useful in describing the mathematical thinking that is actually happening when making projects using the tools found in a makerspace. We may need to expand our thinking about what mathematics actually means in the modern world.

The students identified the use of mathematics concepts during the modeling and production processes and their perceptions aligned with what was identified in the preliminary study. The next step of this study is to systematically organize these issues so that they can be explored in an objective way when the student carries out projects in the makerspace, so that what is applied and learned from the discipline, during the modeling and production process, can be evaluated. The result of this new research will be published in the future.

References

Blikstein, P. (2008). Travels in Troy with Freire: Technology as an Agent for Emancipation. In P. Noguera & C. A. Torres (Eds.), Social Justice Education for Teachers: Paulo Freire and the Possible Dream (pp. 205-244). Sense Publishers.

Brasil. (2018). Base Nacional Comum Curricular. Brasília: Ministério da Educação

Fernandez, C., Hochgreb-Haegele, T., & Blikstein, P. (2021). From "Playful Activities" to "Knowledge Building": A Case Study about a Teacher's Percpetions on the Role of Experiments. Proceedings of the 15th International Conference of the Learning Sciences-ICLS 2021.,

Gavassa, R. C. F. B. (2020). Educação maker: muito mais que papel e cola. Tecnologias, Sociedade e Conhecimento, 7(2), 33-48. doi.org/10.20396/tsc.v7i2.14851

Niss, M., Bruder, R., Planas, N., Turner, R., & Villa-Ochoa, J. A. (2017). Conceptualisation of the role of competencies, knowing and knowledge in mathematics education research. Proceedings of the 13th International Congress on Mathematical Education: ICME-13,

Papert, S. (1980). Mindstorms: Children, Computers, and Powerful Ideas. Basic Books.

Papert, S. (1993). The Children's Machine: Rethinking School in the Age of the Computer. Basic Books.

Wing, J. (2011). Research Notebook: Computational Thinking — What and Why. thelink, 6, 20-23.

Ziegler, G. M., & Loos, A. (2017). "What is Mathematics?" and why we should ask, where one should experience and learn that, and how to teach it. Proceedings of the 13th International Congress on Mathematical Education: ICME-13,

Weekend Makercamps for Students

by Mathias Wunderlich

In January 2021 we had a strict lockdown in Germany due to COVID-19. This was a hard time for students, parents, and for the school staff. But, at our school it also was the time when we established our Weekend Makercamps for students on a regular basis.

Seeing kids were frustrated and sometimes isolated at home on one side, and our school makerspace somewhat abandoned on the other side, we came up with the idea to make our own "bubble" for a weekend.

At the end of 2020 the first commercial COVID-19 rapid tests became available in Germany, and our school decided to buy them long before the tests became common in education. So we got the opportunity to organize the event safely. A lot of kids showed interest, but many of the parents were undecided if our plan was safe or not. Finally, just three boys took part in the event which made it easy to handle. So we had a start! It was big fun for all of us, both for the students and for me as host and facilitator.

Over the past two years, we have repeated the event several times with an increasing number of participants. The organization became a bit more routine, and we were able to host both boys and girls when some female teachers joined in to support the overnight stay at the school. In Fall 2022 we visited maker friends in another FabLab about 150 km north of us over the weekend and shared our different experiences. We opened the weekends for kids from 5th grade on and saw increased participation among girls.

At our most recent Makercamp, we had 16 students, exactly half of them girls, half boys. We also added an "event within the event" for the first time. We opened the space for a special maker activity for kids from 1st to 4th grade. Meanwhile, one former student participant became an adult and returned in a new role as a facilitator.

We are hopeful that we can continue expanding our events to accommodate more participants and even more schools. Every time we do this, we face very different situations and see unique student projects. We learn from one event to the next and hopefully get better in supporting the activities of interested maker kids.

The idea for such events goes back well before the COVID-19 pandemic. Several times we announced plans for weekend or holiday activities with kids — but for some reason just two or three smaller events took place. The idea is very simple, our makerspace with its terrific possibilities is present 24 hours a day, 7 days a week, 365 days a year. The school is heated anyway, has water and electricity, a kitchen, cozy rooms, and even showers! Why leave all this unused during weekends while a lot of kids are sitting at home bored? If they enjoy a happy family weekend, fine! No need to disturb that with other group activities, it's just an offer for the students. In fact we saw several families who were very happy to support their kids by coming along for a while during the weekend, joining us in tinkering and making stuff, and bringing food to share.

Student projects

According to the low floor/high ceiling principle we have almost no formal requirements for students to take part in a Weekend Makercamp. We only ask that they have a project idea. We want to discourage the idea that this is just a sleepaway pizza party. That's why we ask that they come prepared with an idea for a project.

This can change as the weekend goes on. It's absolutely OK to join a different project, participate in multiple projects, to give up a project which gets too difficult, even invent a completely new project during the weekend.

We invest quite a time prior to the weekend to be sure the projects of the participants are roughly matched to their abilities. They should be at least a little bit too hard to handle. If a kid's choice seems to be too close to their comfort zone, we ask questions and discuss the individual goals of the weekend. This is a very valuable process, sometimes learners would like to make the tenth remix of a simple Scratch game, while others have really big ideas, like they plan to build a real Mars rocket during one Saturday afternoon. The planning process requires staff to provide guidance and consulting, with knowledge of the big picture and knowing the students from their daily school life.

The agenda — structured but flexible

Weekend Makercamps usually start Friday afternoon with a group meeting where all participants present their planned projects, sometimes by showing prepared materials (although that is not required). We make sure that all speakers get enough time to present and that they have a friendly and supportive audience. Sometimes collaborations between projects start right here, or participants get valuable suggestions from the group, and sometimes wild discussions generate crazy new project ideas.

After this start, the participants set up their individual workplaces. This is one of the most important differences between working in the school makerspace during the week and taking part in the Weekend Makercamp. Unlike the rushed school schedule, Makercamp students have a lot of uninterrupted time so they can persist in their working process over many hours if they want. We as hosts just ask them to respect the group agenda for eating and reporting progress.

At our first Friday night dinner we check in with all participants to make sure they have found a place to start their work. We have found it valuable that all participants — without any exceptions — are present, to make their plans public and have a voice within the group. Whatever develops during

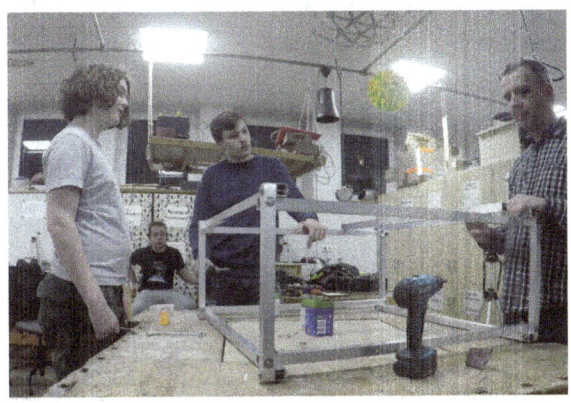

Three very interested boys + one adult coach + one weekend = our very first Weekend Makercamp

the weekend — which collaborations develop, which projects fail, or which get fame — it's meaningful to make the starting point visible in order to see the progress within the next 48 hours.

Saturday is a full work day, with students continuing work on their projects during the day.

We know that eating together is no longer the common thing in many families any longer. We insist on doing so because we see this as an important way to promote collegiality and avoid the kids splitting into isolated groups. On Saturday, we have a nice and relaxed social encounter with a pizza and movie night where all participants are asked to put the tools down and just enjoy.

Sunday after lunch we ring the finish bell. All participants are strongly invited to present their projects, completed or not.. Just like the starting session, we try to provide a calm and supportive atmosphere with plenty of time for all projects to be seen and admired. Even failed projects can be useful as a lesson learned, and should take place within the presentation. After that we facilitate an additional reflection session where all participants are asked what they liked and what to improve next time. Criticizing is highly welcome here, but we also ask for concrete suggestions for improvement. My favorite feedback from one of the "art girls" was, "Why isn't there a Weekend Makercamp every weekend?"

All participants are responsible to tidy up their working spaces, to take or properly store their projects, and to help with the cleaning. Parents usually help with the cleaning of the kitchen and sleeping rooms when they come to pick up their kids. So far these organizational processes were very smooth every time, there has been no need for big planning and formally distributing responsibilities.

Above all, we strive for flexibility. The schedule of the weekend is subject to negotiation with the group. We as facilitators give them room and allow a wide range of possibilities. We just demand a minimal standard for participating in group activities — eating together, reporting progress, and presentations. What we see is that this develops a unique "group feeling" in every single Makercamp — no matter the wide variety of participants creating extremely different projects.

Makercamp participants

From the start, the offer to participate in a Makercamp was only shared with students of our school. Sometimes a best friend of a student asked to participate, and we accommodated these infrequent requests. At our school we work closely with parents, so we know the students, but also their parents. And this is reciprocal — they know us, and they trust in what and how we do such projects. This is a low budget, cost-free, and strictly by choice activity. This creates a high level of engagement by the parents and they help out with resources like food and other support for the event.

There is absolutely no connection between the Makercamp and school tests, grades, or certifications — the participation is really free, no strings attached. Challenges or issues a student may have during the week play no role for the Weekend Makercamp.

All these conditions form a trustful, relaxed, and fearless environment where participants can really focus on creating things.

Rules and guidelines

There are just a few hard rules of course — no drugs, no alcohol, no tobacco, but this so far has not been a problem. Other guidelines are the subject of discussion with participants. These tend to be things like no strong energy drinks, limiting sweets and sugar, no excessive gaming, and getting a minimum amount of sleep. We see these discussions as a part of the educational process, kids must have opportunities to test out their limits. In their families they may or may not have particular rules but at the Weekend Makercamp they have to follow the rules of this temporary setting and community. For some of them this means extra limitations, for some it's a rare opportunity for new experiences.

Our school is safe and comfortable, which makes staying over the weekend easy to organize. We have a fenced school ground and we lock the doors during night time. We are located in a small one-horse town with just about 20,000 people with no serious crime issues. In the building we have several smaller classrooms with carpets, kids bring their own camping mats and sleeping bags, some of them big cozy pillows or their favorite teddy bear. We organize separate rooms for boys and girls along one corridor, and adults sleep in small group rooms nearby. We take care that at least one female and one male adult is present during the nights, so we are (hopefully) prepared for any kind of incident. Interestingly, during school trips with kids we have been seeing increasing homesickness, but in our Weekend Makercamps we have had just one single case which was handled easily without involving the parents.

We ask that students attend the entire weekend, we don't want a continuing coming and going as this may disturb the group processes. Nevertheless we make individual exceptions when kids have commitments to sports clubs or family obligations. The Makercamp is transparent in the sense that parents are invited to come along and see what (their) kids achieve during the weekend. But we ask that they not disturb the atmosphere. Most of our parents are familiar with this approach from our regular school — they are very welcome, but ideally they should be largely invisible. We appreciate their support in all forms. Some help with material and food, some offer guidance to the kids, some act as parent taxis — but most of them are grateful for the extra learning opportunities for their kids.

Working and learning

Most of the time we just let the students do what they want. They need time to think, to discuss, to try, to fail, and to start again. They don't need an advisor stepping in during every situation. They must experience problems on their own. Ideally, we as facilitators are just present as observers, to simply watch and later reflect on the process. In fact we typically do not have one free minute to sit back and watch. There are a thousand questions, material demands, organizational issues, sometimes quarreling, or frustration. Although we are not in our everyday teacher roles, we are professionals and can handle all that. Our school takes a Montessori or maker approach, so we know not to answer every simple question or help too

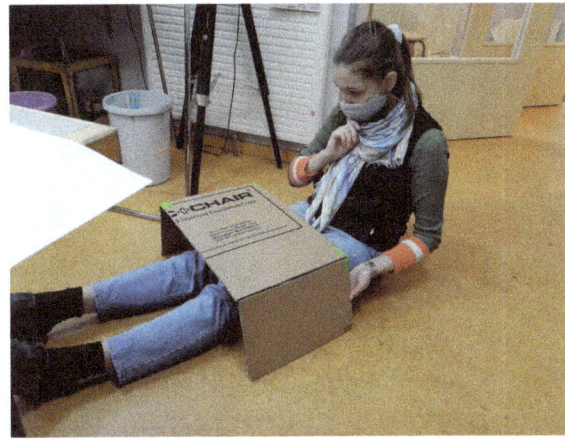
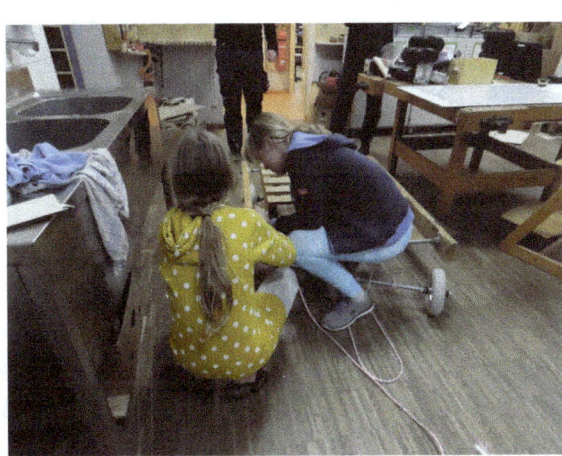

Weekend Makercamps are growing. More participants, more projects, more girls, more professional organization, more routines..

fast with an easy solution. Instead, a student's question generates a counter question, the offer of a hidden clue, or an invitation to ask a peer.

One of the most important advantages of the Makercamp setting in comparison to the normal school setting is time. During the week, everyone is in a permanent hurry — educators and students alike. During school, moments to focus longer than half an hour on complex challenges are rare, if not impossible. During Makercamps, students have this time. They have a real supportive environment where ideas can grow, can be discussed without rush and urgency, can be seen from different points of view, and sometimes can be instantly tested. Students can explore their ideas over hours and hours. Nowhere in formal educational contexts do adolescents have this calm atmosphere, most of the time they are pushed and pulled through the obligations of their job as a student.

During our very first Makercamp I had an experience which I had never before had in my decades as a teacher. It was 10 pm on Friday, and I was tired, planning the next day in my head. What I didn't know was that three boys had a hidden supply of double caffeine cola and several disgusting chips and sweets. At 11 pm I was nodding off, but didn't want to disturb their motivated and excited discussion about 3D modeling. During the next three hours these teen boys dropped into a real workflow! They were nice to each other, joking around and sharing a bunch of clever ideas, even as one of them dove deeply into 3D modeling using Fusion360 for the first time. Only at 2 am I realized that this is them being their normal selves. They are not bored kids in a science class, they were in their Friday night computer game mode where they usually play, discuss, joke and enjoy their lives. This time, they didn't play computer games but learned new things! Without any intervention from adults! How cool is this, colleagues?

Shortly after that insight I decided to leave them and went to my camping mat for a sleep. I was absolutely sure that nothing bad would happen, even without my presence. The next morning I found a bunch of complex aluminum pieces ready to mount and it was clear that the 3D models were far beyond my own capability. The experience of this night is one of my motivations for repeating these events over and over again.

As an educator, it's interesting to observe the development that occurs during the weekend. We see shy kids become empowered, interesting group dynamics, supportive social interactions, incredible project progress, and so much learning. We are able to attend to our students and learn more about them — much more than during the week.

The first weekend Makercamps attracted exclusively tech nerds, mostly boys who haunt the school makerspace during the week. Since then, these weekend events attracted more girls, younger students, and kids who are art enthusiasts. Last time we had six girls painting in the art room. They explored different techniques and completed several creative pieces — without any intervention from adults.

Other makercamps

Some of our students have started a small company delivering food and other goods by cargo bikes. A second student company produces wooden toys, furniture, and Montessori learning material for kindergartens and other local customers. To support these entrepreneurs, we attended workshops at professional makerspaces in the cities of Hamburg to build a second cargo bike, and in Hamm to build a CNC machine that our makerspace needed.

While we went to these workshops with a set project goal in mind, the rest was very similar to the Weekend Makercamps — the same kids, working and learning in their spare time, and social interaction. While we could have purchased the cargo bike and the CNC machine, we believe the experience of building your own tools not only creates ownership, but a deeper understanding of how they work and how to maintain them.

Funding

Often when it comes to Repair Cafés, tours to Maker Faires with kids, or Weekend Makercamps, there is a question about how this is funded. The answer in our case is very easy, there is no funding! My school supports the Weekend Makercamps with supplies and infrastructure. We have our mini school bus on hand for free, we have dry and safe space, energy, water, sometimes a part of the food, and we can use all the rooms, tools, and supplies, so we don't need a fee for supplies from the participants or from other sources. If it is for a useful purpose, the material expenses are covered.

The educators who participate in Weekend Makercamp are all volunteers, although we are allowed to take a half day off if we need it during the following week. People usually decide and act responsibly for themselves and the team.

For me as initiator and organizer of such activities it's an honorary post. I do it by choice, without any salary. I'm paid relatively well in comparison to many other jobs around me. I feel it's beneficial to me as a person and as an educator. And I enjoy these weekends as I am doing things I like anyway – tinkering, creating, learning, exploring, and supporting people doing the same – exactly like professional athletes who like to run a triathlon over the weekend. On Sunday night after a Weekend Makercamp, I'm full of new thoughts and experiences, and I start the next school week enlightened and refreshed. I know that many colleagues over the world act in the same manner, and I would like to see Weekend Makercamps become a movement with real impact for the next generation, and for a better future for all of us.

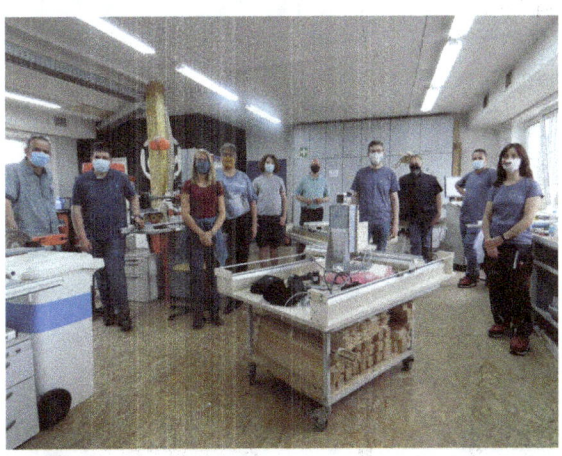

We took part in two offsite makercamps at professional workshops to support growing student businesses. Students built a DIY cargo bike and a CNC machine..

Projects in Depth

The projects in this section give the reader a lot to think about, try, and adapt for one's own situation. In contrast to standard lesson plans, these projects are more fully described and often feature interesting reflections and course corrections from the authors.

Cultural Making: Storytelling through Kalamkari

by Safoura Seddighin

Fabinnov Digital Design and Fabrication Lab was established in 2017, as part of the innovation zone of Isfahan University in the city of Isfahan, Iran. The name was chosen to express our excitement for starting a new movement and inspired us to use the term "nov" which means new in Farsi, as part of the title. The Fabinnov mission is to serve both adults and children by providing access to tools, machines, and specialists from different fields (electronics, robotics, mechatronics, polymers, and education), to bring their ideas to life.

While the industrial section of the lab served university students and startups that were interested in creating MVPs for their services and products, the educational section of Fabinnov focused on serving schools (educators and children) and parents by providing meaningful learning opportunities.

Over the past seven years, Fabinnov has supported summer camps, youth clubs, after school and enrichment programs, and an online platform for virtual learning during the COVID-19 pandemic. Fabinnov provides the materials needed for each course delivered to the participants' doorsteps, and professional development workshops for educators, promoting hands-on and project based learning through a wide variety of projects!

As a co-founder, learner, educator and program designer, one of the common complaints from the educators, parents and administrators was about the kids slowly departing from many of the cultural values of Iran. While the problem of our youth and their identities today is not solely limited to Iran, what makes this subject more worrisome in Iran, is fading of a culture and history that goes back to more than 3,000 years ago.

The city of Isfahan is known for having more than 100 historical buildings and structures. While maintaining the awareness about the history plays an important role in one's identity, our youth are not interested in learning about the rich history and culture!

What adds to the challenge is an educational system that has invested in pure academic achievement as the main path of success for students. This creates a strict, and impossible to challenge list of actions and accomplishments that parents want for their children to have success in life! Graduating with honors, passing the national entrance exam, and getting accepted to a desirable university and major leaves no room for any extra-curricular activities that do not meet the success agenda. As a result of such strict expectations, and despite everyone's concern about the gaps in our children's knowledge of their identity, no one seems to be willing to invest in anything that would change the situation. The parents know what they want and schools can only do their best to keep the parents happy and in case of the private schools, keep the money flowing.

STEAM education and making have been giving us hope that we can meet this challenge and create learning opportunities that connect to what matters and is real! Designing a unit that happens to connect cultural elements with curricular topics would be the closest the learning of a topic could get to reality and life.

One of my friends who is a literature teacher has been working with youth for some years to find ways to connect culture with their experience of learning literature. As part of his efforts, he held his classes inside Isfahan historical buildings twice a month. This experience is so different than what students did on an everyday basis, it opened whole new sets of topics to explore. When a poem was studied, there were history, architecture, and social science units waiting to be explored.

My friend's attempts inspired us to explore the intersection of identity and making for our youth club. Since we had access to a good selection of machines including a laser cutter, CNC milling, vinyl cutter, wood working and workshop tools, we looked for the right physical product to make that was interesting to the students, and connected to culture. In addition to that, as we were exploring the implementation of entrepreneurship for youth in some of the informal settings, having a final product seemed even more ideal.

Kalamkari is the art of painting or printing on fabric that has been practiced in the city of Isfahan for more than 300 years. The art was perfected during the Safavieh period in Iran, when most men's and women's clothes were made from Kalamkari fabrics.

The high demand created a need for increased speed in the production of the fabric, and the use of wooden printing blocks to stamp the designs and motifs became common. These engraved patterns and the art of making these stamps became a profession and the expertise was highly prized. These stamps, usually made of pear or hawthorn wood, are used to print up to four colors on the fabric.

As patterns, fabric, and colors are selected, the application of the wooden stamp on the fabric creates beautiful pieces like music for eyes.

The final products come in many forms including curtains, cloths and table covers, etc., and different sizes and patterns as well.

Creating a unit based on making these stamps and printing patterns on fabric allows connections to amazing topics such as history, math, geometry, the science of paint and fabric, and digital design and fabrication. The project can feed a classroom centuries of knowledge, culture, and pride!

In the lab, the students worked in groups to research different types of patterns, and learned about the difference between natural and chemical paints. They also got the chance to create their own paint from natural materials to use along with the paint provided for them. It was amazing to see their innovative ways of combining the new and old patterns to create the designs to be digitally fabricated and turned into wooden stamps. The stamps were used to print patterns on fabric to make products. The final products of the unit included items such as table covers and curtains. These were put on display, advertised, and sold to the community members by the students themselves.

This experience was an attempt to close the gap between the young generation and their cultural identity. The sense of accomplishment and confidence experienced by the students left no need to convince the students that this was important. The student's themselves drove the process. Throughout their research and in each

Kalamkari block printing

phase of the process from creating the stamps to turning the patterns into the desired results, the students had many meetings with the art masters residing in the old bazaars of Isfahan. Those interactions created unforgettable memories for both adults and children involved in the project.

Although this unit has only been implemented once so far, it has brought so many ideas and generated much excitement in other schools and educators in the district.

While I was working on writing this article, I received an email from Sylvia Martinez about a "Turtle Art Tiles Project" from a book called *The Invent to Learn Guide to Fun* by Josh Burker. This project uses code to create geometric patterns, including Islamic tile patterns, which are then 3D printed to press into ceramic tiles.

It is so beautiful and inspiring to see other educators designing projects that combine cultural artifacts and expertise with modern digital technology. Seeing others doing similar things and watching all the possible connections that making brings gives me hope and the passion to continue this work. Fabinnov looks forward to benefiting from such meaningful connections in the close future and in working with more educators and parents across the country.

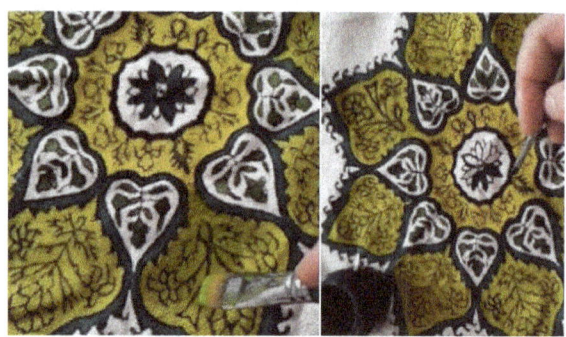

Kalamkari pattern painting

Making in China or Made in China?

by Xiaoling Zhang

Living in Hong Kong is a consumer's dream. A report from 2017 ranked Hongkongers' consumption habits among the unhealthiest in the world. The excessive consumption of goods indicates that one can literally buy whatever they can or even can't imagine here, needed or not. But lately, after spending more time doing projects in the makerspace, I've begun to see the world around me through the lens of a maker and not just as a consumer.

Tinkering with 3D printing and laser cutting, as well as seeing the amazing work of my students and fellow teachers, has changed my perceptions and my consumption habits. When I see an interesting product in a shop, I now stop and think about how it was made, and how I might try to make something similar.

What makes making worth it?

If one can spend a few hundred Hong Kong dollars to buy a cool designer product (about 1% of an average monthly income, so, quite affordable), would one still want to make it?

I often wonder if students think the same way after they become familiar with maker tools and materials. Do they understand that there is additional value to making?

In the midst of developing not only a maker mindset, but a maker educator mindset, I also always pause and ponder: what learning goals am I trying to achieve? As an educator, of course there is value in the act of creation to better understand the process.

I wrestle with these questions and also the implications of what Paulo Blikstein called, "the keychain syndrome" (Blikstein, 2013). He identified a situation in makerspaces where students who are successful at making simple things do not progress to making more complex things, preferring to stay in a comfortable cycle of downloading 3D objects without ever designing them or laser cutting simple designs like keychains and nametags. For me, the question remains: how does one make projects more meaningful which in turn involves longer and deeper learning experiences?

Making and craft culture rooted in Chinese history

Long before "Made in China" became a well-known label world-wide, Chinese had a rich history of invention. From the compass (invented during Han Dynasty, 206 BC – AD 220), to movable clay type printing from the Northern Song dynasty (960 – 1127), and the invention of gunpowder (invented during the Tang Dynasty 618 – 907), inventions have advanced Chinese culture. The exquisite craft-making culture and fabrication deeply rooted in our history has enriched people's lives in China and around the world. A vast body of evidence confirms the importance and sophistication of traditional science and technology in pre-modern China (Needham, 1954–2003).

Inventions first seen in Hong Kong are also rooted in Chinese culture yet at the same time firmly planted in the modern world. Hong Kong is not just a famous tourist destination, but it was the home of the first modern millionaire from the manufacturing industry. Hong Kong's well-known magnate Li Ka-shing owes his wealth to the plastic flower business he started in the years after World War II.

Some of the most distinctive home-grown products such as mosaic tiles, big-character signs, and neon lights have came to define a uniquely Hong Kong aesthetic, a combination of hand-made and manufactured.

Neon Signs in Portland Street, Hong Kong.
Photo credit: See-ming Lee (CC BY-SA 4.0)

Manufacturing and consumerism

How did we lose sight of this maker mindset when everything is "Made in China"? Recognition of Chinese crafts and artisanry has been drowned out by the impression of low-quality mass production. In this modern world, we always want everything to be quick and get the results immediately. But for learning, the process matters, because that's when creativity has a chance to grow. Not being able to create will create students who only know how to be a passive recipient.

Making in the Chinese classroom

For learners, the meaning of what they are learning matters. The aim of maker education should not be to just make something with modern technology, but to give learners an experience that has the potential to create deeper understanding of our unique culture through making.

In 2021, our school launched a new course called *Haoxue*. Haoxue in Chinese means "eager to learn." Haoxue courses are a half year long and a new group of students can take the class each semester. It allows subject teachers to design curriculum based on their own interests and passion.

I found it a perfect chance to make it an extension of my Chinese language class. The goal was for students to experience the beauty and joy of Chinese culture through authentic, meaningful experiences that also supported the normal language curriculum. I was inspired to put into practice "a model in which students work on personal or community-meaningful interdisciplinary projects, often freed from a scripted curriculum, empowered to make choices about their own learning, and using technologies to externalize their ideas in sophisticated ways" (Worsley & Blikstein, 2016).

Students rotate every half of the school year so this course has now been offered four times, allowing for iteration in the course design that is shared here.

Course design and iterations

I named my course "The Chinese Fashion of Life." It was designed mainly for Grade 6 students. In the first class, I asked my students to share their expectations of what they were going to learn in this course based solely on the name. They guessed that it might be about Chinese traditional clothes or art appreciation. In a brief introduction, I explained that the title of the course would actually mean Chinese style and ways of living. Students were asked to document things in their daily lives that show traits of Chinese culture. They immediately came up with the porcelain plates they use, bamboo tea coasters, "good luck fish" decoration, Chinese calligraphy, and painting decoration. They became more aware that their modern life is also surrounded with a lot of local culture.

The design of the course was semi-open as this was its pilot stage. We wanted to leave flexibility to adjust based on student reactions and their ideas of what they might be more interested in. Below are two highlighted projects from each of the four iterations of the course: "The Chinese way of leisure, playing, and games" and "Chinese traditional clothes."

First iteration (Sept to Dec 2021)

The project "The Chinese way of leisure, playing, and games" was inspired by an online question, "Would people be 100% devoted to their work/study if there were no computer, video games, or TV shows?" Instinctively I would say "NO" because leisure time is a crucial part of work-life balance. But another question popped up in my mind. If there were no computer, video games, or TV shows, what would we do? Do we still know how and what to play? So, I decided to explore the answer with my students by learning from our ancestors. We tried to make and play games of arrow tossing, leaf battle, mini sandbags games, and Luban ring locking puzzles. Students created

Projects in Depth

Iteration 1: Students designed instructional posters and invited peers to play the games.

their own "leaves" using recycled paper instead of fallen leaves, reworked some of the rules for the sandbag games, and created instruction posters. Afterwards, they invited another class to enjoy the games with them.

The project "Chinese traditional clothes" was based an essential part of Chinese culture, the magnificent designs of apparel of different dynasties that have been shared and passed down for generations. After many trials with 2D design platforms, we decided to use Gravit, a web-based design tool. Students came in with different levels of previous experience with 2D CAD design, but we felt Gravit would be a good tool to start with for everyone. As a novice myself, I had several sessions with Mr. Pang, our Fablearn liaison engineer teacher, through video calls as well as bringing him into the classroom to answer questions and help students. Because of the limited time and unstable learning environment during the COVID-19 period, we needed to complete this project quickly. Therefore, we decided to make simple stickers and keychains as these were the quickest and easiest to laser cut.

We were soon faced with signs of students developing the "keychain syndrome" as predicted by Blikstein (2013), while literally making keychains.

With more time and without the disruption of COVID-19 to consider, we would have likely pursued other avenues, such as rubber stamps, but in the end, we decided to proceed with the keychain and a plain style of sticker.

Although some students said this was their most well-made and satisfactory product so far, I often ponder if it could have been a more meaningful project that included more complex facilitation, curriculum re-design, and other equipment rather than just making trivial objects like keychains. Bearing this in mind, I asked students if they would be interested in making their own games (vessels for the arrow tossing game, sandbags, etc. All the students answered yes.

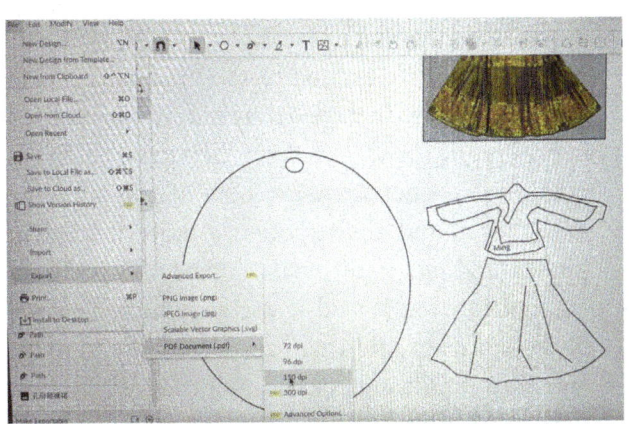

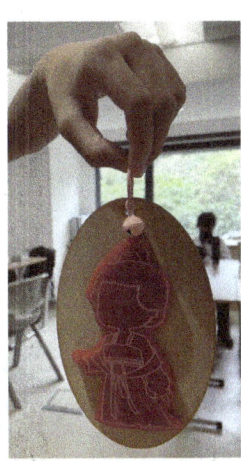

Iteration 1: Fashion project designs

Second iteration with a new group of students
(During a period of online instruction due to COVID-19. Jan. to June, 2022)

The Chinese games project asked students to design their own arrow tossing game using Gravit. To learn to use the online CAD program, Mr. Pang created a study kit for students to practice the basic techniques of 2D CAD design in Gravit. I was getting more familiar with the software which made it possible to facilitate students' learning by giving them guidance and instructions in small online groups.

However, online learning has its pros and cons. In the post-project questionnaire, 70% of the students found the biggest challenge was that they were not familiar enough with the software, and 20% said their original ideas were too complicated to realize in Gravit. 40% of the students said that during online lessons, the whole process of asking questions and getting answers took so much time that they couldn't finish in time.

However, 90% of the students answered that they would want to finish the design and laser cut their own product if more time was allowed.

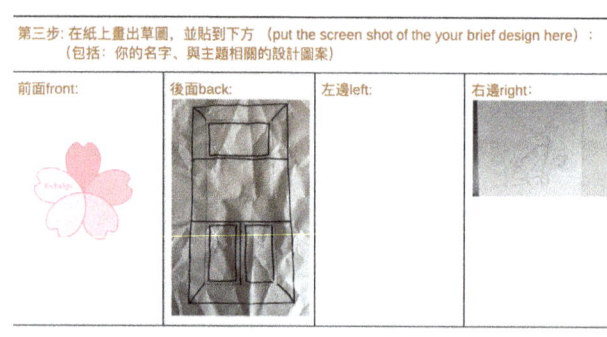

Iteration 2: Laser cut games

Iteration 2: School uniform stickers

This semester, the Chinese traditional clothes project was changed based on an inspiration of my co-teacher Ms. Lin. We decided to introduce a more authentic, modern approach — designing a set of school uniforms with elements of traditional Chinese clothing designs. As a bilingual school, a modern Chinese uniform could represent school spirit and perhaps could actually be turned into reality one day!

In this project iteration, students used the UV sticker printer machine and vinyl cutting machine. With these simpler machines, the technology barrier was lowered and the stickers better represented student designs.

Students were excited to see their work made into tangible products and thus were more engaged in presenting the ideas behind their designs. In the post-project questionnaire, 60% of the students said they found the experience quite helpful in understanding traditional clothes design, and an additional 20% said it was very helpful. 100% of the students said that they would like to make authentic traditional clothes with fabric, if given the opportunity.

Third iteration with a new group of students after lockdown ended (Sept. – Dec 2022)

The Chinese game project went back to "normal" conditions as students came back to the classroom post lockdowns. As I was now a lot more familiar with Gravit, it was easier and more efficient to teach the students how to use the software, although I was much busier going around the classroom and helping them solve their problems. We ran into technical problems when we found out that the Gravit platform had changed its policies. Students realized that in this modern world, I, like them, am also learning these skills in real time so we can learn and help each other. Once we figured out a way to continue, several students learned the new process very quickly, and with that new expert knowledge helped others and made the whole process smoother than expected. With the technology problems out of the way, students were more focused on the requirements that the design would need to be related to Chinese culture.

The Chinese traditional clothes project was divided into several smaller groups based on students' interests: miniature traditional clothes, real traditional clothes, embroidery, and traditional clothes stickers.

Fourth iteration with another new group of students (Jan. – June 2023)

We are currently in our fourth iteration, with students designing an arrow tossing game as well as hands-on projects such as sewing mini sandbags from upcycled clothes and filling them with expired rice. One of our goals this semester is to minimize the use of purchased materials in favor of using second-hand and upcycled materials.

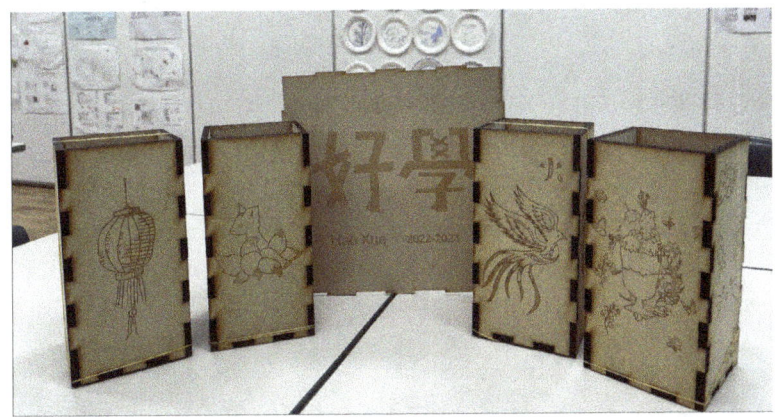

Iteration 3: Games incorporating "dragon boat racing" and "four Chinese ancient mythical beasts" into the design of the arrow tossing game vessel

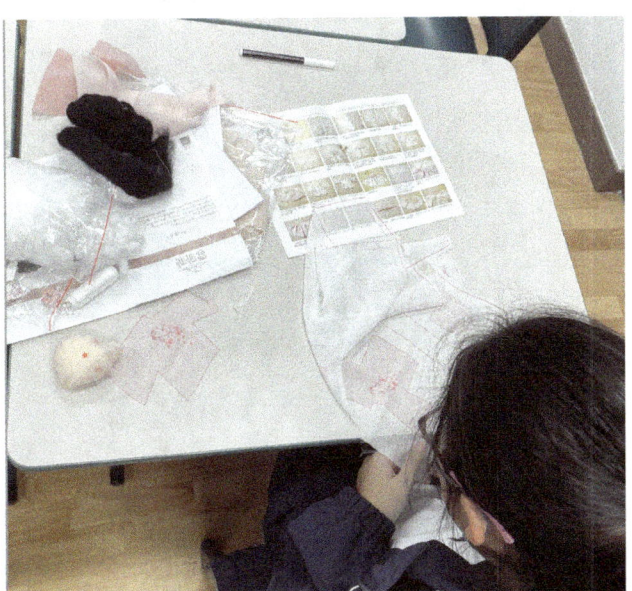

Iteration 3: Various Chinese clothes projects

Student responses to the courses

Students really enjoyed the course. There were students who came to the first class without knowing exactly what they were about to learn and are now excited to ask, "What are we going to do today?" They got to experience and have a deeper understanding of Chinese culture through the process of making, instead of just being lectured. They had a chance to explore with their peers and to discover things they previously thought they might not be good at. It has been a meaningful experience for them to learn about Chinese culture as well as the new technologies through 2D and 3D design as well as using the materials around them in daily life.

Here are some comments from our students:

"I have learned that even without computer games, we can still play happily."

"The games were interesting and were very different from our current games."

"The meaningful part of the Chinese games was that we did our research and made posters and instructions so that I learned more about them."

"I think that ancient people were really smart. They managed to use the simple materials around them to make games."

"The games seemed to be a bit boring at first glance, but I became more interested once we got started."

"I learned how best to introduce the games to those who don't know them. I also learned how to break down a project into smaller tasks and how to cooperate."

"I learned more about history."

"The course was well-designed and very interesting. We had the chance to learn in groups, and through videos. And we also got to try what ancient people played. It was an authentic experience."

Conclusion

Designing and implementing these courses gave me new insight into the difference between making and consuming. Students experienced a unique sense of ownership pf the projects and had "hard fun." Hard fun is one of the "eight big ideas" espoused by Dr. Seymour Papert when he documented a constructionist learning experience (Stager, 2006).

After finishing the half-year course, some students would still come to me and ask if they could continue to laser cut their arrow tossing vessel. Students often mention the experience whenever they see me. They also told me that although learning the 2D software was tough, the

Iteration 4: Projects in process

final product meant more to them than just buying a similar toy because they put effort and their personal ideas into it.

Hearing students articulate this in their own words made me feel like we are on the right track. We must allow students to have meaningful making experiences, while avoiding, as best we can, the "keychain syndrome" which would reduce the process into a one-size-fits-all quick format. We should design projects that take several cycles of redesign and connect the ideas and themes with students' lives, interests, passions, and communities. We need to continue to put more emphasis on the process rather than the product, and to challenge students to realize how far they went outside of their intellectual comfort zones. A last crucial point for us to remember is to let students learn during the process how to work, collaborate, and distribute their efforts (Worsley & Blikstein, 2016). Thus, I find myself moving in the right direction and looking forward to more redesigning and exciting challenges to come.

When we ask students to "make," we are not asking them to do "mass production" or simply learn to use the cool tools. Instead, we are empowering them to think and reflect by connecting clear learning goals and then incorporating the tools to facilitate their imagination and creation. I firmly believe the cultural and historical perspectives of the course added importance to the projects. Last but not least, we must trust students by granting them autonomy in their learning, which empowers both students and teachers to reach their highest potential.

Notes

1. zolimacitymag.com/hong-kong-industrial-history-part-x-how-plastic-flowers-built-global-metropolis/
2. Now called Corel Vector cloud.gravit.io

References

Blikstein, P. (2013). Digital Fabrication and 'Making' in Education: The Democratization of Invention. In J. Walter-Herrmann & C. Büching (Eds.), FabLabs: Of machines, makers and inventors. Bielefeld: Transcript Publishers.

Needham, J. (1954–2003). Science and Civilisation in China 7 vols. Cambridge University Press.

Stager, G. S. (2006). An Investigation of Constructionism in the Maine Youth Center [Ph.D., The University of Melbourne]. Melbourne, Australia.

Worsley, M., & Blikstein, P. (2016). Children are not hackers: Building a culture of powerful ideas, deep learning, and equity in the Maker Movement. In K. Peppler, E. Halverson, & Y. B. Kafai (Eds.), Makeology: Makerspaces as learning environments (pp. 78-94). Routledge.

Robot Art

by Lars Beck Johannsen

I can't think of Seymour Papert without picturing turtle graphics — this little virtual turtle that turns your code into patterns and shapes. This is a classic engaging activity that holds a lot of learning potential. For one thing it gives a tangible outcome to programming, and it makes use of geometry in a way that is challenging and lets you experiment with mathematics.

In his spirit I designed a workshop called Robot Art. The students are told that they will be making art with a robot, by programming it to move with a pen attached to it. I've run this workshop with students ages 9–13. The extra element in this workshop is an activity that is actually more challenging than it sounds: building a pen tool for the robot.

I have used two different types of robots, the LEGO Spike and Cody Rocky. Both are capable of having LEGO bricks attached to it. The students were given access to different LEGO bricks, a rubber band, and a pen. As you can see from the pictures there are a lot of different approaches to this challenge, and I always get surprised by the ingenuity of some kids. But the students did not stop there. Many of the robots became parts of stories that used the robot's behavior as part of the storytelling.

This was not planned for, but just evolved, and made the whole lesson more engaging and meaningful. One of my special needs students, a 10-year-old, amazed me with his robot telling and living out the passion of Jesus. It was about Easter, the topic of a class discussion the day before. His version would most likely be perceived as blasphemous for the average Christian, but nonetheless true to what he had been told.

The drawing process is at least as engaging as the robot-building process. We tell the students that it is art — and let us just say, abstract art — and this frees the students from having to worry about the robot drawing being something naturalistic or pretty. Almost every time students will try to make the robot draw a square. But the difference between coding something that is square in theory and the actual outcome of the robot drawing the square becomes very apparent. Move x, turn 90, repeat 4 times sounds like it should make a square. But real life is not perfect, and usually they don't build a lifting tool so it turns into something more like this in these pictures.

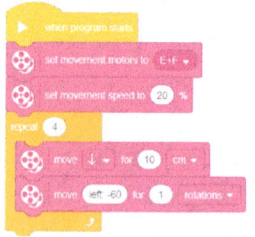

Sometimes students put a lot of effort into drawing a specific shape. Here is a nice example of a group of 10-year-old girls that made their robot draw a flower shape. The robot would start at the bottom, go up and draw the flower and return - not an easy task to get that accurate a result.

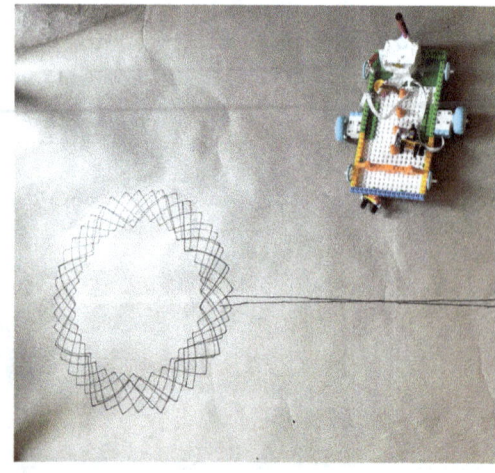

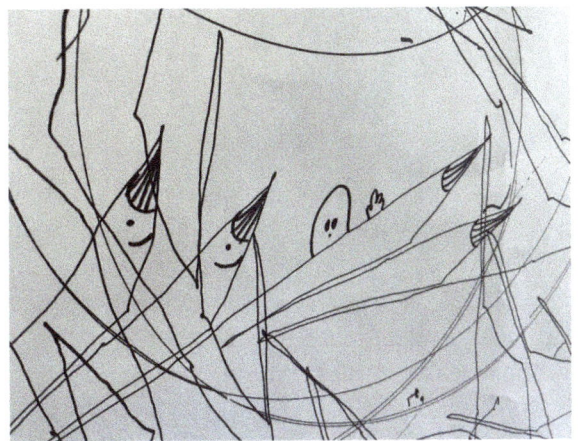 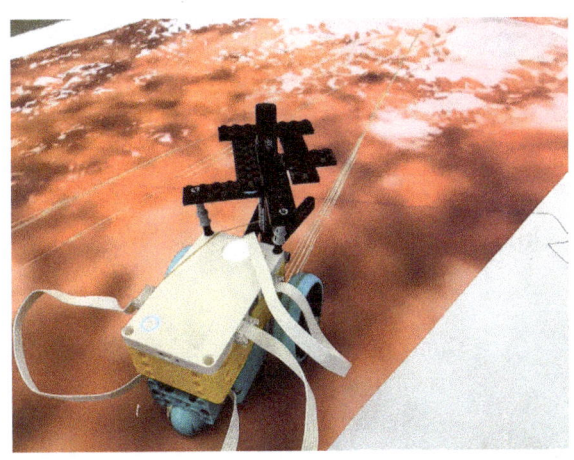

It is important to share the work students do. Making an exhibition with the drawings made by the robots is one way. I like to have the students crop different areas, make them choose a part of work that they find interesting. I encourage the students to draw on top of the robots lines, putting their own imagination into the lines generated. It is a way of having an analog conversation with the digital output of the robot.

Another option is to let the robots draw on printouts. I save failed prints from the large format printer in our Fablab, which gives an extra dimension to the artwork and also a sustainable way to reuse the paper.

Making art with robots is an engaging activity that develops storytelling, imagination, aesthetic senses, ingenuity and involves a lot of programming.

Robot Art Gallery

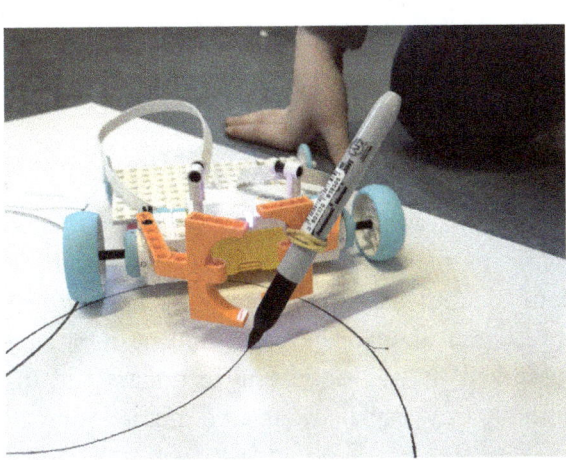 

Biotinkering 101

by Lina Cannone

> Our biggest challenge in this new century is to take an idea that seems abstract—sustainable development — and turn it, too, into a daily reality for all the world's people.
> —Kofi Annan

Over the years I have tried to work sustainably in fablabs and makerspaces. Last year I discovered the DIY Bio movement and became interested in creating activities for students. What is DIY Bio? According to Wikipedia, it is "a growing biotechnological social movement in which individuals, communities, and small organizations study biology and life science using the same methods as traditional research institutions." I searched online for some time but I hesitated in proposing this type of activity because the processes I found often used special tools and required specific knowledge.

I took courage after discovering the activities of Corinne Takara and her Nest Makerspace.[1] Following her activities, I discovered that in addition to Biohacking (scientific experiments with biological material, especially genes), there are also options to engage in Biomaking and Biotinkering (building or tinkering with biological materials). Biotinkering was just what I was looking for to be able to learn with my primary school students.

It was shortly after this that our first classroom biotinkering experiment started and we produced a bioplastic with sodium alginate and calcium lactate. Both are safe, easy to find sustainable materials. Sodium alginate is a material extracted from the cell walls of brown algae and used in the kitchen as a gelling agent, and calcium lactate is used as a leavening and acidity regulator in pastry.

It was around this time that Gary Stager was a guest in our FabLearn Fellow webinar. I have been following his work for some time but I had never had the opportunity to meet him personally. He was a great inspiration and insisted on a fundamental concept that I repeat to myself from time to time: Make it happen! Children learn even if they are not taught.

With this phrase in my head, I went to school, knowing only what I found on the TheTechInteractive website: how to make algae strings that can be a substitute for petroleum-based plastic.[2] I was in the same condition as my students, in the full exploration phase with the willingness to learn with them.

First, we prepared materials, using sodium alginate to gel in distilled water and adding food coloring to taste. We prepared a calcium bath to turn the gel into strings and started this messy experience.

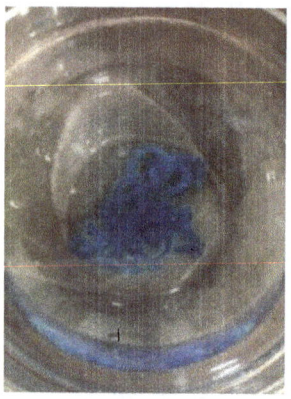 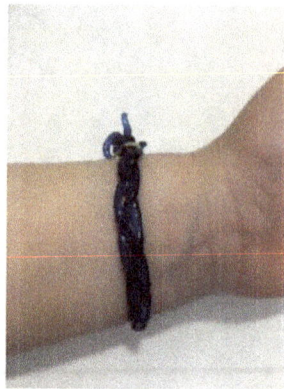

Algae strings and bracelet made with algae strings

The results were fascinating! Children started trying to make shapes, but they were not well defined until one of them thought of trying to spread the alginate gel in a silicone mold, and it worked! It was wonderful to understand that without any explanations and guided only by collaboration, curiosity, and creativity kids created wonderful works. We discovered later that this technique is used in molecular cooking for spherification, for example, bubble tea!

Next Steps

In the next experiments we would like to:
- Try to incorporate objects into the bioplastic or create a film that can be used for decoration
- Improve the conductivity of the bioplastic — we have formulated a hypotheses that we might use lemon juice or add salt to the water
- Create 3D printed customized molds to shape the bioplastics

Notes

1. nestmakerspace.weebly.com/
2. thetechathome.org/algaestring

Stitching Roots: Exploring Family History through Biomaking, Coding, and Stitching

by Lina Cannone

My school is a primary school located in a peripheral neighborhood of Rome, Italy. The area is characterized by a constantly increasing population, both from non-EU immigration and from internal immigration of families who move to this area for work. There is a lack of structured opportunities or places to socialize. The origin of the inhabitants is heterogeneous and often there is no family support network. As a periphery of the metropolis of Rome, it attracts families, even multi-problematic ones, and commuters who travel in and out during the day for work or study.

In this context, I decided to experiment with a path of self-production and biotinkering (as described in my article "Biotinkering 101" in this volume) with the girls and boys in the fourth grade, one hour a week. Kids involved in the learning activity didn't have previous experience and one of the first challenges was to find good materials to use. They needed to be low-cost, easy to grow, should not be frightening, and should stimulate creativity and curiosity.

The material I selected is kombucha leather. Kombucha is a fermented beverage enjoyed for its unique flavor and powerful health benefits. The fermentation process creates a SCOBY — a thick, rubbery, cloudy mass.[1] Drying the SCOBY creates kombucha leather, a flexible material that can be used like fabric. We then embroidered the leather with designs created in Turtlestitch.[2]

The production of kombucha, like other biomaterials, requires patience and care. Before using the material, children need to wait, observe, and understand whether the conditions are right to grow and harvest the material. This leads to a twofold outcome: caring for something so that it can develop, and scientific observation of variables to assess the best conditions for growth and/or production of the material.

After growing kombucha leather, we learned to create a simple project in Turtlestitch. Turtlestitch is a Logo-based block coding language that outputs to an embroidery sewing machine. Using this web-based application, everyone can create an embroidery pattern to stitch.

Practicing with TurtleStitch

I asked them to create a little design that represents their family, something that they view in their home in a quilt or a blanket. As the kids' families are from different countries, they all have different roots, creating a wide variety of patterns.

The project was not simple due to the kids' age but, helped by imported procedures that created modular objects, we were able to complete the project.

At the end of the lessons, students shared what they did in a group, explaining what activities they plan to do in the next lesson and analyzing what they felt satisfied with. They compared their stitched kombucha leather patterns to others and we noticed that in some way all the projects were similar even if different. They were a representation of individuals, united by deep but unique roots. A floral theme was the most common.

The first observation I can make about the experience is an increased awareness by students. They have become more aware of the sustainability of a biodegradable product instead of products with a negative environmental impact. Another observation is that students became aware of the time and effort needed to produce the kombucha leather, with consequent attention to its consumption. I noticed a great deal of attention to minimizing waste because the children knew very well the time it took to produce it.

As a teacher, I can say that this was an enriching experience. It is not easy to manage biotinkering activities at the organizational level because you often need a heat source for the production of bioplastics, with consequent challenges related to the safety of students. You may need to set up special spaces for the culture of materials such as kombucha so they are out of the way of day to day classroom activity. On the other hand, it's great to experiment and learn with my students. As is the case every time I offer tinkering activities, I also challenged myself on my ability to facilitate group work and to handle frustration with an activity that did not turn out as well as the students expected. I hope that the work started at school will be a starting point for conversations at home and with classmates. For the children, bringing home a product made entirely by them is the best way to get them involved and give them ideas to perhaps reproduce the activity with their families and raise awareness in the community about using sustainable products that are linked to their own culture.

Biotinkering is still a very new activity in schools and for this reason, is still not well known. Thanks to the community of educators on social networks, I came into contact with pioneers in this field who gave me many ideas and support. I was able to ask for information, suggestions, and clarifications from people from all over the world and I am sure that without a group of teachers with the same goals and interests I would not have been able to find the keys to make this experiment so successful. I hope that this article can be a starting point for other teachers who are looking for more sustainable experimentation linked to the culture and the territory in which they live.

In the future, I hope to expand the trial to more girls and boys. Tinkering and making have taken off in Italy in recent years and many educators have embraced its potential. The commitment is to be able to support the emergence and contribute to the construction of a local community around the themes of constructionism and pedagogy as a practice of freedom.

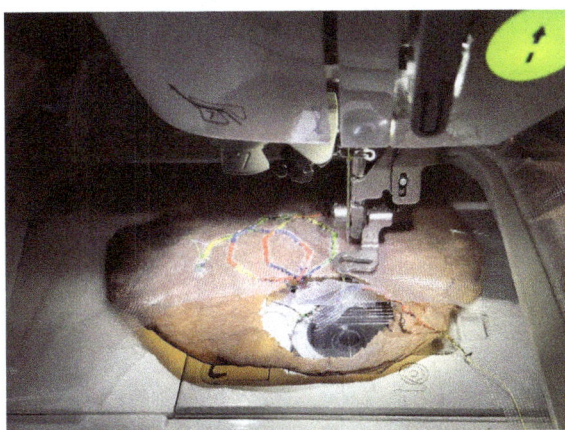 

Coded patterns stitched on kombucha leather using a programmable embroidery machine

Cherokee Language Syllabary Using 3D Design in Tinkercad

by Josh Ajima

The purpose of this article is to present an approach to incorporating indigenous languages into the teaching of 3D printing design. This work is theoretical in that I do not teach or work with students studying the Cherokee language or culture. Rather the Cherokee font is intended to be representative of non-Roman character sets not currently incorporated into 3D design tools.

Frequently, the first 3D printing design challenge presented to students in design software such as Tinkercad is to customize an object with their name. Creating a name tag keychain familiarizes students with navigating the 3D design environment and basic tasks such as adding, moving, and resizing geometric primitives. A library of capital letters enables students to easily add each letter to their project. When the design is 3D printed the student leaves with a personalized object connecting the student to the digital fabrication process.

Converting non-roman character sets into a library of 3D glyphs allows students to easily create their name in their language of choice. The UN Declaration on the Rights of Indigenous Peoples recognizes the right to languages as an inherent right for indigenous peoples.[1] Furthermore, the United Nation recognizes language rights as the direct application of basic human rights such as freedom of expression.

I've saved a Tinkercad project for the Cherokee Language Syllabary.[2] You can make a copy of this design to use for your own projects. Each character represents a syllable in the Cherokee language.

Creating design aids such as the Cherokee Language Syllabary in programs such as Tinkercad works to promote and normalize these rights in the 3D design world.

In creating the Cherokee Language Syllabary for Tinkercad, I referenced the Unicode Standard Version 13.0 Cherokee documentation for organization.[3]

The font file used was Plantagenet Cherokee as packaged in MacOS 10.15.7, designed by Ross Mills of Tiro Typeworks. Another font option is Noto Sans Cherokee.[4]

Notes

1. social.desa.un.org/issues/indigenous-peoples/united-nations-declaration-on-the-rights-of-indigenous-peoples
2. tinkercad.com/things/j3LfzeEOhm8
3. unicode.org/charts/PDF/U13A0.pdf
4. fonts.google.com/noto#sans-cher

Converting Cherokee Font to Tinkercad Workflow
- Open Illustrator document 200mm x 200mm
- Insert Text- Change font to Plantagenet Cherokee
- Type –> Glyph
- Insert Character
- Type –> Change to Outline
- Resize character to 150mm x 150mm
- Center character on artboard
- Save file as SVG -SVG Profiles: SVG 1.1
    -CSS Properties: Presentation Attributes
    -Decimal Places: 3
    -File name = (Unicode Standard Number)
    -CHEROKEE-LETTER-(Letter Name)
- Open Tinkercad file
- Import
    -Center on: Art
    -Dimensions: Length: 11.44mm
    -Change height of character to 4 mm

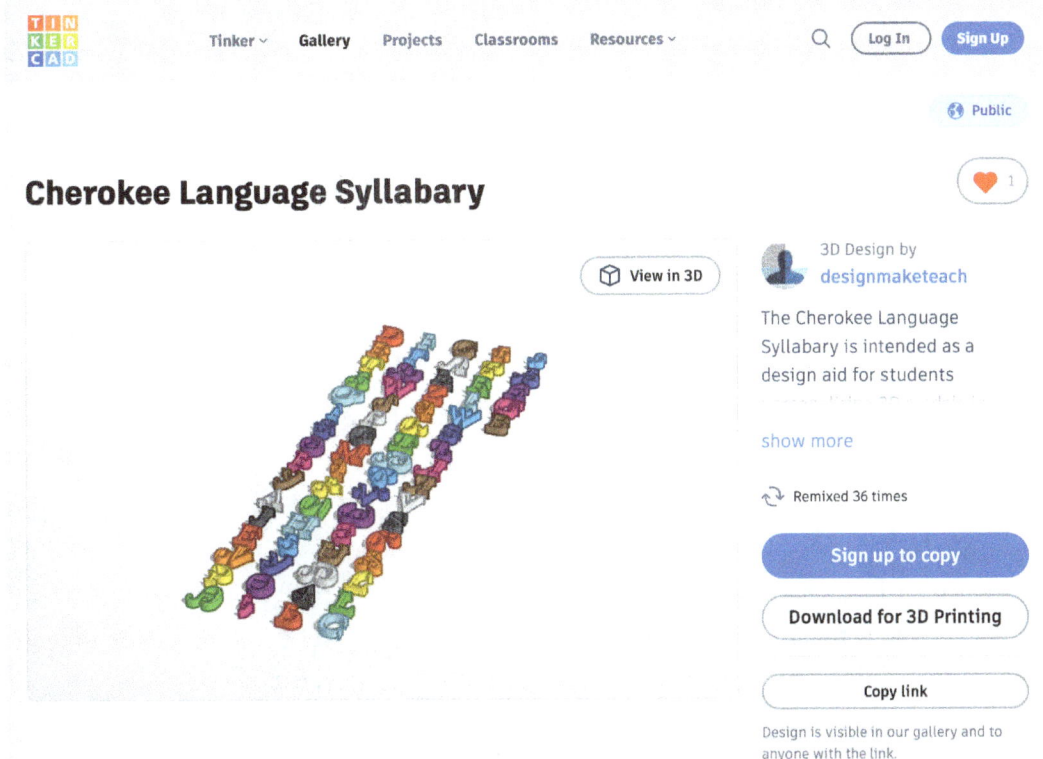

Making Puppets Come Alive

by Ridhi Aggarwal

Activity objective

Students will observe the movement of animals, insects, and birds around us and make a puppet of that animal, insect, or bird with similar movement.

Origin of this activity

Our learning center puts on puppet shows in government schools. Our students are a part of the volunteer team who make puppets and also perform in the shows. In previous years we had done many shows based on animal stories and had made many puppet animals, but their movement was limited to only neck and mouth movement. We had not tried to do anything more complex, but the children decided that the time between school sessions would be a good time to explore this idea which we have been pondering over for a long time. So, this is how I asked the students to plan a session on the movement of animals.

Sessions

This activity lasted five sessions with 11 children mostly in grades 9–11.

Session 1:

To get the momentum going we did a little exercise where all of us had to think of an animal and act out its movements and others had to guess. I gave everyone a *duppata* (a long scarf) and they had to manipulate it to suggest the movement of an animal. Doing movements with their own bodies was easy and it was easy to guess, but there was a lot of thinking when trying to move the duppata and many struggled in the beginning to depict an animal. Then one girl made a caterpillar with the duppata and this gave everyone the impetus to start trying various things.

In our reflection circle at the end of this session, it came out that we have certain ideas of each animal in our minds due to what we have read or seen in pictures — but the movements of a particular animal only comes with observation and spending time with them. Two of the children had cows at their houses and they were able to get the sitting postures right as they had spent time with them.

We discussed the importance of observation and we decided that we should each observe an animal and then see how it changes our perspective. But then the question was which animal? So, to decide on the criteria someone said that since we have to make puppets eventually, we should choose animals whose puppets we haven't made before. But someone else suggested that we should only choose animals which we had made earlier as it would give us better movement in our current shows. The conversation went on for some time, and then one boy suggested that why don't we make a measurement criteria? That sounded interesting, so everyone decided that they would observe an animal that is not bigger than their hands. After this session they all took two days to observe an animal, insect, or bird.

Session 2:

Everyone came back with a sketch and a video of the animal they had observed to show the group. They all had observations and discoveries to share.

One girl said that she observed for the first time how a bee keeps rotating in place and it looked like the earth rotating.

Another boy said he had never imagined that a ladybug had such big wings and it was amazing how it folds its wings inside its upper body.

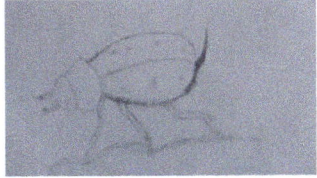

This discussion went in many directions but then someone said that because snakes slither it would be easy for them to go inside their holes. And this was the right time for me to pop in with a question, so I asked them, "What do you think affects the movement of animals? What are the reasons that they move in a specific way?" This discussion brought a lot of ideas about habitat, adaptation, and the limbs, muscles, and structure of the animals. Everyone got curious about this and wanted to research a bit about their animals and see if there was a link between their movements and their habitats, so they decided to read a few articles and come for the next session the next day.

At the end of the session in the circle of reflection we discussed that every animal or human movement has a purpose. Someone shared that there is a reason why we walk on two legs and why some animals walk on four legs, and some don't have legs — every structure is there to suit the climate and the environment of that person or animal. One child shared that we often comment on someone's skin color but that is also a reaction to the environment they live in, and this was an interesting angle about how we all are different because we ought to be.

Session 3:

This session started with everyone excited to share their research. I asked them to share in groups that would explore one movement which their animal, insect, or bird makes. So after much discussion they chose their groups, three groups of three children and one group of two.

1. Wings of a bee
2. Wings of a ladybug
3. Neck of a bulbul bird
4. Ant leg movement for walking and carrying food

When they were in their groups, I asked them to think about two things: first what materials they would need for that movement and second that it's just exploration and not a final puppet that we are making so we should really explore a few mechanisms. I also joined the ant leg group.

They discussed for about 15 minutes and then went to collect some materials for their group. They explored the materials for some time and then we all came together to share what we had done.

In the sharing, the bee group was making wings with paper only, while the ladybug group was using paper and thread. We came to the conclusion that we were not pushing ourselves, but were going back to mechanisms which we already knew, and this would not give us the exact movement of the animal. So, we needed to focus on the movement and then think about the mechanisms. A question also came up that how do we know about new

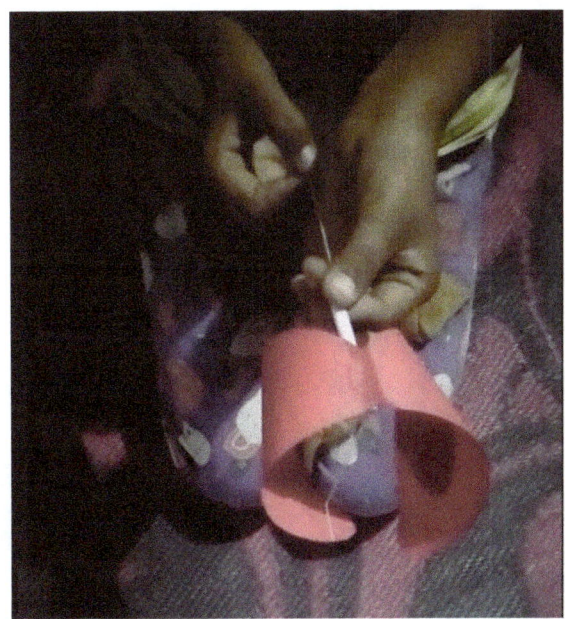

mechanisms to try, and a student suggested that we had not done any toy or object takeaparts for many days, which used to give us some ideas.

This was important feedback for me as I had not done many exploratory sessions. So, we all decided that we would have one such session every month.

Session 4:
This session began with everyone trying different options for the movement.

The bee group tried making wings with a cardboard using an L shaped movement with a hinge, but it was not going sideways. Then they used cardboard to try attaching a P and reversed P shape with four hinges on four corners of a rectangle but this was giving them one-sided movement.

While I thought that it was a good movement they were not satisfied. They mentioned that bee wings move up and down but also have a rotation movement which was not getting achieved by this mechanism. They also realized that they wings of a bee are very tiny in comparison to its body so if they used cardboard it would be too bulky.

The ladybug group had a lot of difficulty as they had to fold the wings and then build a mechanism to open them to full size. They tried doing it with cloth, but the folding part was not very smooth. They had a tough time thinking about options as cardboard was out of question as the wings had to fold in a delicate manner and the wings were thin too. Finally, one of the team members thought of origami as an option and they tried to make folds and open it by pulling one end of the paper just like a beak of a bird would move if made from paper. This was working well but they were not very convinced that it would work when attached to the body.

The bulbul bird group worked with some paper at first and tried getting the movement with only crumpled paper but then they felt it was just waving, and did not look like what they had observed. They had noticed a sudden motion of the neck to check if someone is coming, where the bird moves its neck 180 degrees and then also moves it front and back. They took inspiration from the bee group's rectangle hinged P shapes and built the same thing with some setha sticks (thick sticks from a plant) and attached a rubber band to pull it. They tried it and it worked well.

The ant leg group couldn't meet as both members weren't able to come for the sessions, so I tried some options with wire and cloth but it did not work very smoothly as coordinating all the wires together was difficult.

So, at the end of this session one group was able to get the movement they wanted. This motivated the others to work on their movements again the next day. The bird group also thought that they would now install a face and try to move the puppet. One thing which came from the reflection from all of them was that the observation and research pushed their thinking. Getting one movement with so much detail was so intriguing that now they wanted their puppets to be even more alive.

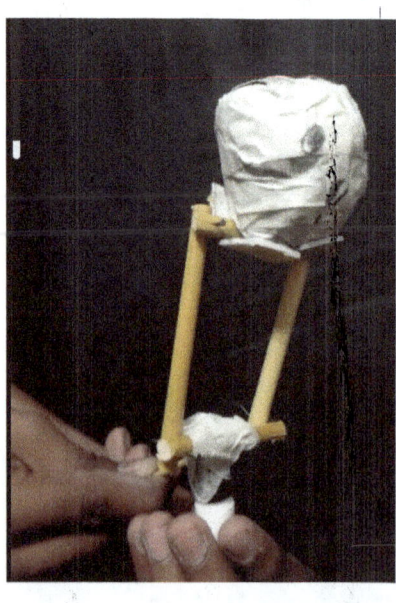
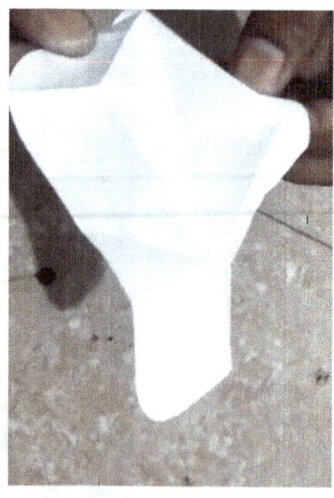

Session 5:

The exploration continued and every group got some of their movements working. They each made a quick body to see if the attachments worked with the body or not.

The bee team used transparent thin plastic bags over a wire frame to make the wings. They got the wings attached and moving up and down, but there was an imbalance between the two wings and the rotational movement didn't work.

The ladybug group was able to use their origami idea and make transparent paper wings that opened automatically when the top part was opened.

When the bird group attached cloth to the body of the bird, they realized that the head was too close to the body, so they used a syringe to increase the length of the neck.

Reflections

After our five building sessions were over, we sat together and reflected on how much we learned from each other, both from our own team members and from other teams. We discussed how observation gave us the eye for details and how we needed time for trial and exploration through the whole process.

This is not the end of the larger work of putting on a puppet show as they will have the opportunity to continue work on their designs and make a puppet with which they will perform. One of the children compared it to dance, as in dance we move our bodies and we have to learn the rhythm and details just like we observed and explored the movements of the bird.

The project raised a lot of questions about how things move, such as how the bee has such thin, small wings but carries nectar? The children had lots of questions and things they were interested in exploring further.

At the end I felt that the whole process gave me so much insight as a teacher, puppeteer, and as a maker. I emerged from this project thinking that when we have real things which add to our own work or knowledge, children enthusiastically explore and find solutions for their problems.

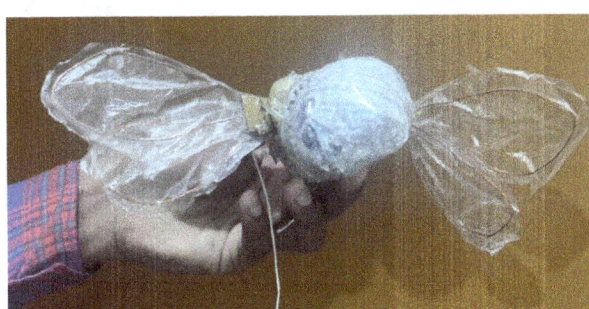

Imagine Anything: 3D Design without a 3D Printer

by Lars Beck Johannsen

This past year I was invited to different schools to lead sessions with their students to do 3D modeling. There would not be enough time to 3D print the models, but I've been successfully using a virtual tool called CoSpaces in these sessions.[1] CoSpaces is a kid-friendly webspace for 3D creation and coding. These kids make 3D models that are filled with story and emotion. Why not bring them to life through code and a virtual environment?

Start with a story

It usually starts with a story or a theme the class has been working with. I introduce Tinkercad, and a short 5 to 10 minute introduction to modeling. I practice this introduction to make it as short as possible, only showing the essential basics. The rest they will discover and share among each other as they model. The sharing and helping is important, and I make a point to emphasize it during the introduction. After about half an hour, we pause the session and share tips & tricks in front of the class by the different students who discovered something.

Make a model

The next step is exporting the model. This is often a bit tricky for some students, because a lot of the Danish pupils use tablets or smartphones and therefore have little or no knowledge about file handling. But there are always some who get it quickly or know a bit already and they help the rest.

One thing that I learned throughout this process is that the orientation of the model can be important for the later work in CoSpaces.

The exported file needs to be an OBJ file since it has colors, which STL files don't have. You can even have semi-transparent parts in your design.

If you group shapes in Tinkercad they will get the same color. Ungroup to get the colors back or lock the shapes in place instead of grouping them.

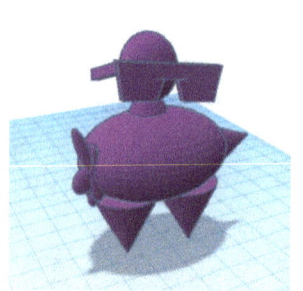
Don't group objects

Ungroup to get colors back

Workplane direction with arrow when exporting OBJ

Workplane direction (from side) when exporting OBJ

Make a scene

When the model is exported it is time to import it into CoSpace. Danish schools have a special access to CoSpaces to ensure GDPR rules. But it is free to set up a teacher account and make a class code so students can use the teachers class code to join their class. In the free version, you are limited to the basic coding blocks and do not have the option to code with Python.

Students can collaborate in a CoSpace or work alone. I usually do not have more than 4 students in one space, because the individual scene is not that big. You could have multiple scenes, but that might get a little complicated. A scene in CoSpace is a space to put your 3D models. A scene can have an environment, additional 3D objects and always has a camera, which represents the initial viewpoint of the user.

Bring the story to life

Once you get your model imported into the scene, the fun begins! You can code your model to move and to be interactive. Bringing your models to life and building a story, a game or whatever you can imagine is really engaging. You can even have multiple scenes to create more complicated stories. You can shift between scenes by creating interactive objects, so that clicking on it switches to another scene.

You can share your work as a 3D environment for others to explore, show it as an AR through a smartphone, or experience it through a VR headset.

It is always a good sign when the students do not want their usual breaks during the day. I usually make this a one-day event that lasts 3–4 hours, but it can be done in shorter periods of time spread over a few days just as well.

Example projects

Here are some examples of what different age groups can do. In these groups, there are usually a few students who have tried a bit of Tinkercad beforehand, but that is not always the case, and it is not a necessity for success.

8–9 year-olds collaborated on building houses to create a scene. This works well with a theme, for example, around Christmas it was Santa's Village, where they used the premade models to bring the scene to life. Another class made a village on a distant planet inhabited by aliens of their own design.

Students discussed what their own city would look like. What different buildings did they think a city should have? Should it have shops, public buildings, government, leisure, housing, etc.? Each student then chose a building to model.

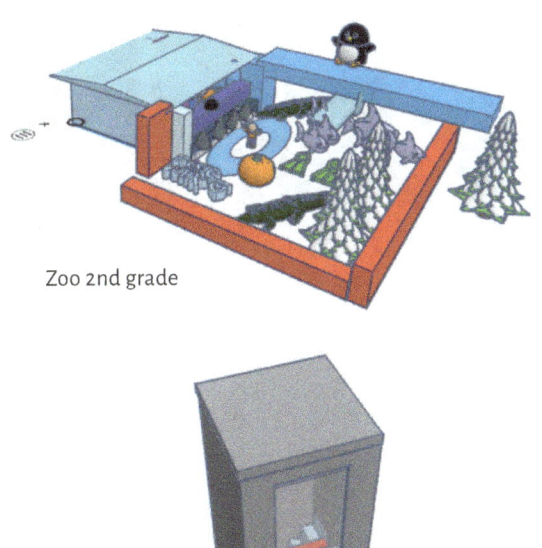

Zoo 2nd grade

Cafe 2nd grade

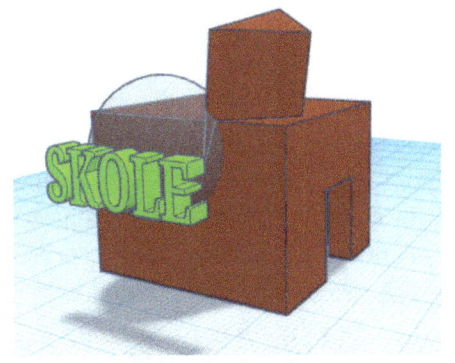

IT department 2nd grade

School 2nd grade

A class of 11-year-olds had read a lyrical novel about a bird and they were assigned to model their own bird and make it interactive in the CoSpace. The bird would either recite a part of the story or show text when clicked on. Of course, they wanted their bird to fly around as well! This was done by setting up a path that the model followed. It was at this point that we discovered that the orientation in the export from Tinkercad is important. Otherwise, it would fly sideways or backwards.

Bird projects 5th grade

Bird project code 5th grade   Bird project with visible path 5th grade

Several classes of 13-year-olds spent a week making their own projects. Some of them wanted to show a different way of using their school's cantina using CoSpaces while others designed a whole new school. Many of them had modeled beforehand and had made some really good models they wanted to print. But they did not have experience in 3D printing, so it would have been really difficult to do, time consuming, and not a good way to present their work.

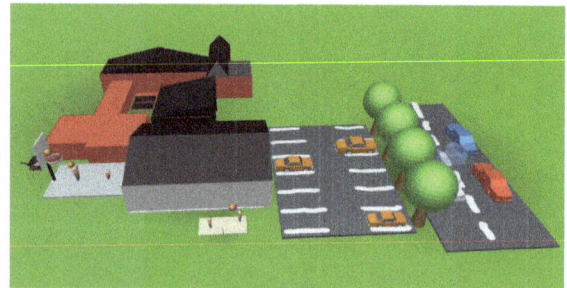 

School redesign 7th grade   New cantina 7th grade

Use the best tool for the job

3D printing is still a slow production method and on many occasions, it is not necessarily the best tool for the assignment given. As a teacher you should always give thought to which tools you have students use. Sometimes the pencil is more powerful than drawing with a mouse. The best tool is the one that supports learning and gives students creative agency over their work.

Notes

1. CoSpaces - cospaces.io/edu/

GoGo Board in Brazil: The Engine of Digital Inclusion

by Charles Pimentel

The GoGo Board is an open-source electronic board developed for schools for robotics, environmental sensing and the Internet of Things (IoT).[1] Using the GoGo Board for low-cost science, computer science, and robotics experimentation has the potential to democratize STEM education in public and private K12 schools in Brazil and around the world.

GoGo Board 6

Background

Brazilian schools are looking for ways to promote active and meaningful learning activities to meet the needs of the current generation of students.

In the last century, when information did not travel so quickly, most young people only had access to knowledge at school through their teachers. Current K–12 students, most of them born in the 21st century, are digital natives who have access to real-time information in the palm of their hands through their mobile devices.

So we must consider that when teaching and learning activities do not take this change seriously it results in a lack of interest in school as a relevant place in students' lives.

In the last century, researchers and educators such as John Dewey, Paulo Freire, and Seymour Papert proposed ways that education could be more active and meaningful, yet this has not happened in many schools. But the technological advances of the last few decades, combined with a networked and connected society, show that we can no longer wait for such ideas to be put into practice.

This is especially true for academic subjects related to STEM careers. Classes that are purely theoretical discourage students and make the lack of interest even greater.

A possible way for education in Brazil to be redirected is through the introduction of new technologies in the classroom, through hands-on experiments and creative activities. We can have students participate in real research, or explore student entrepreneurship opportunities. We can explore their interests. In STEM areas, for example, robotics, automation, programming, digital games and the inclusion of Artificial Intelligence (an increasingly ubiquitous technology in society), are means to attract interest and develop the potential of young people who are in school and, in the future, will join the workforce in these areas that are so important for the development of the country.

The challenge of Digital Inclusion

However, some educational institutions, as well as some educators, face another challenge: Digital Inclusion.

Digital Inclusion is the process of democratizing access to technologies (Freire, 2004), but some educators and school managers think that this access is only possible through expensive resources, such as robotics and electronics kits from large companies, which makes it unfeasible, for most Brazilian schools.

Many Brazilian educators have sought to

overcome these difficulties. The work of the Brazilian teacher and FabLearn Fellow Débora Garofalo, in the State of São Paulo, stands out. Ms. Garofalo popularized the inclusion of technology in public schools in São Paulo through the Robotics with Scrap Project (Garofalo, 2019). Using electronic waste and recyclable materials from around the school where she worked, she awakened in Brazil a change in the mindset of educators and school managers who previously understood that Digital Inclusion was only done with a lot of money.

Digital Inclusion with the GoGo board

Another project that supports Digital Inclusion is the development of the low-cost robotics kit GoGo Board, a project developed by the Transformative Learning Technologies Lab (TLTL), coordinated by Professor Paulo Blikstein, at Columbia University in the United States, and the Learning Inventions Lab (LIL), coordinated by Professor Arnan Sipitakiat, at Chiang Mai University, Thailand.

> "The GoGo board allows computer programs to interact with the physical world. The GoGo board shares its fundamental functionalities with other devices in the programmable brick family. Users can connect various sensors and actuators to the board and write programs to read the sensor data and control the behavior of various physical objects using motors, small lamps, LEDs, and relays." (Sipitakiat & Blikstein et al. 2003)

The GoGo Board is an open-source electronic board for robotics, environmental sensing and IoT. The current version, GoGo Board 6, can be understood as the union between the BBC micro:bit, Lego EV3, and Arduino and, even with all these characteristics, is financially accessible.

If any educator wants to develop activities focused on Science, Engineering or Mathematics, GoGo is a technological resource that easily allows people who have never built or programmed robots to develop meaningful projects.

Designed for learning programming and electronics

The GoGo board was designed to support both learning programming and electronics. The programming dashboard is available not only in the computer-based programming environment[2] but also on the device's integrated screen.

Even before the automation and robotics project is developed, the user can try out the electronic circuits, even actuators and sensors that will be used in the project, without necessarily having to create a circuit and program the resources.

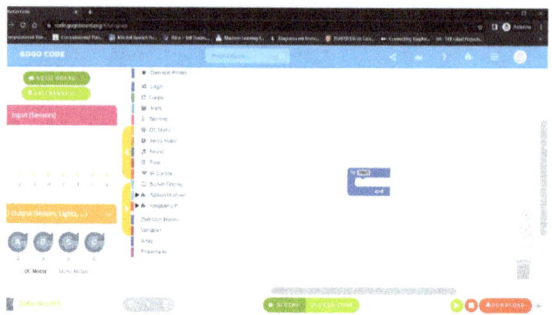

GoGo board block-based programming environment

Dashboard in the programming environment and on the integrated screen

Case studies

Two case studies from Brazil provide evidence of the usefulness of the GoGo board to implement robotics, automation, and programming, using the STEM approach. The first is with high school students in a private educational institution, and the second is in a Brazilian public middle school.

Case Study 1 – Polo Educacional Sesc STEM Club

Polo Educacional Sesc is a high school in Rio de Janeiro, Brazil, that promotes free and quality education for students, preferably from public schools and low-income families. Polo is a place where innovative educational actions are developed, with the aim that these innovations can be replicated in other educational institutions, through technical cooperation and teacher training.

At Polo, I participated in the implementation of a mathematics course where the curriculum is fully taught with hands-on GoGo Board projects. This class was developed through a partnership with the TLTL group at Columbia University in the US.

For this course, the traditional classroom is transformed into a space for innovation. Students have low-tech tools and recyclable materials at their disposal, in addition to scissors, box cutters, glue, tape, and clamps, among other resources. These materials can be connected to actuators that respond to sensors, all programmed by the students with the GoGo 6 Board.

Currently, the course includes 13 students. It is a mixed-grade class, with five 10th year students, five 11th year students and three 12th year students. For the first month, students are incentivized to explore the board and its features. Thus, after three weeks of work, the young people are already programming the board, its actuators, and sensors.

Next, the students were introduced to two classic robotics projects: a traffic light with LEDs that responds to traffic, and an autonomous car programmed to avoid obstacles, lighting up LEDs when identifying them.

During these activities, the visual/block programming language used by the GoGo Board 6 is being explored, and students are encouraged to implement logic, loops, and mathematics, and to use sensors in their projects.

STEM Club participant Nicolly Figueiredo, a student participating in the classes with the GoGo 6, said, "My first programming experience was with GoGo Board, which increased my interest in robotics a lot. Especially for those who are starting in this field, it is important to have a simple, dynamic, and interesting tool that can be used for multiple projects." A video of Nicolly speaking about the GoGo 6 board is on YouTube.[3]

Case 2 – Computer Lab of a public school in the Municipality of Tanguá – Summer Course

The second case study focused on the transformation of a computer lab into a space for innovation in a public middle school located in a small Brazilian municipality, Tanguá using the GoGo 6.

Most Brazilian K–12 schools have computer labs, which are used as the main means of introducing technology into the school curriculum. The computer labs are spaces with computers connected to the internet, organized in rows, where instructors teach students how to use an operating system, browse the internet, create and send messages and e-mail, in addition to covering topics related to word processing, image editing, spreadsheets, and presentations.

However, with the popularization of personal computers and mobile devices, skills such as word processing, image editing, and video editing have become common, especially among young people

Traffic light

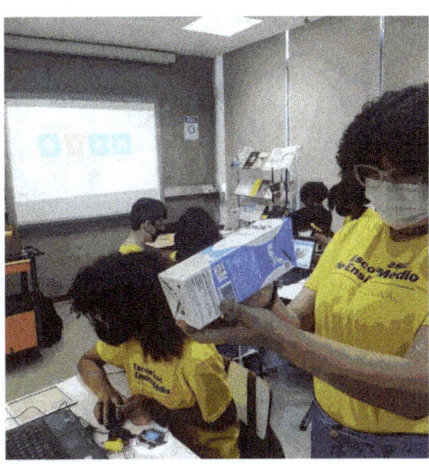

Autonomous car

who are currently in K–12 education schools.

Thus, although computer labs maintain their importance, the democratization of technological resources points to the need for these rooms to expand to include other, more relevant topics such as computational thinking and robotics.

Based on this reflection, we planned a workshop called Educational Robotics in Tanguá, with middle school students from a municipal public school using the GoGo Board.

Tanguá is a small rural Brazilian municipality, located 70 km from the city of Rio de Janeiro. The municipality has 35 thousand inhabitants and is known as the capital of oranges. Many families have small fruit plantations, which contribute to their livelihood.

Through a partnership between the Tanguá Municipal Department of Education, the Federal University of Rio de Janeiro (UFRJ) and TLTL, for three days, a computer lab was transformed into a space for innovation and creativity using the GoGo Board as the educational robotics resource.

For this activity, recyclable materials and low-tech tools were made available.

The activity was carried out with the participation of 10 students from the last year of middle school, 6 girls and 4 boys, in addition to 3 volunteer teachers who, for the first time, guided students in maker education projects.

The activity was organized into three three-hour meetings. In the first meeting, the students were introduced to block programming through the Code.org platform. In this way, the students were led to understand, through playful activities, how to use blocks of logic and loops of repetition. It is important to highlight that the recreational feature of Code.org activities are powerful ways to generate student engagement.

At this same meeting the students tried out the GoGo Board actuators and sensors through its dashboard. As mentioned above, the dashboard is an important feature of the GoGo Board 6, as it allows students to recognize the functions of actuators and sensors, without having to create an electronic circuit or write code.

In the second meeting, the students assembled and programmed a car that would move when triggered by the gesture sensor (a feature integrated in the GoGo 6). Programming the DC motors and the sensor was a challenging activity,

Tanguá workshop

Meeting 1 - Introducing GoGo 6

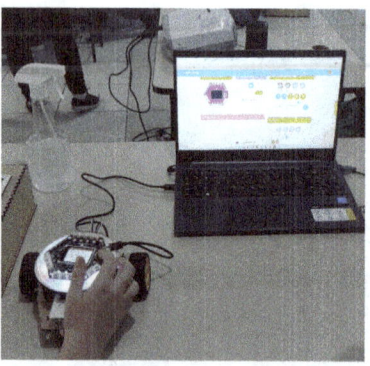

Meeting 2 - Car guided by gestures

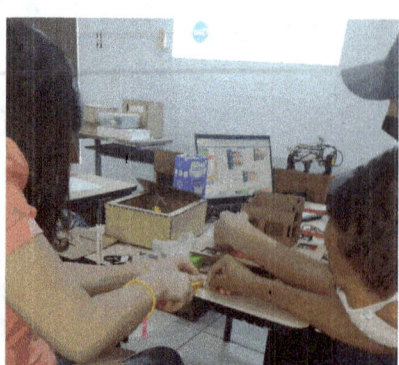

Meeting 3 - Automated house

but the students were engaged with the project and were successful.

At the third meeting the challenge was to automate a house. Proximity sensors, light sensors, LEDs, and servo and DC motors were made available and used in the students' projects.

At the end of each meeting, the educators who participated in the activity reported how easy it was to guide students in the use of the GoGo Board. The fact that, they experienced immediate success with the GoGo in activities with students in the Summer Course became the first step for the municipality of Tanguá, through its Municipal Department of Education, to implement robotics and programming classes in the curriculum.

The report of Professor Érika Soares, one of the educators of the municipal school system, who participated as a counselor in the Summer Course, stands out. She said that:

> "From the observation in the Summer Course and feedback from the students, I can say that the GoGo 6 is extremely accessible, from acquisition to use."

Conclusion

These two case studies demonstrated the ease of implementation of GoGo with Brazilian students from middle and high school, both in the public and private schools.

The small learning curve required allowed both students and educators to feel confident about developing robotics, automation and programming projects for the teaching of science and mathematics.

As we move on with this project, some innovative features of the GoGo 6 will be explored, such as IoT and the Data Laboratory (DataLab). The DataLab, in particular, is one of the new features of the board that will contribute to interdisciplinary classes, as this resource allows a wide variety of data collection that will be useful in many subject areas.

Thus, the possibility of integrating curricular subjects is expanded through projects with GoGo 6. For example, history and sociology educators can use the resource to discuss technological advances and their impacts on society, in the discussion about employability and new professions. Philosophy and computing teachers can use GoGo projects to explore issues, for example, of ethics in obtaining and using data.

These are practices and initiatives that faculty, not just from STEM areas, can take ownership of because of the ease of use of the GoGo board.

Special Thanks: I would like to thank Professor Érika Soares, English teacher in the Municipality of Tanguá, Isaac D`Césares, Analyst of Educational Technologies at Polo Educacional Sesc and Walter Akio, researcher at TLTL, for their invaluable contribution in reviewing this article.

Notes

1. gogoboard.org
2. code.gogoboard.org
3. youtube.com/watch?v=182RLkwgiKg

References:

Freire, I. M. (2004). O desafio da inclusão digital. Transinformação, 16, 189-194.

Garofalo, D. D. (2019). Robótica com sucata. Revista Brasileira de Pós-Graduação, 15(34), 1-21.

Pimentel, C., Castro, B. B., Rodrigues, E. G., Almeida, G. H. A., Schaedler, L. S., & Pereira, M. A. (2018). Programação Visual em Blocos e Letramento Digital: Uma Investigação Realizada por Meio de Um Programa de Iniciação Científica na Educação Básica. In III Congresso sobre Tecnologias na Educação (Ctrl+ e), Fortaleza, Brasil.

Sipitakiat, A., Blikstein, P., Cavallo, D. P., Camargo, A., & Alves, R. D. D. L. (2003). A placa GoGo: robótica de baixo custo, programável e reconfigurável. XIV SBIE: Simpósio Brasileiro de Informática na Educação, 73-92.

Ideas about America: Making in History Class with Fabric Collage

by Heather Allen Pang

This project started out as a fun activity for online learning when we went into the fall semester of 2020, starting fully remote. Our school had students pick up bags of supplies, and I wanted to be able to have some fun crafty projects to stimulate historical thinking and provide all the materials to students. Using recycled materials from FabMo, a local non-profit that rescues fabrics and other materials from design showrooms and sells them to teachers and crafters, I put together bags for each student with a random range of fabric and paper materials.

Version 1.0

The prompt was both simple and complicated:

> "Using the fabric and other recycled materials (and the envelope), you will create a collage that represents something you want to say about the United States (today or historically or both). You may not add any additional materials other than glue (or other fastening materials) to the materials you have been given. Use the envelope as the BASE for your artwork. Your message may be political, cultural, historical, or symbolic, but it should include some of the ideas from your alphabet chart, your freewriting, or your homework brainstorming."

The alphabet chart, the freewriting, and the brainstorming had included simpler versions of the prompt: What do you think about when you think about US history?

Although remote learning ended, I have kept the project because I have found students not only enjoy the novel art form and working with a new material seems freeing to some. When I have done projects that involve other forms of art, especially drawing, I have noticed some students go into the work thinking that they "can't draw"

or that "my drawing won't be good enough." With fabric collage, I have yet to find any students who are already familiar with the format, or who come to the project with any pre-conceived notions about who is good at it and who is not. When they don't assume they are "bad" at it, they let their imagination fly.

Over the last few years, I have changed the

warmup and the brainstorming, but I have kept the limitation of using only the materials from the bag. Sometimes limitations are great for creativity.

Version 2.0

This year I followed my normal plan for the first version, but in the second semester, I revisited the project. The instructions stayed the same, but the materials were much freer. I put out all the fabric scraps, and they picked their own after they did some design brainstorming.

Students had almost a full year of American History to think about. We had studied the Constitution, read *Stamped from the Beginning* by Ibram X. Kindi and Jason Reynolds, and done deep dives into topics students chose for National History Day. We also spent some time thinking about other ways to think about symbols, current events, and protest movements. The second set of collages showed that more detailed understanding of the United States. Students were eager to get going, and less worried about not being able to do it.

Sometimes students wonder why we are doing so much "art stuff" and not learning more history. As I listened to a group of students brainstorm for their fabric collages, I again heard the evidence for deep historical thinking in their design work. One student wondered how to show statistics about immigration in their fabric collage. Another answered by suggesting a bar graph made out of gray felt. A third observed that the different colors should be meaningful, they should represent something the student wanted to say.

As I moved to the next table, I reflected that this little snipit of conversation confirms how deep the thinking can be, when students engage in meaningful "art stuff" through making in the history classroom. The conversations I listened in on included deep historical thinking, analysis, and creativity.

Found Object Puppetry

by Ridhi Aggarwal

Art expresses the soul of human civilization as does making. In today's ever-evolving environment it is important for the fields of art and making education to continue defining and redefining their versatility and malleability in the education of children. As per Marshall (2014), art integration should be framed as a trans-disciplinary paradigm which meets the current needs of education. In this article I discuss how the art of puppetry acts as an integrated tool for exploratory making. The hybrid nature of puppetry provides many opportunities for merging of various disciplines, learning styles, and pedagogies to create a comprehensive learning experience. In addition, puppetry is a natural bridge to play, imagination, experimentation, storytelling, and collaboration.

Found object puppetry

Found object puppetry uses everyday objects to build puppets and create a story around them. These examples are from primary and upper primary classrooms.

One of the roles of the puppeteer is to listen to and work with the materiality of things. Objects inform us, which involves more than merely hearing the imaginary voices of things. Listening to a thing involves holding it and turning it this way and that — an exploration of its unique materiality. Learning to explore the materiality of things and see things with fresh eyes is also an important aspect of a makerspace.

The upper primary school learners started the project by exploring cardboard as material for making puppets. But, as they were making puppets for a show about Savitribai Phule (an Indian social reformer, teacher, and poet), the students discovered that cardboard is not an exciting material to work with. It is monotonous and lacks interesting properties that engage learners. Also, the availability of cardboard is restricted to urban areas. The facilitator asked the students, "Are there any objects around us which can help in making puppets differently?" This was the beginning of exploration with found objects.

Artists want to use materials that have interesting properties and "listen" to what the material is saying. The learners started to explore with materials such as paper, bamboo, corn-leaves, sticks, and rice husks to make puppets. They combined these with found objects like brooms, buckets, tires, spoons, shoes, clothes, etc.

Gosden (2005) argues in his essay "What do Objects Want?" that objects have agency and can be "socially powerful." The kinds of questions the puppeteer might ask of material might include: "What does it want?" "Which way does it want to go?" "What story does it want to tell?"

The learners explored materiality of paper from various sources — paper from their old notebooks, textbooks, newspapers, and other sources. They tried to crumple, wet, soak, dry, make some marks, and change the texture of paper. During this exploration they reached a point where they actually discovered the process of making paper-mache puppets. While they were making puppets for the Savitribai Phule show using this technique, they found out that there is an issue with respect to weight and density of the puppet, so they mixed paper pulp with husks and mud from the pond to make it heavier to bring stability into the puppet. The size, shape, texture, weight, age, and density of matter can dictate the flow of movement that gives each character life on stage. In this unit, the learners were also given perspective about how paper puppets can be animated, when the facilitators showed students the work of some artists of the Little Angel Theatre group as examples.

In another example with Grade 5 students, while exploring a theme around re-purposing, the learners were asked to bring one object to class which they thought might have the potential to be re-purposed. They were given the task to transform their objects into a person and represent a whole person metaphorically. So, they had to think about personality, occupation, and their role in the family as they explored their object. The learners used old shoes, pliers, suitcases, bottles, and hasia (a small scythe) to put on a puppet show about the life story of the object. The learners also identified the designed injustices in the objects, for example, the chappals (sandals) of all females had heels so the chappal represented the discomfort that women have when they walk for long time, and metaphorically represented gender inequality. This also initiated a discussion on equality and discrimination.

This experience had a huge impact on the learners, and on Teachers Day the learners presented a puppet show "Mr Phunsuk Lal ki Bagia," a story of a grumpy old man who has to make peace with a mole that invades his garden. They made Phunsuk Lal using shoes and wool and the mole was made of scissors and hasia.

The materiality and expressiveness of puppets offers a range of entry points to inquiries from practical to metaphorical, even to something as complex as designed injustices of objects and their politics. It not only serves as a tool for building imagination and creativity, but also serves in building decision-making competencies like which object to use, how to use it, and so on. Language development is nurtured by connecting with the outer world, using and building vocabulary in context.

Through such experiences, the puppeteer can create a puppet character that is a metaphor for human experience. The performer also steps into a new reality, looks around, explores what this new reality looks like, moves on, and makes connections on the way which are extremely creative and imaginative. The learners move into a powerful micro-world of imagination and form a micro-identity while performing the show. This enhances the power of thinking both for primary and upper primary learners.

Two observations came from this experience. One is that the integration of art and making in found object puppetry requires close observation that supports both art and making education. The second is that there needs to be time spent on iterations of the puppets to develop a deeper understanding of how small changes can impact the ability to tell a story. Found object puppetry provides multiple opportunities for facilitators to design explorations that provide excellent stimulus for imagination and learning.

References

Gosden, C. (2005). What do objects want? Journal of archaeological method and theory, 12, 193-211.

Marshall, J. (2014). Transdisciplinarity and Art Integration: Toward a New

Understanding of Art-Based Learning across the Curriculum. Studies in Art Education, 55(2), 104-127.

Mole Day in the Makerspace

by Josh Ajima

Happy Mole Day!

Mole day is an unofficial holiday celebrated on October 23rd between 6:02 am and 6:02 pm. The time and date are based on Avogadro's number, 6.02×10^23, which is the number of atoms/molecules in one mole of a substance. A mole is one of the seven base units of the International System of Units (SI) that defines the amount of a substance.

Mole Day and Pi Day are staples of STEM school culture that add fun and festivity into the school day. STEM educators love a good pun so of course Mole Day is filled with images, jokes and activities related to the small mammal. However, I was feeling like a Mole Day Scrooge because I didn't want to join in on school activities like making a decorative stuffed mole. I realized that if I was going to make something, I wanted it to be connected to the actual science and mathematics behind the mole as a unit. I wanted to make something that helped me learn more about the mole. I wanted to celebrate Mole Day in the Makerspace!

The first thing I wondered was, what does a mole of something look like? There is lots of aluminum stock available in my makerspace so that seemed like a good starting point. The atomic mass of aluminum is 26.981539 u. This means 1 mole of aluminum has a mass of 26.981539 grams according to the formula **atomic mass * molar constant (1 g/mol) * moles (mol) = mass (g)**. Then it was a simple matter of machining down a block of aluminum to a rough size, weighing and then filing and sanding until hitting the target mass.

And just like that we have a Mole of Aluminum! I upped the level by using a small CNC machine to engrave a mole icon and the atomic symbol of aluminum.

Increasing the challenge

This could be a challenge for an engineering student — fabricate a one mole object out of aluminum or mild steel. I used mass to determine the amount of material, but students could also make their object by calculating the volume of one mole of the material.

An activity like this is a great way to take an abstract concept and bring it to a human scale object that students can design and fabricate. Of course, distance learning makes this activity impossible but CAD tools like Fusion 360 give a virtual option for exploring mole concepts in human scale dimensions.

When creating bodies in Fusion 360, students can select a physical material, including a range of metals. Once the body is made, students can look at the properties of the objects to see the mass and volume of the object. This can make for an interesting exploration as students create objects of different materials. In the images below, the bodies modeled are one mole of aluminum, gold, titanium, and steel.

Now you too can celebrate Mole Day in your makerspace.

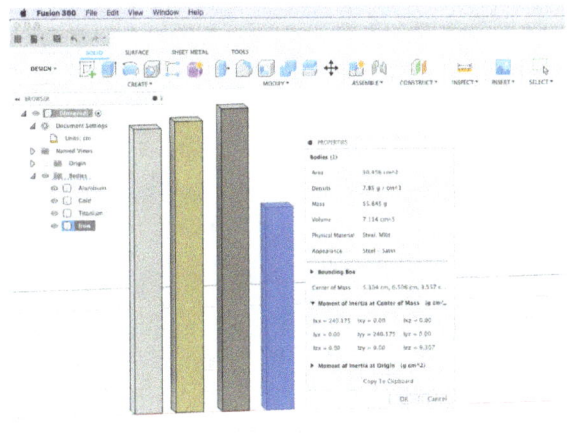